Cognitive Linguistic Approaches to Text and Discourse

Cognitive Linguistic Approaches to Text and Discourse
From Poetics to Politics

Edited by Christopher Hart

EDINBURGH
University Press

Edinburgh University Press is one of the leading university presses in the UK. We publish academic books and journals in our selected subject areas across the humanities and social sciences, combining cutting-edge scholarship with high editorial and production values to produce academic works of lasting importance. For more information visit our website: edinburghuniversitypress.com

© editorial matter and organisation Christopher Hart, 2019, 2021
© the chapters their several authors, 2019, 2021

Edinburgh University Press Ltd
The Tun – Holyrood Road, 12(2f) Jackson's Entry, Edinburgh EH8 8PJ

First published in hardback by Edinburgh University Press 2019

Typeset in 11/13pt Adobe Garamond Pro by
Servis Filmsetting Ltd, Stockport, Cheshire

A CIP record for this book is available from the British Library

ISBN 978 1 4744 4998 4 (hardback)
ISBN 978 1 4744 4999 1 (paperback)
ISBN 978 1 4744 5000 3 (webready PDF)
ISBN 978 1 4744 5001 0 (epub)

The right of Christopher Hart to be identified as the editor of this work has been asserted in accordance with the Copyright, Designs and Patents Act 1988, and the Copyright and Related Rights Regulations 2003 (SI No. 2498).

Contents

List of Figures and Tables	vii
Notes on Contributors	ix

Introduction   1
Christopher Hart

1   Shelley's Dominion: Subliminal and Ambient Tonal Effects Across a Literary Work   20
Peter Stockwell

2   A 'Half-Remembered Quality': Experiencing Disorientation and Claustrophobia in *The Goldfinch*   37
Chloe Harrison

3   Creativity and Cognition in the Discourse of National Trust Holiday Cottage Guestbooks   54
Joanna Gavins and Sara Whiteley

4   Metaphorical Descriptions of Pain on a Trigeminal Neuralgia Forum: Pushing the Boundaries of Cognitive Linguistics   73
Elena Semino

5   Simulation in Deictic Space: Scenes and Episodes in the Lord's Prayer   93
Jeremy Holland

6   Cultural Responses to 9/11 and the Healing Power of Songs: A Text-World-Theory Analysis of Bruce Springsteen's 'The Rising'   111
Laura Filardo-Llamas

7   'A Nation Divided': Metaphors and Scenarios in Media Coverage of the 2016 British EU Referendum   131
Veronika Koller and Josie Ryan

8 'That's Just What We Hear on Telly All the Time, Isn't It?'
   Political Discourse and the Cognitive Linguistic Ethnography of
   Critical Reception   157
   Sam Browse
9 Spatial Properties of ACTION Verb Semantics: Experimental
   Evidence For Image Schema Orientation in Transitive Versus
   Reciprocal Verbs and Its Implications for Ideology   181
   Christopher Hart

Index   205

List of Figures and Tables

Figure 1.1	Dominion	23
Figure 1.2	Dominion chaining	24
Figure 3.1	Holiday guestbook	60
Figure 5.1	Basic deictic space model	101
Figure 5.2	Deictic space of Matthew 6: 9–13	103
Figure 6.1	Components of text-worlds and context models as mental spaces	116
Figure 6.2	Summarised text-worlds in Springsteen's 'The Rising'	118
Figure 6.3	Conceptual blending in 'The Rising'	123
Figure 6.4	Proximity and distance in Springsteen's 'The Rising'	124
Figure 7.1	A model of metaphor and scenarios in discourse	136
Figure 8.1	A model of critical reception	161
Figure 8.2	Annotations on the speech	167
Figure 8.3	The immediate and maximal scope of arm and hand	169
Figure 8.4	Focusing on the level of the clause	171
Figure 8.5	Cat circles the passives	171
Figure 8.6	The conceptual substrate of 'demand' and its 'thing-like' construal	174
Figure 9.1	Example of questionnaire in Experiment 1	185
Figure 9.2	Visual depiction of mean axis angles for transitive versus reciprocal verbs	187
Figure 9.3	Left–right orientation of transversal schema for reciprocal verbs	188
Figure 9.4	Front–back orientation of sagittal schema for transitive verbs	188
Figure 9.5	Stimulus images used in Experiments 2a and 2b	195

Figure 9.6	Blame allocation in transversal versus sagittal images	197
Figure 9.7	Spatial discrimination in perception of aggression	198
Table 1.1	Keyness words in Shelley's text	28
Table 3.1	Linguistic creativity and communicative situations (adapted from Carter 2004: 165)	68
Table 6.1	Textual and knowledge-determined activity schemata in 'The Rising'	122
Table 7.1	Overview of the data	138
Table 7.2	Metaphoric expressions for the electorate	150
Table 7.3	Metaphoric expressions for the UK political establishment	153
Table 9.1	Percentage of participants choosing each image schema orientation	186
Table 9.2	Mean axis angles for transitive versus reciprocal verbs	187

Notes on Contributors

Sam Browse is a Senior Lecturer in English Language at Sheffield Hallam University, UK. His research uses ideas and concepts from cognitive stylistics, classical rhetoric and cognitive and social psychology to investigate audience responses to political discourse. He is the author of *Cognitive Rhetoric: The Cognitive Poetics of Political Discourse* (John Benjamins, 2018) and has published on the reception of political text and talk and the language of the new British left.

Laura Filardo-Llamas is Senior Lecturer in English Linguistics at the University of Valladolid, Spain. Her main research area is discourse analysis and conflict resolution. Her research has been recently applied to ethno-nationalist conflicts and to domestic violence. She is also interested in the study of songs as socio-cultural communicative practices. She has attended several international conferences and she has published in journals such as *Ethnopolitics*, *Peace and Conflict Studies*, *CADAAD Journal* and *Critical Discourse Studies*.

Joanna Gavins is Professor of English Language and Literature and is Chair in English Language and Literature at the University of Sheffield, where she teaches courses in cognitive linguistics and stylistics. She is the author of *Text World Theory: An Introduction* (Edinburgh University Press, 2007), *Reading the Absurd* (Edinburgh University Press, 2013) and co-editor (with Gerard Steen) of *Cognitive Poetics in Practice* (Routledge, 2003) and (with Ernestine Lahey) of *World Building: Discourse in the Mind* (Bloomsbury, 2016). She is the Director of the Text World Theory Special Collection at the University of Sheffield and Editor of the John Benjamins *Linguistic Approaches to Literature* book series.

Chloe Harrison is a Lecturer in English Language and Literature at Aston University. Her research interests include cognitive stylistics, reader response studies, and contemporary and postmodern fiction. She is the author of *Cognitive Grammar in Contemporary Fiction* (John Benjamins, 2017) and co-author of the textbook *Cognitive Grammar in Stylistics: A Practical Guide* (Bloomsbury, 2018).

Christopher Hart is Professor of Linguistics at Lancaster University where he teaches courses in cognitive linguistics and critical discourse analysis. His research investigates the link between language, cognition and action in social and political contexts of communication. He is author of *Critical Discourse Analysis and Cognitive Science: New Perspectives on Immigration Discourse* (Palgrave, 2010) and *Discourse, Grammar and Ideology: Functional and Cognitive Perspectives* (Bloomsbury, 2014).

Jeremy Holland is a Philosophy Lecturer at Northeast Texas Community College in Mt Pleasant Texas. In 2018, he received his PhD in applied linguistics from Lancaster University. He has published articles on political and corporate texts in the journals *Discourse & Society* and *Semiotica*. His research concerns the way language is used to mobilise people into groups and the central role of language in the formation of geo-political worldviews.

Veronika Koller is Reader in Discourse Studies at Lancaster University. Her research interests comprise various domains of discourse (business, healthcare, politics), as well as language and sexuality. A particular focus in her work is metaphor. She has published widely, including the research-based textbook *Language in Business, Language at Work* (with Erika Darics; Palgrave Higher Education, 2018) and the edited volume *Discourses of Brexit* (Routledge, 2019).

Josie Ryan is a postgraduate researcher and English teacher at Bangor University. Her PhD project uses cognitive linguistic approaches to discourse analysis to investigate discourses of national identity.

Elena Semino is Professor of Linguistics and Verbal Art in the Department of Linguistics and English Language at Lancaster University, and Director of the ESRC Centre for Corpus Approaches to Social Science. She holds a Visiting Professorship at the University of Fuzhou in China. She specialises in health communication, medical humanities, corpus linguistics, stylistics, narratology and metaphor theory and analysis. She has (co-)authored over eighty academic publications, including *Metaphor in Discourse* (Cambridge

University Press, 2008) and *Metaphor, Cancer and the End of Life: A Corpus-Based Study* (Routledge, 2018).

Peter Stockwell is Professor of Literary Linguistics at the University of Nottingham, and a Fellow of the English Association. He has published twelve books and over eighty articles in stylistics, sociolinguistics and applied linguistics, including *Cognitive Poetics* (Routledge, 2002), *Texture: A Cognitive Aesthetics of Reading* (Edinburgh University Press, 2009) and *The Language of Surrealism* (Palgrave, 2017). He co-edited *Contemporary Stylistics* (Continuum, 2007), *The Language and Literature Reader* (Routledge, 2008) and *The Cambridge Handbook of Stylistics* (Cambridge University Press, 2014). His work in cognitive poetics has been translated into many languages, including Chinese, Japanese, Polish, Persian and Arabic.

Sara Whiteley is Senior Lecturer in Language and Literature at the University of Sheffield, UK. She specialises in cognitive discourse analysis and the cognitive stylistics of contemporary literary texts. She co-authored *The Discourse of Reading Groups: Integrating Cognitive and Sociocultural Perspectives* (Routledge, 2016) and *Contemporary Stylistics: Language, Cognition, Interpretation* (Edinburgh University Press, 2018). She also co-edited *The Cambridge Handbook of Stylistics* (Cambridge University Press, 2014).

Introduction

Christopher Hart

Throughout the twentieth century, predominant models of language have viewed the language system (langue, competence) as something that can be studied independently of language use or practices (parole, performance). In Generative Linguistics, language is treated as an instrument of computational thought rather than an instrument of communication (Chomsky 1965). In this tradition, linguistic knowledge, reduced to a set of syntactic 'rules', is seen as biologically preordained, represented in the mind by a dedicated language 'module' (Chomsky 1986; Pinker 1994; Pinker and Jackendoff 2005). In the twenty-first century, Cognitive Linguistics presents a radical revision of linguistic theory in which language is seen as usage-based and experientialist. The primary object of investigation in Cognitive Linguistics, however, has remained the language system, with a focus on lexical and grammatical phenomena, rather than realisations of that system in texts and discourse.

To say that language is usage-based is to say that the structures and organising principles that constitute a speaker's linguistic knowledge emerge through language use. Linguistic structure develops in the way it does to fulfil, and is therefore reflective of, the communicative needs of speakers (Givón 1979). From this perspective, alternative linguistic formulations are functional in communicating different meanings. To say that language is experientialist, in Cognitive Linguistics, is to claim that language is simultaneously embodied and socio-culturally relative. Many of the meanings associated with linguistic forms develop pre-linguistically out of the experiences we have with our bodies and our interactions with, and observations of, the physical environment and are only later co-opted by language (Johnson 1987). Other meanings associated with linguistic forms are more encyclopaedic, derived from experiences we have as members of a particular culture or community of speakers (Fillmore 1982; Lakoff 1987).

From these basic epistemological commitments, a number of significant corollaries arise (Croft and Cruse 2004). For example, it follows that the language system is not represented by a dedicated language module. Rather, language is distributed, exploiting multiple extant cognitive systems. It also follows that the processes involved in language are not special to language. Rather, language makes use of underlying cognitive processes that are also found to function in other domains, like memory, reason and perception. Many of these processes are conceptual in nature. The structures and processes of language, accordingly, are not purely propositional or computational in form but conceptual and imaginative. Moreover, since the same conceptual processes seem to account for meaningful distinctions at different levels of linguistic description – phonological, semantic, syntactic – it further follows that language itself should not be treated as modular, made up of specific sub-components representing phonology, the lexicon, grammar and so on.

A number of conceptual processes are identified as relevant for language. These include categorisation, metaphor, schematisation, selective attention, figure-ground segregation, point of view and deixis. These processes are what structure the meanings associated with linguistic expressions and thus, when different linguistic expressions are selected in discourse, serve to *construe* the designated situation in particular ways. When described in relation to language, these conceptual processes are therefore referred to as 'construal operations' (Croft and Cruse 2004; Langacker 2008).

The notion of construal is a cornerstone of Cognitive Linguistics and what makes Cognitive Linguistics particularly amenable to text and discourse analysis, where it can shed light on the impact that textual choices have on readers' experiences. Construal refers to our 'manifest ability to conceive and portray the same situation in alternate ways' (Langacker 2013: 45). The role of construal in language is most obvious when more than one linguistic formulation is truth-conditionally licensed to describe the same situation. The classic example is deixis. The two sentences in (1) are truth-conditionally synonymous yet clearly they are different in meaning. (1a) construes the scene from inside the building while (1b) construes the scene from outside the building. In other words, the verb choices encode a contrast in perspective or point of view.

(1) a. The man came into the building
    b. The man went into the building

Deixis is just one example of construal, which is in fact ubiquitous in language. Indeed, every aspect of a sentence, from its morphological inflections to its lexical content and syntactic structure, involves construal, such that 'whenever we utter a sentence, we unconsciously structure every aspect of the experience we intend to convey' (Croft and Cruse 2004: 40). From this perspective, then, language is seen as a set of prompts for the construction of meanings which, configured through different construal operations, are jointly attended to in successful instances of communication. The conceptualisations evoked by language usages are semantically rich, dynamic and intersubjectively shared representations of the target situation.

Because the construal operations involved in language are general features of conceptualisation, and therefore manifested in other cognitive domains like memory, reason and perception, semantic characterisations in Cognitive Linguistics are heavily influenced by general psychological research in these areas. For example, Lakoff's (1987) work on lexical semantics is inspired by Prototype Theory (Rosch 1975, 1978) in cognitive psychology, which shows that people categorise objects in their environment in graded rather than absolute ways, with some objects treated as more central members of a category than others. In language, graded categorisation shows up in the meaning of words and accounts for sense relations like hyponymy and polysemy. Similarly, conceptual approaches to grammar (Langacker 1987; Talmy 1983) are motivated by research in Gestalt psychology (Koffka 1935), which seeks to explain the principles of visual perception. Two key principles concern our ability to discern from the world around us single complex objects, distinct from other objects, and our tendency to organise objects into figure-ground relations. Conceptual approaches to grammar argue that language exhibits the same principles, realised through construal operations of schematisation and figure-ground segregation. For example, in expressing spatial relations or motion events, language not only distinguishes two objects but selects one object as the *figure* whose location or movement is described relative to the other, the *ground* (Talmy 1983). For example, in (1) 'the man' is the figure while 'the building' is the ground. Which object is selected as figure and which is selected as ground seems to be based on a number of objective properties like relative size and mobility. Croft and Cruse (2004) organise the construal operations involved in language with respect to four general areas of psychological experience: (i) attention/salience; (ii) judgement/comparison; (iii) perspective/situatedness; (iv) constitution/gestalt.

These construal operations have been proposed to account for a wide range of linguistic phenomena and investigated in detail across different research programmes in Cognitive Linguistics. Several distinct programmes can be identified, including Cognitive Grammar (Langacker 1987, 1991, 2008), Conceptual Semantics (Talmy 2000), Conceptual Metaphor Theory (Lakoff and Johnson 1980, 1999), Frame Semantics (Fillmore 1982, 1985) and

Mental Spaces and Conceptual Blending Theory (Fauconnier 1994, 1997; Fauconnier and Sweetser 1996; Fauconnier and Turner 2002).

Despite the usage-based commitment of Cognitive Linguistics, analyses in these programmes have typically only been made of invented examples that do not extend beyond the level of the sentence and which are decoupled from any specific context of use. As Stockwell (2000: 515) has observed: 'the common method of discussion in Cognitive Linguistics is to examine individual sentences asocially'. However, this does not reflect the way language is really used. Real language usages occur in discourse, as part of texts.

At this point, a note is needed on the terms 'discourse' and 'text'. Discourse has multiple definitions coming from different disciplines across the arts and social sciences. In linguistics, discourse is most commonly understood as the dynamic, unfolding activity of producing and interpreting language in context. Text is the material product or 'trace' of that process (Brown and Yule 1983). Texts, therefore, represent (constellations of) attested language usages which are bound together by principles of cohesion and coherence and tied to particular occasions. Outside of theoretical linguistics, discourse is seen as more than just a verbal activity; every act of discourse is seen not only as a linguistic practice but as a form of social or cultural practice too (Fairclough 1989).

Texts and discourse, then, are always spatio-temporally situated but they are also always socio-culturally situated, where the contexts in which discourse takes place extend beyond the immediate situational coordinates of 'here' and 'now' to incorporate the wider institutional settings and the shared systems of knowledge, beliefs, values, norms, expectations and conventions that lie behind discourse (Flowerdew 2014) and where the texts produced in discourse instantiate different genres – recognised communicative activity types, such as poetry, prose or news reporting (Swales 1990). As socio-culturally situated language instances, texts are both reflective and reifying. Texts are constituted by and constitutive of the social contexts and communicative genres in which they are produced (Fairclough 1989).

Discourse does feature in cognitive linguistic theories. For example, Mental Spaces Theory (Fauconnier 1994, 1997) offers a model of how meaning is constructed and managed in ongoing discourse and specifically aims to account for discourse problems like reference, presupposition and counterfactuality. Langacker (2001) explicitly addresses the relationship between expressions in usage events and their structures as characterised by Cognitive Grammar. Here, Langacker identifies two forms of context necessarily apprehended in discourse as part of the ongoing process of conceptualisation: (i) the 'ground', comprising the speech event, the speaker and the hearer; and (ii) the 'current discourse space', comprising 'those elements and relations construed as being shared by the speaker and hearer as a basis for communication at a given moment in the flow of discourse' (p. 144). In both theories, however, discourse is conceived primarily only as the highest rank level of linguistic structure. That is, as language 'above the sentence'. Discourse is seen as a dynamic unfolding verbal activity but it is not seen as a form of social or cultural practice. In Langacker's treatment, context remains an abstract theoretical construct. Authentic textual material, produced in real social contexts and representing specific communicative genres, is not analysed.

The focus in Cognitive Linguistics on non-attested examples places it, somewhat ironically, in the same precarious position as Generative Linguistics, where the models of language it espouses may only account for highly idealised instances, which have been invented for the purpose of illustrating a particular theoretical point, and may not provide any analytical handle on the way people actually speak or write in genuine communicative encounters. Where better, then, to test the viability of cognitive linguistic theories, as models of natural language, than in analyses of authentic texts and discourse? If a linguistic model or framework works in accounting for natural language usages then that in itself is evidence to support the validity of the model. Of course, the linguistic data analysed in this volume can hardly be described as 'natural' in one sense of the term – the texts investigated involve highly creative, carefully crafted, multi-authored, institutionally or sometimes computer-mediated forms of language use. However, the data does represent real language usages produced and interpreted as part of communicative activities that seem to come naturally to humans. Moreover, there are no grounds on which to postulate a specialised cognitive capacity for literary or political language that is distinct from our capacity for 'everyday' talk. Rather, literary, political and other forms of genre-specific language rely on the same underlying mechanisms as 'ordinary' language. Their study can therefore reveal something about the human linguistic capacity in general.

In this way, Cognitive Linguistics and applied forms of Cognitive Linguistics enter into a dialogue with one another. Cognitive linguistic approaches to text and discourse can shed light on the utility of particular frameworks when they are applied to authentic textual data and feed back theoretical refinements and methodological innovations which emerge through empirical analyses. Many of the chapters in this volume contribute to Cognitive Linguistics in this way.

Frameworks in Cognitive Linguistics are now increasingly extended to analyse texts and discourse in different social contexts and communicative genres (e.g. Dancygier 2015, 2017; Dancygier et al. 2012; Dirven et al. 2003). And some frameworks have been developed specifically with textual analysis in mind (Chilton 2004; Werth 1999). Much of this work is carried out in the traditions of stylistics (Dirven et al. 2007; Gavins 2013; Gavins and Steen 2003; Giovanelli and Harrison 2018; Harrison 2017; Harrison et al. 2014; Nuttall 2018; Semino and Culpeper 2002a; Stockwell 2002, 2009a) and critical discourse analysis (Chilton 2004; Hart 2010, 2011, 2014; Hart and Lukeš 2007; Koller 2004, 2005a; Musolff 2004, 2006, 2012). Indeed, realising Turner's (1991: vii) pre-emption that 'humanistic studies will be centred once again upon the study of the human mind', cognitive stylistics and cognitive critical discourse analysis (CDA) now stand as important strands of applied Cognitive Linguistics research, which receive independent entries in recent handbooks and companions representing the state of the art in the field (Harrison and Stockwell 2014; Hart 2015a; Koller 2014; Stockwell 2015).

Stylistics and CDA share a common ancestry with both having roots in the forms of literary criticism and critical linguistics pioneered by Roger Fowler (Fowler 1977, 1986, 1991; Fowler et al. 1979), for whom it was Halliday's systemic functional linguistics that provided a model for systematically describing the way texts create meaning. In the preface to *Linguistics and the Novel*, for example, Fowler (1977: ix) noted:

> Halliday's 'functional' approach encourages us to think about *why* a language-user chooses one sentence-structure rather than an alternative, and Halliday provides some valuable terminology for our answers to such questions. I will be using these modes of linguistic description to focus particularly on the ways individual sentences add up to a larger textual shape.

However, in the years that have since intervened, stylistics and CDA have developed in divergent directions. While taking context seriously, stylistics has remained focused on the text and committed to linguistic methods of analysis. CDA, by contrast, has become more concerned with contextual aspects of discourse and less interested in textual analysis per se, with linguistic theory, as a result, taking something of a back seat (Jeffries 2010). Cognitive stylistics and cognitive CDA represent a convergence once again of these two fields, with Cognitive Linguistics providing the common toolkit for close, linguistically motivated, textual analysis.[1] Indeed, in their cognitive guises, stylistics and CDA share much in the way of common ground and researchers in one stand to benefit from analyses and advances made within the other.

Epistemologically, cognitive stylistics and cognitive CDA inherit from Cognitive Linguistics a view of language as usage-based and experientialist. They thus aim to account for meaning construction in discourse in terms of general psychological processes in a way that is reflective of principles in contemporary cognitive science. The embodied basis of language, its distributed nature in cognition, and the role of metaphor and other imaginative processes in language understanding are all central to both cognitive stylistics and cognitive CDA. What is 'cognitive' about cognitive stylistics and cognitive CDA, then, is a principled concern for the mental processes at work when we encounter and experience texts.

Theoretically, both cognitive stylistics and cognitive CDA apply the same frameworks and theoretical constructs sourced from Cognitive Linguistics, including image schemas, profiling and other attentional and perspectival phenomena, frames, conceptual metaphors, and mental spaces or worlds, to account for the way that texts create meanings for their readers. Departing from Cognitive Linguistics, however, both cognitive stylistics and cognitive CDA use these notions to account for the 'higher-level' effects of language usages on readers' experiences, whether these are literary, rhetorical or ideological effects.

The earliest and most prominent forms of textual analysis based in Cognitive Linguistics applied Lakoff and Johnson's (1980) Conceptual Metaphor Theory (CMT) or Fauconnier and Turner's (2002) development of CMT in 'Blending' or 'Conceptual Integration' Theory (e.g. Chilton 1996; Dirven et al. 2003; Freeman 2002; Hamilton 2002; Koller 2004; Musolff 2004; Santa Ana 2002; Semino 2002, 2006; Steen 2002; Turner 1991, 1996). Metaphor theory remains a central feature of cognitive linguistic text and discourse analysis and figures comprehensively in this volume in chapters by Elena Semino, Laura Filardo-Llamas, and Veronika Koller and Josie Ryan. However, as noted by Dirven et al. (2003: 4), Cognitive Linguistics has more strings to its bow than its know-how on metaphor. Also of notable significance, playing a prominent role in the development of cognitive stylistics especially, but also applied in cognitive CDA, is Text World Theory (Gavins 2007; Werth 1999). Text World Theory, briefly, is a cognitive model of discourse processing, the key postulate of which is that the scenes and states-of-affairs described in a text are represented in the mind by different 'worlds' made up of 'world building elements'. As discourse unfolds, and prompted by certain textual triggers, readers dynamically switch between relevant worlds. Text World Theory has much in common with Chilton's (2004) Discourse Space Theory developed in cognitive CDA. According to Discourse Space Theory, discourse establishes an abstract, deictically anchored, three-dimensional mental space. As discourse unfolds, readers reconstruct the 'discourse-world' envisioned by the text by positioning textual elements at locations in this mental space along three axes – space, time and modality – relative to a deictic centre. Text World Theory and Discourse Space Theory have been successfully applied to account for meaning construction and various literary and ideological effects in a range of discursive contexts and genres (e.g. Cap 2013; Cruickshank and Lahey 2010; Dunmire 2011; Filardo-Llamas 2010, 2013, 2015; Gavins 2000, 2013; Hart 2014; Hidalgo Downing 2000; Nuttall 2017; Semino 1995, 1997). In this volume, analyses of worlds and spaces feature in chapters by Joanna Gavins and Sara Whiteley, Jeremy Holland, Laura Filardo-Llamas and Sam Browse. More recently, key notions in Langacker's (1987, 1991, 2008) Cognitive Grammar, including action chain models, dominion, profile-base relations, scanning, and viewing arrangements, have been extended to account for various aspects of textuality in both literary and political genres (Harrison 2017; Harrison et al. 2014; Hart 2013, 2014, 2015b; Marín Arrese 2011; Nuttall 2018; Stockwell 2009b, 2014). In this volume, analyses based on concepts in Cognitive Grammar are presented by Peter Stockwell, Chloe Harrison, Sam Browse and Christopher Hart.

Methodologically, cognitive stylistics and cognitive CDA both proceed in a way that can be characterised as 'artful science' (Stockwell 2015). Semino and Culpeper define cognitive stylistics as follows:

> Cognitive stylistics combines the kind of explicit, rigorous and detailed linguistic analysis of literary texts that is typical of the stylistics tradition with a systematic and theoretically informed consideration of the cognitive structures and processes that underlie the production and reception of language. (2002b: ix)

Exactly the same characterisation could be offered of cognitive CDA replacing 'literary texts' with 'political texts' and 'the stylistics tradition' with 'the CDA tradition'. Cognitive stylistics and cognitive CDA are scientific in so far as they deal with quantifiable and measurable effects of textuality on cognition. They therefore adhere to general methodological principles of science. These include: (i) the object of investigation (whether it is a textual feature or a textual effect) must exist or potentially exist so that it can be subject to analysis; (ii) analyses must be motivated, that is conducted against a theoretical background that gives cause to the investigation; (iii) analyses must be systematic and rigorous, exploiting theoretical frameworks faithfully and consistently; (iv) analyses must be supported by evidence; and (v) analyses must be transparent such that they are either replicable or refutable. At the same time, however, Cognitive stylistics and cognitive CDA are artful or humanistic endeavours. Analyses remain exercises in interpretation which rely on the researcher's own engagement with the material in question, as well as their own knowledge and understanding of the contexts behind it, in order to deal with effects that are subjective, often difficult to characterise, and perhaps only accessible by introspection (Stockwell 2015: 441).[2]

Cognitive stylistics and cognitive CDA have also evolved in parallel new directions, reflecting new empirical trends in Cognitive Linguistics (Gonzalez-Marquez et al. 2007). For example, in both it is now common to find corpus linguistic techniques deployed in evidence of one's analyses (O'Halloran 2007; Stockwell 2014; Stockwell and Mahlberg 2015). In this volume, such an approach can be seen in chapters by Peter Stockwell and, to a lesser extent, Veronika Koller and Josie Ryan. Cognitive stylistics and cognitive CDA have also begun to exploit empirical methods in various kinds of reception study. This work tends to fall into one of two paradigms: using experimental methods to collect reader response data 'in the lab' (e.g. Fuoli and Hart 2018; Hart 2018a, 2018b) or using more ethnographic methods to obtain naturalistic response data from (internet) discussion groups (e.g. Nuttall 2015, 2017; Whiteley 2011).[3] In this volume, these approaches are reflected in the chapters by Christopher Hart and Sam Browse respectively. All three methodological orientations are regarded as empirical because they seek to evidence claims about reader responses using data (Whiteley and Canning 2017: 78).

Perhaps, then, the primary difference between cognitive stylistics and cognitive CDA lies in the type of textual material analysed. While the former tends to focus on texts that belong to literary genres, such as poetry, prose and drama, the latter is concerned with texts that can broadly be characterised as political, including political speeches, parliamentary debates and hard news reports. Even here, though, we are on slightly shaky ground, for what counts as a 'literary' text and what counts as a 'political' text is open to question. Some texts, such as protest songs, bear features associated with both literary and political genres. It is no coincidence that in this volume, Laura Filardo-Llamas' chapter analysing Bruce Springsteen's 'The Rising' occurs around the midway point, marking a transition from ostensibly non-political to political data. There are also, of course, great swathes of text-types out there, from recipes (Fischer 2017) to religious ceremonies (Chilton and Cram 2018), which do not typically fall within the purview of either cognitive stylistics or cognitive CDA but which can nevertheless be informedly analysed from a Cognitive Linguistics perspective. For these reasons, I would prefer to see cognitive stylistics and cognitive CDA as part of a broader approach to text and discourse analysis emerging within Cognitive Linguistics.

This volume brings together nine original case studies which together serve to showcase and celebrate this budding form of applied Cognitive Linguistics research. The nine chapters target a wide range of text genres including novels, poems, health fora discussion threads, holiday guestbook entries, prayers, political songs, hard news reports and opinion pieces. Extending Cognitive Linguistics to text and discourse analysis, the chapters not only contribute new insights into the workings of linguistic and conceptual features like metaphor, transitivity or event-structure, viewpoint, deixis and other attentional or perspectival phenomena but also help to shed light on the more elusive, epiphenomenal features of language such as a text's ambience, atmosphere, tone, resonance, valence, power, ideology or persuasiveness. The volume, further, takes new strides in cognitive text analysis by exploiting experimental and ethnographic methods to empirically investigate readers' reception of, and resistance to, texts. This volume, then, is intended to represent the state of the art in the rapidly expanding area of cognitive linguistic text and discourse analysis. What the nine chapters have in common is (i) an interest in some specific feature of language and/or textuality; (ii) a focus on a specific social context and/or communicative genre; (iii) a concern for the cognitive processes involved in the way texts create meaning; (iv) a commitment to the general principles of Cognitive Linguistics; and (v) a claim that frameworks in Cognitive Linguistics are particularly well-placed to account for processes of meaning construction in texts and discourse.

Of course, this is not to claim that the volume is without limitations or that the field itself is without scope for continued development. Most strikingly, in this volume, all of the texts analysed are produced in English. It is clearly important that future work in cognitive linguistic text analysis covers languages other than English and, further, considers culturally situated communicative activities that extend beyond Western genres. Another limitation is that the textual material analysed is all restricted to the linguistic modality. Theories in Cognitive Linguistics have been extended to account for processes of meaning construction in encounters with multimodal texts (e.g. El Refaie 2003; Forceville and Urios-Aparisi 2009; Gibbons 2012, 2016; Hart 2017; Koller 2005b; Pleyer and Schneider 2014). Unfortunately, however, this work is not represented here.

Finally, cognitive linguistic approaches to text and discourse analysis depend on, and must be responsive to, the most recent research in Cognitive Linguistics. As Cognitive Linguistics continues to evolve, then, so too must cognitive linguistic approaches to text and discourse analysis. One recent finding in Cognitive Linguistics pertains to the role of 'simulation' in language understanding. In line with principles of embodiment, it has been found that we understand language by running a perception- or motor-based mental simulation of the scenes or actions described in sentences (Bergen 2012; Gibbs 2006; Glenberg and Kaschak 2002; Stanfield and Zwaan 2001; Zwaan 2004). Simulation Semantics, in particular, seems to offer new insights into the way that texts create meanings for their readers (Hart 2016). Future work in cognitive linguistic text and discourse analysis will need to incorporate this newly flourishing framework.

Outline of Chapters

In Chapter 1, Peter Stockwell examines the subliminal sense of ambience created in Percy Shelley's celebrated poem 'A Summer Evening Churchyard'. Ambience covers a broad range of qualities such as sense of pace, urgency or suspense, feelings of immersion or alienation, impressions of atmosphere, tone and poignancy, and intuitions of fear, dread, foreboding or joy, optimism and satisfaction. Drawing primarily on Cognitive Grammar, Stockwell theorises that ambience arises as a function of 'dominion chaining'. Here, following Langacker, the meaning of a given word or larger unit extends beyond its immediate denotation to include a cascading set of associated concepts, feelings and experiences. For Stockwell, the ambience of a text arises cumulatively as these 'residues' are repeatedly accessed by semantically related reference points in the text.

In Chapter 2, Chloe Harrison similarly makes use of Cognitive Grammar to explore atmosphere and tone in Donna Tartt's 2013 novel *The Goldfinch*. Harrison focuses on one pivotal scene known as the 'gallery scene'. She shows how conflicting stylistic choices in specification, subjectification and action chain models within this passage contribute to feelings of fear, narrational disorientation and claustrophobia.

In Chapter 3, Joanna Gavins and Sara Whiteley analyse entries made in National Trust holiday cottage guestbooks. Their focus is on guestbooks as complex sites of social and linguistic interaction in which inscribers create transient identities for themselves and fellow holidaymakers who read the entries. Gavins and Whiteley work with Text World Theory to show how meaning is created – how experiences of the momentarily inhabited environment of the holiday cottage are conceptualised – between participants in this socially complex and temporally disjointed communicative situation.

In Chapter 4, Elena Semino analyses conceptualisations of pain in an online health forum for patients with Trigeminal Neuralgia. She focuses on metaphorical conceptualisations of pain indexed by similes containing the words 'feels like'. Semino identifies three types of metaphor in her data which lend themselves to different types of analysis. These are (i) embodied primary metaphors which can be accounted for within Conceptual Metaphor Theory; (ii) more creative metaphors that rely on cultural elaborations and which are best understood in terms of Conceptual Blending Theory; and (iii) metaphors in which the source domain is less familiar than the target or which give rise to implausible scenarios. This third type, Semino argues, presents a challenge to standard cognitive linguistic accounts of metaphor which can be partially met by adopting a dynamic systems approach instead.

In Chapter 5, Jeremy Holland takes up and further develops Discourse Space Theory in an analysis of the Lord's Prayer as found in the Gospel according to Matthew. Holland's aim is to show how the internal scenes and episodes of a religious text are simulated by image-schematic structures operating inside a dynamic, deictically defined, three-dimensional mental space.

Chapter 6 bridges the stylistic and more critical analysis of text as Laura Filardo-Llamas explores the healing power of a politically motivated song: Bruce Springsteen's 'The Rising'. In common with Chapters 3 and 5, Filardo-Llamas uses a combination of Text World Theory and Discourse Space Theory to show how the complex layering of meaning within the text as well as the proximal/distal relations between elements in the text-world function to heal and energise audiences. Drawing further on Conceptual Metaphor Theory and Conceptual Blending Theory, Filardo-Llamas demonstrates the positive evaluations, energising forces and healing values evoked by spatial metaphors and religious imagery contained within the text.

In Chapter 7, Veronika Koller and Josie Ryan return to metaphor but in the context of overtly political discourse. Koller and Ryan investigate metaphors that appeared on the UK's most popular national news websites the day after the 2016 Brexit vote. They focus on spatial metaphors for the UK electorate and the political establishment, using a metaphor identification procedure to obtain their data. Metaphors retrieved are then subject to qualitative analysis where the most predominant spatial metaphors are found to construct 'divisions' and 'distances' both within the electorate and the establishment as well as between the two. Like Semino in Chapter 4, Koller and Ryan argue that standard theories of metaphor found in Cognitive Linguistics are not always able to satisfactorily account for usage patterns in their data. In order to better explain spatial metaphors in discourse, they further develop the notion of 'metaphor scenarios' to show how spatial and ontological metaphors interact at various levels.

Chapters 8 and 9 return to Cognitive Grammar. Chapters 8 and 9 also take new steps in cognitive text analysis by adopting mixed methods approaches which combine textual analysis with ethnographic and experimental methods respectively. In Chapter 8, Sam Browse investigates the critical reception of texts using concepts from Text World Theory and Cognitive Grammar. As part of this investigation, Browse conducts a kind of cognitive linguistic ethnography in which he analyses the responses (elicited by means of 'think-aloud' tasks, focus group discussions and interviews) of three participants to a section of a 2015 Conservative Conference speech by then British Home Secretary Theresa May. All three participants were municipal politicians and members of the Labour Party. Browse begins by developing a model of oppositional reading based in Text World Theory in which there is a clash between the proffered text-world and the pre-existing conceptual frames of critical audiences. He goes on to show some of the ways in which audiences resist representations in the proffered text-world. These fall into two general strategies: reject or reconstrue. The second type of resistance, for Browse, is the most interesting because it relates less to content and more to linguistic form. Resistance based on reconstrual, Browse shows, is neatly captured using concepts from Cognitive Grammar and in particular the notions of (re)scoping and (re)profiling.

Finally, in Chapter 9, Christopher Hart combines qualitative cognitive linguistic analysis based in Cognitive Grammar with experimental methods. As Bergen et al. (2007: 760) state: 'although cognitive linguistic work is based largely on introspection and text analysis, it provides many useful insights into language use and representation and serves as an extremely rich source for empirically testable potential functions of linguistic items'. Specifically, Hart investigates the ideological functions of transitive versus reciprocal verbs in news reports of violence at political protests. He begins by arguing that the action chain schemas encoded by transitive versus reciprocal verbs are further construed from contrasting viewpoints. He then reports an experiment in the form of a sentence–image matching task which verifies this hypothesis. Results of this experiment show that the actions encoded by transitive verbs are construed along the sagittal axis while the actions encoded by reciprocal verbs are construed along the transversal axis. Differences in information sequence within reciprocal verb constructions are further shown to result in alternative left–right configurations along the transversal axis. From here, Hart speculates as to the ideological significance of these relative spatial orientations and values, drawing on theories of embodied valence, visual semiotics and Conceptual Metaphor Theory. To show that viewpoint is a semiotically significant factor encoded in the meanings of transitive and reciprocal verbs, Hart reports two further experiments which demonstrate convergence between ideological effects for viewpoint in both language usages and images which, by the hypothesis, are congruent.

Notes

1. Some authors prefer the label cognitive poetics in place of cognitive stylistics. However, there does not seem to be any discernible difference in what the two labels signify (Jeffries and McIntyre 2010: 126; Semino and Culpeper 2002b: x). It should also be noted that in both stylistics and critical discourse analysis there are broader 'cognitive' trends which are not based in Cognitive Linguistics (e.g. Tsur 1992; van Dijk 1998). Here, I use 'cognitive' as a modifier to denote areas of applied linguistics approached specifically from the perspective of Cognitive Linguistics (cf. 'Cognitive Sociolinguistics' (Pütz et al. 2014)).
2. Not that introspection should be dismissed as 'unscientific'. Defined as 'conscious attention directed by a language user to particular aspects of language as

manifest in her own cognition' (Talmy 2007: xii), introspection has been central in the development of Cognitive Linguistics and remains its dominant methodology. It is particularly apposite in textual analysis where, as Stockwell (2015: 442) points out, the articulated recount of a reading experience is to all practical purposes the reading in hand. On this basis, analyses arrived at by introspection can be counted as a form of empirical evidence (ibid.). This is even more so the case when the same introspective experiences are shared by multiple readers. Introspection can also be confirmatory where predictions made via systematic linguistic analysis can be compared with the 'sense' one has of a text to see if they match.

3 Steen (2002) is an early empirical approach to cognitive stylistics investigating reader recognition of and response to metaphors.

References

Bergen, B. (2012). *Louder than Words: The New of Science of How the Mind Makes Meaning*. New York: Basic Books.
Bergen, B., Lindsay, S., Matlock, T. and Narayanan, S. (2007). Spatial and linguistic aspects of visual imagery in sentence comprehension. *Cognitive Science* 31 (5): 733–64.
Brown, G. and Yule, G. (1983). *Discourse Analysis*. Cambridge: Cambridge University Press.
Cap, P. (2013). *Proximisation: The Pragmatics of Symbolic Distance Crossing*. Amsterdam: John Benjamins.
Chilton, P. (1996). *Security Metaphors: Cold War Discourse from Containment to Common House*. New York: Peter Lang.
Chilton, P. (2004). *Analysing Political Discourse: Theory and Practice*. London: Routledge.
Chilton, P. and Cram, D. (2018). Hoc est corpus: Deixis and the integration of ritual space. In P. Chilton and M. Kopytowska (eds), *Religion, Language and the Human Mind*. Oxford: Oxford University Press, pp. 407–36.
Chomsky, N. (1965). *Aspects of a Theory of Syntax*. Cambridge, MA: The MIT Press.
Chomsky, N. (1986). *Knowledge of Language: Its Nature, Origin and Use*. Westport: Praeger.
Croft, W. and Cruse, D. A. (2004). *Cognitive Linguistics*. Cambridge: Cambridge University Press.
Cruickshank, T. and Lahey, E. (2010). Building the stages of drama: Toward a Text World Theory account of dramatic play texts. *Journal of Literary Semantics* 39 (1): 67–91.
Dancygier, B. (2015). *The Language of Stories: A Cognitive Approach*. New York: Cambridge University Press.
Dancygier, B. (2017). Cognitive Linguistics and the study of textual meaning. In B. Dancygier (ed.), *The Cambridge Handbook of Cognitive Linguistics*. New York: Cambridge University Press, pp. 607–22.
Dancygier, B., Sanders, J. and Vandelanotte, L. (eds) (2012). *Textual Choices in Discourse: A View from Cognitive Linguistics*. Amsterdam: John Benjamins.
Dirven, R., Frank, R. and Pütz, M. (eds) (2003). *Cognitive Models in Language and Thought: Ideology, Metaphors and Meanings*. Berlin: Mouton de Gruyter.

Dirven, R., Polzenhagen, F. and Wolf, H. G. (2007). Cognitive Linguistics, ideology and critical discourse analysis. In D. Geeraerts and H. Cuckyens (eds), *The Oxford Handbook of Cognitive Linguistics*. Oxford: Oxford University Press, pp. 1222–40.

Dunmire, P. (2011). *Projecting the Future through Political Discourse*. Amsterdam: John Benjamins.

El Refaie, E. (2003). Understanding visual metaphor: The example of newspaper cartoons. *Visual Communication* 2 (1): 75–96.

Fairclough, N. (1989). *Language and Power*. London: Longman.

Fauconnier, G. (1994). *Mental Spaces: Aspects of Meaning Construction in Natural Language*. Cambridge: Cambridge University Press.

Fauconnier, G. (1997). *Mappings in Thought and Language*. Cambridge: Cambridge University Press.

Fauconnier, G. and Sweetser, E. (eds) (1996). *Spaces, Worlds and Grammar*. Chicago: The University of Chicago Press.

Fauconnier, G. and Turner, M. (2002). *The Way We Think: Conceptual Blending and the Mind's Hidden Complexities*. New York: Basic Books.

Filardo-Llamas, L. (2010). Discourse worlds in Northern Ireland: The legitimation of the 1998 agreement. In K. Hayward and C. O'Donnell (eds), *Political Discourse and Conflict Resolution: Debating Peace in Northern Ireland*. London: Routledge, pp. 62–76.

Filardo-Llamas, L. (2013). 'Committed to the ideals of 1916'. The language of paramilitary groups: The case of the Irish Republican Army. *Critical Discourse Studies* 10 (1): 1–17.

Filardo-Llamas, L. (2015). Re-contextualising political discourse: An analysis of shifting spaces in songs used as a political tool. *Critical Discourse Studies* 12 (3): 279–96.

Fillmore, C. (1982). Frame Semantics. In Linguistics Society of Korea (eds), *Linguistics in the Morning Calm*. Seoul: Hanshin Publishing Co., pp. 111–37.

Fillmore, C. (1985). Frames and the semantics of understanding. *Quaderni di Semantica* VI (2): 222–54.

Fischer, K. (2017). Cognitive Linguistics and Pragmatics. In B. Dancygier (ed.), *The Cambridge Handbook of Cognitive Linguistics*. Cambridge: Cambridge University Press, pp. 330–46.

Flowerdew, J. (ed.) (2014). *Discourse in Context*. London: Bloomsbury.

Forceville, C. and Urios-Aparisi, E. (eds) (2009). *Multimodal Metaphor*. Berlin: Walter de Gruyter.

Fowler, R. (1977). *Linguistics and the Novel*. London: Methuen.

Fowler, R. (1986). *Linguistic Criticism*. Oxford: Oxford University Press.

Fowler, R. (1991). *Language in the News Discourse and Ideology in the Press*. London: Routledge.

Fowler, R., Hodge, R., Kress, G. and Trew, T. (1979). *Language and Control*. London: Routledge and Kegan Paul.

Freeman, M. (2002). Cognitive mapping in literary analysis. *Style* 36: 466–83.

Fuoli, M. and Hart, C. (2018). Trust-building strategies in corporate discourse: An experimental study. *Discourse & Society* 29 (5): 514–52.

Gavins, J. (2000). Absurd tricks with bicycle frames in the text world of *The Third Policeman*. *Nottingham Linguistic Circular* 15: 17–33.

Gavins, J. (2007). *Text World Theory: An Introduction*. Edinburgh: Edinburgh University Press.
Gavins, J. (2013). *Reading the Absurd*. Edinburgh: Edinburgh University Press.
Gavins, J. and Steen, G. (eds) (2003). *Cognitive Poetics in Practice*. London: Routledge.
Gibbons, A. (2012). *Multimodality, Cognition and Experimental Literature*. London: Routledge.
Gibbons, A. (2016). Multimodality, cognitive poetics, and genre: Reading Grady Hendrix's novel *Horrorstör*. *Multimodal Communication* 5 (1): 15–29.
Gibbs, R. W. (2006). Metaphor interpretation as embodied simulation. *Mind & Language* 21 (3): 434–58.
Giovanelli, M. and Harrison, C. (2018). *Cognitive Grammar in Stylistics: A Practical Guide*. London: Bloomsbury.
Givón, T. (1979). *On Understanding Grammar*. New York: Academic Press.
Glenberg, A. and Kaschak, M. (2002). Grounding language in action. *Psychonomic Bulletin and Review* 9: 558–65.
Gonzalez-Marquez, M., Mittelberg, I., Coulson, S. and Spivey, M. J. (eds) (2007). *Methods in Cognitive Linguistics*. Amsterdam: John Benjamins.
Hamilton, C. (2002). Conceptual integration in Christine de Pizan's *City of Ladies*. In E. Semino and J. Culpeper (eds), *Cognitive Stylistics: Language and Cognition in Text Analysis*. Amsterdam: John Benjamins, pp. 1–22.
Harrison, C. (2017). *Cognitive Grammar in Contemporary Fiction*. Amsterdam: John Benjamins.
Harrison, C. and Stockwell, P. (2014). Cognitive poetics. In J. Littlemore and J. R. Taylor (eds), *The Bloomsbury Companion to Cognitive Linguistics*. London: Bloomsbury, pp. 218–33.
Harrison, C., Nuttall, L., Stockwell, P. and Yuan, W. (eds) (2014). *Cognitive Grammar in Literature*. New York: John Benjamins.
Hart, C. (2010). *Critical Discourse Analysis and Cognitive Science: New Perspectives on Immigration Discourse*. Basingstoke: Palgrave.
Hart, C. (ed.) (2011). *Critical Discourse Studies in Context and Cognition*. Amsterdam: John Benjamins.
Hart, C. (2013). Event-construal in press reports of violence in political protests: A cognitive linguistic approach to CDA. *Journal of Language and Politics* 12 (3): 400–23.
Hart, C. (2014). *Discourse, Grammar and Ideology: Functional and Cognitive Perspectives*. London: Bloomsbury.
Hart, C. (2015a). Discourse. In E. Dąbrowska and D. Divjak (eds), *Handbook of Cognitive Linguistics*. Berlin: Walter de Gruyter, pp. 322–45.
Hart, C. (2015b). Viewpoint in linguistic discourse: Space and evaluation in news reports of political protests. *Critical Discourse Studies* 12 (3): 238–60.
Hart, C. (2016). The visual basis of linguistic meaning and its implications for CDS: Integrating cognitive linguistic and multimodal methods. *Discourse & Society* 27 (3): 335–50.
Hart, C. (2017). Metaphor and intertextuality in media framings of the (1984-85) British miners' strike: A multimodal analysis. *Discourse & Communication* 11 (1): 3–30.
Hart, C. (2018a). Event-frames affect blame assignment and perception of aggression: An experimental case study in CDA. *Applied Linguistics* 39 (3): 400–21.

Hart, C. (2018b). 'Riots engulfed the city': An experimental study investigating the legitimating effects of fire metaphors in discourses of disorder. *Discourse & Society* 29 (3): 279–98.
Hart, C. and Lukeš, D. (eds) (2007). *Cognitive Linguistics in Critical Discourse Analysis: Application and Theory*. Newcastle: Cambridge Scholars Publishing.
Hidalgo Downing, L. (2000). *Negation, Text Worlds and Discourse: The Pragmatics of Fiction*. Stanford: Ablex.
Jeffries, L. (2010). *Critical Stylistics: The Power of English*. Basingstoke: Palgrave.
Jeffries, L. and McIntyre, D. (2010). *Stylistics*. Cambridge: Cambridge University Press.
Johnson, M. (1987). *The Body in the Mind: The Bodily Basis of Meaning, Imagination and Reason*. Chicago: The University of Chicago Press.
Koffka, K. (1935). *Principles of Gestalt Psychology*. New York: Harcourt, Brace.
Koller, V. (2004). *Metaphor and Gender in Business Media Discourse: A Critical Cognitive Study*. Basingstoke: Palgrave.
Koller, V. (2005a). Critical discourse analysis and social cognition: Evidence from business media discourse. *Discourse & Society* 16 (2): 199–224.
Koller, V. (2005b). Designing cognition: Visual metaphor as a design feature in business magazines. *Information Design Journal and Document Design* 13 (2): 136–50.
Koller, V. (2014). Cognitive Linguistics and ideology. In J. Littlemore and J. Taylor (eds), *The Bloomsbury Companion to Cognitive Linguistics*. London: Bloomsbury, pp. 234–52
Lakoff, G. (1987) *Women, Fire and Dangerous Things: What Categories Reveal about the Mind*. Chicago: The University of Chicago Press.
Lakoff, G. and Johnson, M. (1980) *Metaphors We Live By*. Chicago: The University of Chicago Press.
Lakoff, G. and Johnson, M. (1999). *Philosophy in the Flesh: The Embodied Mind and Its Challenge to Western Thought*. New York: Basic Books.
Langacker, R. W. (1987). *Foundations of Cognitive Grammar: Volume I: Theoretical Prerequisites*. Stanford: Stanford University Press.
Langacker, R. W. (1991). *Foundations of Cognitive Grammar: Volume II: Descriptive Application*. Stanford: Stanford University Press.
Langacker, R. W. (2001). Discourse in Cognitive Grammar. *Cognitive Linguistics* 12 (2): 143–88.
Langacker, R. W. (2008). *Cognitive Grammar: A Basic Introduction*. Oxford: Oxford University Press.
Langacker, R. W. (2013). *Essentials of Cognitive Grammar*. Oxford: Oxford University Press.
Marín Arrese, J. I. (2011). Effective vs. epistemic stance and subjectivity in political discourse: Legitimising strategies and mystification of responsibility. In C. Hart (ed.), *Critical Discourse Studies in Context and Cognition*. Amsterdam: John Benjamins, pp. 193–224.
Musolff, A. (2004). *Metaphor and Political Discourse: Analogical Reasoning in Debates about Europe*. Basingstoke: Palgrave.
Musolff, A. (2006). Metaphor scenarios in public discourse. *Metaphor and Symbol* 21 (1): 23–38.
Musolff, A. (2012). The study of metaphor as part of critical discourse analysis. *Critical Discourse Studies* 9 (3): 301–10.

Nuttall, L. (2015). Attributing minds to vampires in Richard Matheson's *I Am Legend*. *Language and Literature* 24 (1): 23–39.

Nuttall, L. (2017). Online readers between the camps: A Text World Theory analysis of ethical positioning in *We Need to Talk about Kevin*. *Language and Literature* 26 (2): 153–71.

Nuttall, L. (2018). *Mind Style and Cognitive Grammar: Language and Worldview in Speculative Fiction*. London: Bloomsbury.

O'Halloran, K. (2007). Critical discourse analysis and the corpus-informed interpretation of metaphor at the register level. *Applied Linguistics* 28 (1): 1–24.

Pinker, S. (1994). *The Language Instinct: How the Mind Creates Language*. New York: Harper.

Pinker, S. and Jackendoff, R. (2005). The faculty of language: What's special about it? *Cognition* 95: 201–36.

Pleyer, M. and Schneider, C. W. (2014). Construal and comics: The multimodal autobiography of Alison Bechdel's *Fun Home*. In C. Harrison, L. Nuttall, P. Stockwell and W. Yuan (eds), *Cognitive Grammar in Literature*. Amsterdam: John Benjamins, pp. 35–52.

Pütz, M., Robinson, J. A. and Reif, M. (eds) (2014). *Cognitive Sociolinguistics: Social and Cultural Variation in Cognition and Language Use*. Amsterdam: John Benjamins.

Rosch, E. (1975). Cognitive representations of semantic categories. *Journal of Experimental of Psychology* 104 (3): 192–233.

Rosch, E. (1978). Principles of categorisation. In E. Rosch and B. B. Lloyd (eds), *Cognition and Categorisation*. Hillsdale: Erlbaum, pp. 27–48.

Santa Ana, O. (2002). *Brown Tide Rising: Metaphors of Latinos in Contemporary American Public Discourse*. Austin: University of Texas Press.

Semino, E. (1995). Schema theory and the analysis of text worlds in poetry. *Language and Literature* 4 (2): 79–108.

Semino, E. (1997). *Language and World Creation in Poems and Other Texts*. London: Longman.

Semino, E. (2002). A cognitive stylistic approach to mind style in narrative fiction. In E. Semino and J. Culpeper (eds), *Cognitive Stylistics: Language and Cognition in Text Analysis*. Amsterdam: John Benjamins, pp. 95–122.

Semino, E. (2006). Blending and characters' mental functioning in Virginia Woolf's *Lappin and Lapinova*. *Language and Literature* 15 (1): 55–72.

Semino, E. and Culpeper, J. (eds) (2002a). *Cognitive Stylistics: Language and Cognition in Text Analysis*. Amsterdam: John Benjamins.

Semino, E. and Culpeper, J. (2002b). Foreword. In E. Semino and J. Culpeper (eds), *Cognitive Stylistics: Language and Cognition in Text Analysis*. Amsterdam: John Benjamins, pp. ix–vi.

Stanfield, R. A. and Zwaan, R. A. (2001). The effect of implied orientation derived from verbal context on picture recognition. *Psychological Science* 12: 153–6.

Steen, G. (2002). Metaphor in Bob Dylan's 'Hurricane': Genre, language and style. In E. Semino and J. Culpeper (eds), *Cognitive Stylistics: Language and Cognition in Text Analysis*. Amsterdam: John Benjamins, pp. 183–210.

Stockwell, P. (2000). Towards a critical Cognitive Linguistics. In A. Combrink and I. Biermann (eds), *Discourses of War and Conflict*. Potchefstroom: Potchefstroom University Press, pp. 510–28.

Stockwell, P. (2002). *Cognitive Poetics: An Introduction*. London: Routledge.
Stockwell, P. (2009a). *Texture: A Cognitive Aesthetics of Reading*. Edinburgh: Edinburgh University Press.
Stockwell, P. (2009b). The cognitive poetics of literary resonance. *Language and Cognition* 1 (1): 25–44.
Stockwell, P. (2014). Atmosphere and tone. In P. Stockwell and S. Whiteley (eds), *The Handbook of Stylistics*. Cambridge: Cambridge University Press, pp. 360-74.
Stockwell, P. (2015). Poetics. In E. Dąbrowska and D. Divjak (eds), *Handbook of Cognitive Linguistics*. Berlin: Walter de Gruyter, pp. 432–52.
Stockwell, P. and Mahlberg, M. (2015). Mind-modelling with corpus stylistics in *David Copperfield*. *Language and Literature* 24 (2): 129–47.
Swales, J. (1990). *Genre Analysis: English in Academic and Research Settings*. Cambridge: Cambridge University Press.
Talmy, L. (1983). How language structure space. In H. L. Pick and L. P. Acredolo (eds), *Spatial Orientation: Theory, Research, and Application*. New York: Plenum Press, pp. 225–82.
Talmy, L. (2000). *Toward a Cognitive Semantics*. Cambridge, MA: The MIT Press.
Talmy, L. (2007). Foreword. In M. Gonzalez-Marquez et al. (eds), *Methods in Cognitive Linguistics*. Amsterdam: John Benjamins. pp. xi–xxi.
Tsur, R. (1992). *Toward a Theory of Cognitive Poetics*. Amsterdam: North-Holland.
Turner, M. (1991). *Reading Minds. The Study of English in the Age of Cognitive Science*. Princeton: Princeton University Press.
Turner, M. (1996). *The Literary Mind: The Origins of Thought and Language*. Oxford: Oxford University Press.
van Dijk, T. A. (1998). *Ideology: A Multidisciplinary Approach*. London: Sage.
Werth, P. (1999). *Text Worlds: Representing Conceptual Space in Discourse*. London: Longman.
Whiteley, S. (2011). Text World Theory, real readers and emotional responses to *The Remains of the Day*. *Language and Literature* 20 (1): 23–42.
Whiteley, S. and Canning, P. (2017). Reader response research in stylistics. *Language and Literature* 26 (2): 71–87.
Zwaan, R. A. (2004). The immersed experiencer: Toward an embodied theory of language comprehension. In B. H. Ross (ed.), *The Psychology of Learning and Motivation, Volume 44*. New York: Academic Press, pp. 35–62.

1

Shelley's Dominion: Subliminal and Ambient Tonal Effects Across a Literary Work

Peter Stockwell

> Wealth and dominion fade into the mass
> Of the great sea of human right and wrong,
> When once from our possession they must pass;
> But love, though misdirected, is among
> The things which are immortal, and surpass
> All that frail stuff which will be – or which was.
> (Percy Bysshe Shelley, *Fragment: Amor Aeternus*, p. 549)

1. Subliminal Effects

One of the most characteristic but least analysed features of literary discourse is its capacity for inducing emotional, tonal and modal experiences at the lowest but diffused level of conscious awareness – the 'frail stuff' which fades slowly from memory, leaving a cumulative impression. While the impact of character and plot development might seem most prominent, the less definite, ambient qualities of literary texts remain significant: these include a sense of pace, urgency or suspense, a feeling of immersion or alienation, an impression of atmosphere and tone, an intuition of fear, dread, foreboding, inexorability, bleakness, melancholy, or joy, optimism, satisfaction, aptness or poignancy, for example. These subliminal effects are highly valued in literature, and are familiar to almost everyone who has ever read a poem or novel, but the precise workings of such effects have rarely been adequately described nor understood as systematically as narratological plot development nor characterisation. Both scholarly and ordinary conversations about such textured effects of literary works tend to rely on impressionistic metaphors and vague analogues to capture these attenuated, diffused sensations that are otherwise difficult to articulate.

It is worth pointing out that subliminal effects such as these in literary reading are merely a special case of the general phenomenon in which all discourse can generate subliminal experiences. Advertising, political, commercial, persuasive, journalistic and other kinds of texts convey ideological effects at a low or subliminal level of conscious awareness. Indeed, many of these kinds of discourse gain their power principally because of this capacity. A longstanding counter-argument to critical discourse analysis has been the claim that ordinary people do not read texts to the same level of heightened awareness as the analyst, and so critical discourse analysis (CDA) is accused of generating its own artefacts and perceiving ideology where none effectively exists (see Widdowson 1995, 1998, 2005; Breeze 2011). In fact, much of the detailed evidence in cognitive linguistics is at the subliminal or unconscious level. Taken together and cumulatively, however, these local patterns build up into a sustained and consistent effect that can be discerned and measured.

There is a twofold problem in attempting to capture such effects systematically. Firstly, the effects are highly subliminal – so close to the very boundary of conscious awareness that the experiential impact might only be felt cumulatively towards the end of the reading, or retrospectively, or even only upon the feeling being pointed out and given a name. In this last situation, the sense that the analytical comment and labelling has in fact created the effect itself is easy to conclude. Secondly, discourse analysis in various approaches has traditionally not been able to capture these effects for reasons of a deficiency in the theoretical frameworks. Subliminal effects are experiential in the mind and body of a reader or audience, and are manifest textually often as a highly diffused and rarefied patterning across the text in hand. Their inherently dual nature makes both a theoretical approach and a practical analysis problematic.

This chapter sets out an approach for exploring subliminal effects that focuses on a reading experience of a specific literary text: in this case, the effect is a sense of ambience (explained below) and the text is a canonically celebrated poem by Percy Shelley. On the theoretical hand, the effect is modelled drawing on cognitive linguistics. A degree of validity is claimed for this more systematic understanding, arising from the psychological claims made generally by cognitive linguistics (see Evans 2006; Langacker 2008). On the practical, empirical hand, evidence for validating the theoretical approach is sought by drawing on some simple corpus linguistic techniques. Taken together, the theoretical frame from cognitive linguistics and the empirical exploration from corpus linguistics can be regarded as an integrated application of cognitive poetics (Stockwell 2009). My argument overall is that subliminal effects in literary reading are a phenomenon that can only be adequately studied by drawing on this integrative approach. We need our current best understanding of language and mind, working together, to begin a systematic exploration of the power of subliminal and diffused textual patterns.

2. Ambience as Dominion Chain

Ambience, as theorised in cognitive poetics, is a cumulative combination of what is commonly experienced as *atmosphere* and *tone* in a literary work. Atmosphere relates principally to the felt quality of the world being depicted in the text, and tone pertains principally to the quality of voice of the author/narrator producing the depiction (Stockwell 2014, 2017). In cognitive linguistic terms, atmosphere is an effect of objective construal, whereas tone is an effect of subjective construal (Langacker 2008). Construal, in Cognitive Grammar here, is an interanimating phenomenon arising from the reader's subjective interpretation of an objective pattern in the text.

Both atmosphere and tone, of course, implicate the other, since a world requires a consciousness able to perceive and articulate it, and the tone of that articulation can only be conveyed by describing some tangible content. In practice, atmospheric text and tonal text are intricately woven together across a spectrum of ambient effects, and are not entirely separate at the interface. At the tonal end of ambience, the analysis can be conducted largely along traditional text-stylistic lines, with an exploration of modalisation, viewpoint, mind style and perspective, for example. The atmospheric end of ambience is a matter of the quality of world creation and maintenance, and is therefore best explored using cognitive poetic approaches to text-worlds and deictic relations between the reader's world and the setting of the text. At the interface and common to both atmosphere and tone is the importance of diction. The tone of lexical choices constitutes an attitudinal sense of register across a text; atmosphere is conveyed not only by the inventory of objects in the articulated world but also by the manner, connotations and associations of the lexical choices made to denote those objects.

Diction – or lexical choice – is the focus of ambience, then, for this analysis. The problem is that ambient effects are diffused across a text, so a traditional semantic account merely of denoted meanings will not sufficiently capture the delicate, rarefied and diffused impressions that are collectively felt as ambience. Even more problematically, a great deal of ambient effect is achieved when a text seems to gesture towards a set of descriptions either by association, allusively or obliquely – so the actual subliminal effect resides in what is *not* articulated, rather than what is actually lexicalised. How can we suggest a framework for exploring something which is both diffused and unsaid?

The problem can be resolved by appealing to the way several different disciplines deal with non-denotational meaning. My primary approach here

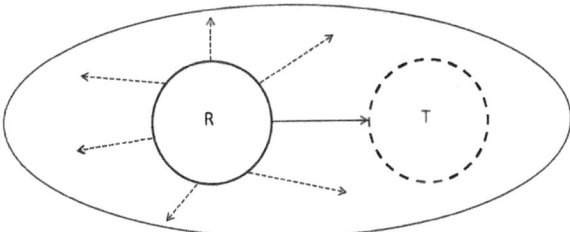

Figure 1.1 Dominion

is Cognitive Grammar (CG; Langacker 2008). CG addresses the question of how the effects of linguistic sequences can feel richer and more informative than the plain denotation of the words and syntactic forms that are presented. Furthermore, it has long been apparent in the field of psycholinguistics that readers and listeners can process linguistic phrases, clausal sequences and longer stretches of discourse far more rapidly and efficiently than can be explained by a simple step-by-step parsing of each incoming lexical element. Some sort of priming of expectations is clearly in operation if we are to explain human language processing: we do not read, evaluate, parse, interpret and denote every incoming word afresh – this would take too long. Instead, it is clear that incoming elements of language prime up certain expectations that restrict the possible meanings of subsequent incoming elements. In other words, we are ready for what is coming next, given a well-formed and coherent text. (Indeed, our sense of incoherence is dependent on this process as well.)

CG models this lexical priming using the concept of *dominion*. Any linguistic unit – such as a lexical item – creates a reference point placeholder in the mind. The instance of a word invokes the meanings of that word not simply in terms of a limited denotation, but an experiential set of the typical usages of that word in various different settings from memory. Every word – not only homophones and homonyms – possesses this rangy set of associated experiences in the mind of every language user. The full potential meaning of a reference point like a word or phrase resides in this large set of past possibilities, which might include not only the denoted meaning but also the feelings associated with the individual's experience of that word in previous encounters. Much of this set will be conventional and socially habitual, but quite a lot of it as well will be idiosyncratic and personal. Any single reference point, such as a word, will have a set of potential concepts attached to it, one of which will turn out to be the linguistic target that becomes manifest in the sequence. The set of possible connections culminating in the target of the reference point altogether constitute that reference point's dominion. Figure

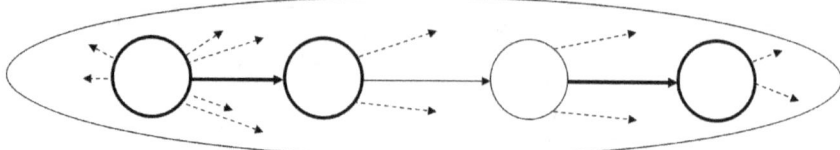

Figure 1.2 Dominion chaining

1.1 shows all of the possible meaningful but unrealised associations of the reference point, and the single association that is actualised by the target point.

This approach to understanding associated meanings below the level of denotation is clearly suggestive for thinking about unrealised, semi-conscious local meanings. If a dominion in this sense exists for each word, phrase or short sequence in a text, then it is reasonable to imagine a chaining of dominions as a reader works through a text. Figure 1.2 represents this graphically.

For each word or phrase, a set of primed meanings and associations is evoked, from which one thread is actualised by the subsequent text. In a cohesive and coherent text, the chain of dominions is likely to be closely semantically related, with threads that remain unrealised repeatedly primed but not articulated. It seems reasonable to propose that all of these unrealised dominion traces, especially if repeated, persist in the mind as the reader progresses through the text. Over a period, all of these micro-instances may well be cumulatively regarded as a macrostructural representation that characterises the unspoken background to the text. This corresponds to its ambience.

3. Mapping the Unarticulated: A 'Lost Wax' Technique

There is, of course, a challenge for the stylistician in locating and specifying what is not actually present on the surface of a text. This is compounded in corpus stylistics where software can only be asked to search for textual elements that exist. What we need to discover is the set of possible semantic associations that might accompany a word or phrase in most readers' minds, but which are not explicitly lexicalised in the text. Producing this for an individual reader, with their idiosyncratic associations and experiential meanings, is probably impossible, but I think we can approximate towards a culturally valid reading-in-common by generalising the problem to massive corpora of the English language (see Mahlberg et al. 2016). A large corpus is treated – for example by lexicographers and grammarians – as an idealisation of societal usage. Regarded in this way, we can treat a large general corpus of English as a proxy instrument for a common reading response.

Inspired by the 'lost wax' technique of metal casting, it is possible to imagine a corpus linguistic process by which the item for study is sacrificed in order to create a mould that approximates to the surrounding shape of the original item. The method can be set out as follows:

1. List the top keywords in the text or passage (set A).
2. Find those keywords in a general English language corpus.
3. Find the highest-occurring collocates of those keywords in the general corpus – this gives a diffused universal dominion chain for the target text (set B).
4. But we are only interested in the words which *do not* appear explicitly in the original target text or passage, so – using the set B list, find which of them also occur in the text or passage, and remove them from set B. Those that are left are set C.
5. Set C gives us the local dominion – the 'lost-wax' version of the text – and a list of unrealised but associated ambient words for the passage under analysis.

The unrealised words in set C constitute the ambient dominion for the target passage. Clearly this cloud of associations will also be psychologically prototyped for strength and weakness of association – certain associations will be personal, but many will be culturally shared; this more subtle semantic arrangement might show up in a more detailed collocation and frequency analysis. The lost wax technique is most effective for extended prose texts, for example as explored by Mahlberg et al. (2016) in relation to Dickensian ambience. Establishing a persisting and sustained consistent sense of ambience is most easily achieved in this sort of extended text such as a prose novel or short story. However, shorter lyric poetry can also achieve a quick power of ambience through intensely crafted linguistic patterning, and here the subliminal effect can be intuited for comparison and validation more conveniently.

4. Shelley's Ambience

The following poem was written by Shelley while visiting the English village of Lechlade in September 1815.

A Summer Evening Churchyard
Lechlade, Gloucestershire

The wind has swept from the wide atmosphere
Each vapour that obscured the sunset's ray;
And pallid Evening twines its beaming hair
In duskier braids around the languid eyes of Day:
Silence and Twilight, unbeloved of men,
Creep hand in hand from yon obscurest glen.

> They breathe their spells towards the departing day,
> Encompassing the earth, air, stars, and sea;
> Light, sound, and motion own the potent sway,
> Responding to the charm with its own mystery.
> The winds are still, or the dry church-tower grass
> Knows not their gentle motions as they pass.
>
> Thou too, aereal Pile! whose pinnacles
> Point from one shrine like pyramids of fire,
> Obeyest in silence their sweet solemn spells,
> Clothing in hues of heaven thy dim and distant spire,
> Around whose lessening and invisible height
> Gather among the stars the clouds of night.
>
> The dead are sleeping in their sepulchres:
> And, mouldering as they sleep, a thrilling sound,
> Half sense, half thought, among the darkness stirs,
> Breathed from their wormy beds all living things around,
> And mingling with the still night and mute sky
> Its awful hush is felt inaudibly.
>
> Thus solemnized and softened, death is mild
> And terrorless as this serenest night:
> Here could I hope, like some inquiring child
> Sporting on graves, that death did hide from human sight
> Sweet secrets, or beside its breathless sleep
> hat loveliest dreams perpetual watch did keep. (Shelley 1970: 524–5)

The poem regularly appears in popular collections of 'atmospheric' writing, such as the Poetry Foundation (www.poetryfoundation.org), Poemhunter (www.poemhunter.com), All Poetry (allpoetry.com) and many others. Indeed, the word 'atmosphere' occurs explicitly in the first line. Similarly, published literary critical work on the poem almost always notes its elegiac tone in the tradition most famously established by Thomas Gray's 'Elegy written in a country churchyard', written in 1750 (see Welburn 1986: 34: McGann 1998). Shelley's poem was first published in 1816 as one of twelve poems in the collection *Alastor, or The Spirit of Solitude*. Most literary scholarship that mentions the poem focuses on this context, on the place of the poem above in relation to the longer poem in the book, and to Shelley's own biography (Bloom and Edmundson 2009; West 2016). Other than noting its atmospheric and tonal qualities, however, there are no detailed accounts of precisely how the poem establishes its general ambience.

Applying the 'lost wax' technique as outlined above produces first a set of key words from the poem. There are several ways in which this could be done. A subjectively valid method might simply be to note down the most personally striking words or phrases across the poem and treat these as the 'set A' key ambient words: this introspective method would be the closest accordance to a personal intuition. A more socially generalisable method would be to use a comparison of all the words in the poem against a representative corpus of the English language, in order to see which words in the poem were key in the statistical sense used in corpus linguistics.

Accordingly, I tested out the keywords in the Shelley text against the British National Corpus (BNC; corpus.byu.edu/bnc), a collection of 100 million words from a range of genres from the late twentieth century. (It should be noted that this means that all steps that follow this method can only entail a modern reading of ambient effects in the poem, rather than one contemporaneous with Shelley – for which an early nineteenth-century reference corpus would be required.) Using the 'key words in context' (KWIC) tool, the search produced a table listing the 153 unique words in the poem, out of a total of 231 ('their', 'in' and 'from' appear five times each, for example). The table arranges the words by their keyness value: how unusual their occurrence is in the given text, compared with 'normal' usage across the BNC. Table 1.1 shows the top twenty-six values.

In the poem, the words 'their' and 'its' are unusually prominent, both in terms of their repeated use and their keyness compared with the language in general. Both signify possession or *part–whole* relationships, and both words are scattered across the whole text. Similarly, 'around' carries an image-schematic structure that signifies the close proximity of main element (figure or trajector) and secondary element (landmark). All three of these items show how the world-building elements of the poem (the noun phrases, mainly) are tightly interrelated and implicated closely with each other. The preposition 'among' has the same image-schematic structure. This pervasive effect can be seen in the fact that the long sentences feature a high number of specifying and locating prepositional phrases: aside from 'around', the poem includes five examples each of 'in', 'from' and 'of', three 'as' and two 'with'. This is a high density of prepositional phrases across the short text, and the effect is a highly grounded, spatially precise lyrical description. It might even be argued that it is significantly this density of prepositional positioning that encourages a perception of the poem as a strongly textured atmospheric piece of writing.

Of course, it is the accumulation of nouns themselves which build up the semantic associations around the poem (the 'set B' field). Here, the most statistically prominent are 'night', 'day', 'death', 'hand', 'silence', 'sleep', 'sound', 'spells' and 'stars'. These align quite well with my own,

No.	Hits	Keyness	Item
1	5	5.939	their
2	4	4.576	its
3	3	4.150	around
4	3	4.150	night
5	3	4.150	they
6	3	3.224	that
7	2	2.767	among
8	2	2.767	day
9	2	2.767	death
10	2	2.767	did
11	2	2.767	half
12	2	2.767	hand
13	2	2.767	like
14	2	2.767	own
15	2	2.767	silence
16	2	2.767	sleep
17	2	2.767	sound
18	2	2.767	spells
19	2	2.767	stars
20	2	2.767	sweet
21	2	2.767	whose
22	2	1.899	still
23	11	1.572	and
24	1	1.383	aerial
25	1	1.383	air
26	1	1.383	atmosphere

Table 1.1 Keyness words in Shelley's text

prior intuitive notes on striking nouns across the poem: the keyness tool picks up 'day' and 'silence' but does not notice the capitalised forms of these and 'Evening' and 'Twilight', which subjectively renders them as striking personifications.

The word 'night' is particularly salient, though it is important to notice that its three occurrences appear only in the last three stanzas. In the BNC, the qualities of *night* are quite low prototypical senses in the dominion: the most common associations are specifications of time such as 'last night', 'Saturday night', 'tomorrow night' and so on. Associations like 'dream' (at nineteenth collocate position), 'moonlit' (at fifty-six), 'starry' (fifty-nine), and 'windless' (208th) are relatively remote in the conventional dominion. However these are more like the senses used in the poem. The poem moves towards these *night* qualities by gradually dimming down the poem, not explicitly but by dominion association: from 'sunset', to 'pallid Evening', from 'beaming' to 'duskier', by diminishment from 'wide' to 'languid'. The quality of *night* is further developed from 'clouds of night' to 'still night' to 'serenest night'.

All of the nouns across the poem are as follows (in sequence):

> wind atmosphere vapour ray Evening hair braids eyes Day Silence Twilight men hand hand glen spells day earth air stars sea light sound motion sway charm mystery winds grass motions pinnacles shrine pyramids fire silence spells hues heaven spire height stars clouds night dead sepulchres sound sense thought darkness beds things night sky hush death night child graves death sight secrets sleep dreams watch

The qualifying or modifying items across the poem, up to the final stanza, are:

> wide sunset's pallid beaming duskier languid unbeloved obscurest departing potent dry church-tower gentle aereal sweet solemn dim distant lessening invisible thrilling half half wormy living still mute awful

The textual cohesion and interpretative coherence of the poem as a description of a churchyard at dusk can be seen clearly across these lists. It should not be a surprise to find that the diction of the poem is consistent in its dominion: after all, the topic of the scene remains constant. However, the effect of the density of consistent description is to build up an intense view of the twilight churchyard scene. This in itself has a sort of 'aura' effect, in that a word in the poem, like 'wind', that might have a particular set of dominion meanings in a different general context, instead takes on a particularly flavoured dominion by appearing specifically alongside, for example, 'vapour', 'braids', 'pallid', 'languid' and so on. In general modern English usage, for example, the BNC gives the most common collocates of *wind* as: 'rain', 'blowing', 'strong', 'cold', 'blew', 'direction', 'wind' itself, 'solar', 'blows', 'speed', with 'sea' at eleventh most common collocate. The first collocate in modern usage that also occurs in the poem is 'swept', at fifty-second position. From this set of collocations, it appears that the most prototypical sense of dominion for *wind* is its strength, storminess and power. Indeed, the first 130 collocations presented by the BNC involve violence and action. However, the poem alters the emphasis across the first two stanzas. The first line – 'The wind has swept' – matches the active prototypical dominion meaning quite well, but then the poem picks out less prototypical senses of the *wind* by slowing it down. The quietening of the wind is a less prototypical sense in *wind*'s dominion (the BNC has 'puff' at 133, 'whisper' at 144 and 'soughing' at 174). The poem activates this less prototypical area of *wind*'s dominion by shifting verb forms from fast associations to slower ones ('swept' – 'obscured' – 'twines' – 'creep'), by picking out a less prototypical dominion trace for *wind* ('breathe'

– 'responding'), and then ending with a stative verb form 'The winds are still', so that they have 'gentle motions'.

The movement from *wind* to *breath* aligns with the movement across the poem from the most encompassing perspective ('the wide atmosphere') to something much quieter, personal and intimate. From *breath*, the poem is able to shift subtly into whispering, hush and silence as if this is a natural progression, because there is a clear coherent dominion chaining involved across these. The overall ambient effect is that the wind has slowed and quietened, the perspective has narrowed from the wide landscape to the intimate graveyard, and the voices of personified abstractions are hushed and silenced.

5. Ambience as Message

The ultimate effect at the end of this dominion chain is of a silence that is palpable – a positive sense of absence that I have elsewhere described as a *lacuna* (Stockwell 2009). The subtlety of this is extremely delicate and difficult to articulate, leaving Shelley reliant on paradox: 'its awful hush is felt inaudibly'. In the final stanza, he deploys another lacuna, 'terrorless', to evoke and disarm the terrible feeling instantly. Indeed, the final stanza has a different ambience from the preceding poem. The qualifying and modifying items from this stanza contrast with those listed above for the preceding stanzas:

> mild terrorless serenest inquiring human sweet breathless loveliest perpetual

This set of items seems to instantiate a different dominion chain from those evoked up to this point. The ambient effect of the first four stanzas of the poem might be summarised as a movement from motion to stillness, from day through twilight to darkness, from a wide perspective to a precise one, from a social landscape to a personal grave-plot, from the sky above down to the earth below, from the personification of abstract qualities to actual bodies, and from noise to quietness. All of the outlines of dominion traces in the foregoing account represent the associative meanings and senses arising in set C from a reading of the poem. We arrive at the beginning of the final stanza in a graveyard that is quiet and peaceful, in a moment of contemplation and reflection, having been removed from the departing wider daylight world to this place and moment of 'awful hush'.

It is quite an achievement of the poem to have brought readers to this point in the graveyard without, I think, disruptively evoking creepiness, spookiness, fear or dread. These ambient effects were all certainly available in the dominion chains that might have been invoked through the poem up to this point. But I suggest that they are not generally primed for most readers because the poem has deployed ambient threads through the dominion chain that are calm and positive in quality, rather than negative or fearful. Certainly this is the most common reading attested in the online contexts that I cited above, where the poem is popularly commented on and discussed. The move from day to night in the setting of a graveyard might have been anxious, perhaps more for us in a post-gothic and urbanised society, but even, I think, for a modern reader, the feeling over the first four stanzas is one of calmness and restfulness.

I would like to argue, for the rest of this chapter, that Shelley's manipulation of many readers' subliminal senses of peace to this point is strategically important not only for the aesthetic pleasure it gives but also for the thematic message that the poem conveys. The perspectival sweep in from the general to the particular is a framing technique that strongly suggests that the focus of the scene is a microcosm and an emblem of the initial perspective. This movement across the poem is even prefigured itself in microcosm in the generic title ('A Summer Evening Churchyard') which is quickly followed by the highly specific cited location, 'Lechlade, Gloucestershire'. Literary critical discussions of the poem are almost always distracted by the biographical observation that Percy and Mary Shelley visited the church with friends while on a boating expedition up the Thames. The path through the graveyard is now called 'Shelley's Walk'. Such accounts rarely engage with the poem itself, or consider it as anything more than a lyrical reflection, or as being overshadowed by the longer poem, 'Alastor', with which it was published (Fraistat 1984).

According to Wroe (2011), the meaning of *night* for Shelley can be traced across his poetry, from earlier work like 'A Summer Evening Churchyard' to his later major writing. Night, in Shelley's writing, evokes not dread but access to the sublime, to a world of dreams and positive, idealistic visions. This certainly accords with the ambient movement from the wild, windy and rainy day at the beginning of the poem to the twilight and then dark churchyard, and indeed the even darker setting of the sepulchre and graves. These 'wormy beds' are not uncanny but are where the dead are restfully 'sleeping'. The calm and stillness of *night* in the poem is an essential part of its message that *night* is a time of revelation and deeper understanding.

We can discern evidence of this progression into revelatory night towards the end of the poem. As set out above, the ambient noise is turned down gradually to the point of 'awful hush' in the last line of the penultimate stanza. That this is a pivotal point in the poem is subtly signalled by the fact that the rhyme that ends this stanza ('mute sky ... inaudibly') is the only imperfect rhyme in the poem – even in Shelley's early nineteenth-century Sussex accent. (It is, of course, iconically neat that this only pararhyme occurs on the word 'inaudibly'.)

The final stanza itself is tonally different from the ambience of the previous part of the poem, as mentioned above, but it is also variant in its

Cognitive Grammar (terms that follow are from Langacker 2008). Here I want to demonstrate Shelley's alignment of the ambient progression with the text's use of grammatical construal. Up to this point in the poem, the scene itself is unpopulated by any living people, but the qualities of the scene have been highly animated and given apparent agency throughout. Initially this is conventional ('The wind has swept'), but it moves swiftly into a full personification: 'pallid Evening twines its beaming hair in duskier braids around the languid eyes of Day'. Similarly, 'Silence' and 'Twilight' are personified not only by the capitalisation but also by the fact that they are made the agents who 'Creep hand in hand' and are 'unbeloved'. These, and other aspects of the landscape, are given agent participant roles that are often further strengthened by being experiencer or mover roles as well: 'They breathe', 'Light, sound and motion own', 'Responding' and the 'dry church-tower grass Knows not'. At the same time, those elements that are being diminished or de-figured in attention are placed in patientive roles as they are removed from readerly consciousness: the clouds (vapours) and rays are swept by the wind and 'obscured', the 'beaming hair' becomes 'duskier', and Silence and Twilight creep away 'from yon obscurest glen'. Similarly, in the second stanza these patient grammatical roles are lexicalised iconically with the vocabulary of departure, increasing distance and diminishment: 'the departing day', 'the earth, air, stars, and sea', 'their gentle motions'.

In the middle stanza of the poem, there is an explicit switch from a construal pattern that seems objective and descriptive (though the metaphoricality of the animation is clearly implicitly perceptual by the narrating observer). Here, the vocative address ('Thou too, aereal Pile!') draws attention to the viewing perspective. This shift, in alignment with all of the aligned shifts already mentioned, moves from an objective construal to a subjective construal, and thus subtly indicates a move into the observing consciousness and ideological mind of the poet in the second half of the poem.

Up to this point, all the verbal action chains have been unmodalised: *swept, twines, Creep, breathe, own, are still, Knows not, point, Obeyest, Gather, are sleeping, stirs, is felt*. Of these, only the negated 'Knows' is not a directly forceful action chain, and even here the negating particle is diminished by being placed after the verb. The negation is also a neat normalisation of the personification up to this point, as if the shift to subjective construal is mirrored by an emerging self-consciousness that the first two stanzas have been too poetically overblown. It is literally true that the dry grass does not know anything, but the negation acts to draw attention to the positive absence of personification at this point. The effect is highly subtle, though, as also in the passive 'awful hush is felt', where the experiencing subject is ambivalent between the overhearing dead bodies sleeping or the observing poet. It is a transition point.

The final stanza introduces the first modalisation: 'Here could I hope'. It is also the first explicit mention of a subjectivity, and the general movement of the poem from distance to particular culminates in the proximal deictic 'Here'. The subjective construal in evidence in this part of the poem is further reinforced by the experiencer roles lexicalised with 'hope' and 'inquiring'. Furthermore the two remaining verbs that are subordinate to the poet's hope as we move into his interior thought each receive the auxiliary 'did': 'death did hide ... sweet secrets' and 'loveliest dreams ... did keep [watch]'. As action chains, the modal 'could' and the auxiliary 'did' both serve, to a greater or lesser extent, to block the straightforward transfer of energy along the action chain. Modalisation is a slowing factor on the grammatical construal; it deflects the construal of agency (Langacker 2008: 303–9), in the case of *could* to an unreal potential but positive future. 'Could', in the poem, has ambivalence, however, because of the nature of this obstructed construal. And this is the crux of the poem's subliminal meaning, I think.

The poem is generally taken as an atmospheric lyrical reflection and plain description. However, the ambient progressions as outlined in this chapter suggest a subliminal readerly positioning to the point at which a reader is potentially open to a revelatory moment. The subtlety of its articulation, however, renders this moment less than epiphanic, and more delicate and uncertain. The precursive 'Elegy' by Thomas Gray ends uncomplicatedly and uncompromisingly in 'The bosom of his Father and his God'. Shelley, of course, was a notorious atheist. One of his most famous acts was to arrive in Chamonix below the sublime and spiritual majesty of the Alps, and write (in Greek) in the hotel register next to his name: 'Democrat, humanitarian, atheist'. To guarantee the social outrage, he also added 'L'Enfer' (Hell) as his destination (see Jager 2010).

Given this biographical context, few have counted 'A Summer Evening Churchyard' as a comforting Christian or religious poem in itself, treating it instead as a plain lyrical description or even reading the ending as a ridicule or scorning of religious comfort ('like some inquiring child'). This is the writer who co-wrote *The Necessity of Atheism* (Hogg and Shelley 1811), after all, for which he was expelled from Oxford University. However, several have argued that even this tract is more agnostic than atheistic (Baker 1948; Magarian 1993; Bloom 2001), and indeed I think that the subliminal and delicate movement of Shelley's poem disposes a reader principally towards this more ambivalent meaning. The 'hope' that is presented at the end, though deflected by modalisation, morphological negation ('terrorless'), semantic negation ('hide', 'secrets') and ontological switch ('like some inquiring child'), is nevertheless softened, mild, sweet and ending in 'loveliest dreams'.

The comfort, calm and peace by the end of the poem are principally an effect of its ambience. Death, at the end, is left only suggestively personified: not capitalised, not highly agentive, with weak cognitive capacities 'mild' and 'terrorless', and in the end hidden 'from human sight'. Personification is replaced by a person ('I', 'child' and 'human'), though even here the definite child is rendered indefinite ('some') and is an unreal participant in a hoped-for modalised world. There are layers of subtle ambivalence all around this final stanza. The poem, throughout, draws on religious diction that surely has a subliminal associative dominion effect: supernatural senses of 'spells', 'charm', 'potent', and religious feelings from 'church-tower', 'shrine', 'obeyest', 'solemn spells', 'clothing in hues of heaven', 'spire', 'invisible', 'sepulchres', 'awful', 'solemnized' and 'perpetual watch'.

Of course, Shelley necessarily has to use lexical fields from religion when describing a church and its graveyard, and so the religious ambience is perhaps unavoidable – a necessary consequence of his choice of scene rather than his beliefs. Nevertheless, he chose the scene to depict, and he could have set it in a daytime atmosphere, a wedding, a christening, a picnic scene and so on. And the ambience, it seems to me, though subtle and subliminal and difficult to articulate, is definitely there.

6. Subliminal Effects at Large

In this chapter, I have traced the presence and possible effects of one type of subliminal patterning: ambience. Of course, there are many varieties of subliminal phenomena, ranging from the purely emotive and aesthetic through to sub-conscious effects on meaning. In the Shelley reading, above, I have tried to show how, in a case like this, the ambient sense that can simply be enjoyed can also serve to predispose a reader to construe the text in a particular meaningful way.

This has obvious applications more widely, not only in poetic, literary and other artistic texts. Persuasive and political discourse of all kinds often draws additional power from its subliminal effects. Where these are deployed with great technique – as in the Shelley example – the overall effect on the meaning, significance and impact on the audience can be exponentially greater than the simple denotational value.

The integration of approaches from critical discourse analysis, cognitive poetics and corpus linguistics goes some way to addressing the introspection problem in research on subliminality. The obvious problem is in validating a subjective sense that is difficult to articulate in your own experience in the first place. Introspective reflection is always necessarily an act of retrospection, but when even the initial cognition that is being recalled is sub-cognitive in some delicate, subtle way, the difficulty is obvious. How do you know that the general, accumulated or vaguely global feelings you have about a text have arisen specifically from these or those particular patterns? The first step is to acknowledge that those vague, delicate, rarefied and diffused senses are real and shared. The next step – as in this chapter – is to try to pin down likely models for exploring these delicate effects, and bring them to conscious awareness. The final step is to present these findings for recognition or rejection, and to develop new methods for exploring subliminality further. The act of faith is in believing that subliminal effects are amenable to exploration, but the proof of this belief lies in the practice of analysis.

References

Baker, Carlos (1948). *Shelley's Major Poetry*. Princeton: Princeton University Press.
Bloom, Harold (ed.) (2001). *Percy Bysshe Shelley*. New York: Chelsea House.
Bloom, Harold and Edmundson, Melissa (eds) (2009). *Percy Shelley*. New York: Bloom's Literary Criticism.
Breeze, Ruth (2011). Critical discourse analysis and its critics. *Pragmatics* 21 (4): 493–525.
Evans, Vyvyan (2006). *Cognitive Linguistics: An Introduction*. Edinburgh: Edinburgh University Press.
Fraistat, Neil (1984). Poetic quests and questioning in Shelley's 'Alastor' collection. *Keats-Shelley Journal* 33: 161–81.
Hogg, Thomas J. and Shelley, Percy B. (1811). *The Necessity of Atheism*. Worthing: C. & W. Phillips.
Jager, Colin (2010). Shelley after atheism. *Studies in Romanticism* 49 (4): 611–31.
Langacker, Ronald (2008). *Cognitive Grammar: A Basic Introduction*. Oxford: Oxford University Press.
McGann, Jerome (1998). *The Poetics of Sensibility: A Revolution in Literary Style*. Oxford: Clarendon Press.
Magarian, Barry (1993). *Indeterminacy in Some of Shelley's Major Poems: A Critical Discussion*. Unpublished PhD thesis. Durham University, <http://etheses.dur.ac.uk/5719/> (last accessed 29 November 2018).
Mahlberg, Michaela, Stockwell, Peter, de Joode, Johan, Smith, Catherine and O'Donnell, Matthew (2016). CLiC Dickens – novel uses of concordances for the integration of corpus stylistics and cognitive poetics. *Corpora* 11 (3): 433–63.
Shelley, Percy B. (1970). *Poetical Works* (edited by Thomas Hutchinson). Oxford: Oxford University Press.
Stockwell, Peter (2009). *Texture: A Cognitive Aesthetics of Reading*. Edinburgh: Edinburgh University Press.
Stockwell, Peter (2014). Atmosphere and tone. In Peter Stockwell and Sara Whiteley (eds), *The Cambridge Handbook of Stylistics*. Cambridge: Cambridge University Press, pp. 360–74.
Stockwell, Peter (2017). Poe's Gothic ambience. In Linda Barone and Alfonso Amendola (eds) *Edgar Allan Poe Across Disciplines, Genres and Languages*. Newcastle: Cambridge Scholars Publishing, pp. 7–24.

Welburn, Andrew J. (1986). *Power and Self-Consciousness in the Poetry of Shelley*. Basingstoke: Macmillan.
West, Sally (2016). *Coleridge and Shelley: Textual Engagement*. London: Routledge.
Widdowson, Henry G. (1995). Discourse analysis: a critical view. *Language and Literature* 4 (3): 157–72.
Widdowson, Henry G. (1998). Review article: the theory and practice of critical discourse analysis. *Applied Linguistics* 19 (1): 136–51.
Widdowson, Henry G. (2005). *Text, Context, Pretext: Critical Issues in Discourse Analysis*. Oxford: Blackwell.
Wroe, Ann (2011). Shelley and night. *The Keats-Shelley Review* 25 (1): 55–67.

2

A 'Half-Remembered Quality': Experiencing Disorientation and Claustrophobia in *The Goldfinch*

Chloe Harrison

1. Introduction

The examination of how readers experience fictional worlds is gaining attention and interest in contemporary stylistic and cognitive poetic research. This idea has always been at the centre of Text World Theory applications (Werth 1999; see also Gavins 2007; Gavins and Lahey 2016), for example, and is also a preoccupation that underpins the renewed focus on 'real readers' and situated reading experiences (Burke 2011; Stockwell 2013; Whiteley 2011). Increasingly, these studies are drawing on ideas from Cognitive Linguistics to explore the mechanisms that establish readerly experiences with a text. Such approaches have shown how these 'cognitive considerations are enhancing our understanding of both specific linguistic choices and general conceptual strategies involved in the construction of meaning' (Dancygier 2007: 133).

In line with this emphasis on readers and cognition, this chapter applies cognitive linguistic concepts, and in particular ideas from Cognitive Grammar (Langacker 1987, 1991, 2008), for literary linguistic analysis. Cognitive Grammar is a theory of grammar that is premised on the notions that grammatical choices are inherently meaningful, and that cognition itself shapes language. Studying patterns of language and structure in texts through a Cognitive Grammar perspective therefore offers a bridge between the text on the one hand, and our embodied experience of reading it on the other. Consequently it satisfies the contemporary concerns of cognitive poetics in that it enables an analysis of fiction that is both text-driven and, simultaneously, readerly.

Alongside other applications, it has been observed that a Cognitive Grammar analysis can shed light on how readers experience texts that represent contrasting styles. Stockwell's (2014a) chapter on H. G. Wells' *War of the Worlds*, for example, considers how a 'grammar of anticipation' is established in the scene from the novel, which brings about feelings of anxiety in readers, and how this is then followed by a 'grammar of action' when the Martians are revealed for the first time. Pursuant to Stockwell's study, this chapter explores contrasting patterns of grammar in a pivotal scene from a novel: the 'gallery scene' in Donna Tartt's (2013) *The Goldfinch*. While this scene is regarded as a central and particularly memorable one by many readers, as the next section of this paper observes, it also complicates a 'grammar of action' and a 'grammar of anticipation' by representing conflicting style choices within the same passage.

With ideas from Cognitive Linguistics and cognitive poetics, this chapter draws on Cognitive Grammar's 'specification', 'subjectification' and 'action chains' in order to explore this stylistic contrast, and to consider how it generates feelings of narratorial 'disorientation' and an increasing sense of 'claustrophobia' (Taylor 2013) in this scene. The analysis in this chapter observes that 'spatial immersion' (Ryan 2001) impacts on how atmosphere (Stockwell 2009) is created in the text, and concludes that it is the complicating and contradictory style choices that play a key role in readers' immersion into – and subsequent cinematic experience of – this extract.

2. *The Goldfinch*

Published in 2013, *The Goldfinch* is Donna Tartt's long-awaited third novel. Amongst some critical dispute (its reception is described by Peretz [2014] as 'polarized'), it won a Pulitzer Prize in 2014. Following *The Secret History* (1992) and *The Little Friend* (2002), *The Goldfinch* is contemporary realist novel of epic proportions. The novel is a 771 pages-long first-person narrative told from the perspective of Theo Decker. Set in New York, it tells the story of how Theo gains possession of a priceless work of art, 'The Goldfinch', by Carel Fabritius.

It is argued that the *Bildungsroman*-style means that 'Dickens has swiftly emerged as the kneejerk comparison for this novel' (Tonkin 2013). The polarisation of *The Goldfinch*'s critical reception, however, can be traced to the reviewers' responses to the style of writing itself. One reviewer argues that the 'chief complaint about the novel is that it represents itself as serious fiction but really it merely mimics serious fiction', and that the novel's provenance is 'movies' rather than Dickens (Perry 2014). The reviewer makes this parallel by describing the compulsion he felt to continue reading:

> Because movies keep going, going, going -- it's not like a novel where you can go back and reread a section or a paragraph . . . You kept going, going,

going, as if someone were about to snatch the book from your hands. (Perry 2014)

In this review, Perry clearly draws on one of several metaphors frequently used by readers to account for the felt experience of reading: 'reading as control' (Stockwell 2009; see also Gerrig 1993). Specifically, he describes the experience of reading this novel as a *lack* of control; the style has somehow removed the opportunity to 'go back and reread a section or a paragraph', and instead readers are forced to 'keep going, going, going', 'as if' at the demands of an external force.

While Perry implies that such a style of writing falls within the domain of 'movies', and not 'serious fiction', other reviewers describe this as a positive, immersive experience. In defence of similar reviewer criticisms that have branded the novel as 'children's literature' (Wood 2013) and commented on the 'movie-style' writing style of the novel, for example, a Huffington Post reviewer argues that,

> Tartt's light language ... reels you into the world she's created, and immerses you fully in her character's experiences. Because it's not especially complex, the barrier of entry into the world she's created is low. Readers can mosey into Theo's consciousness, and embody his hardships and feelings and lessons and extrapolated philosophies (which, by the way, *are* complex) for the length of the novel. (Crum 2014)

In this review, Crum again evokes the 'reading as control' metaphor (she argues, for example, that the narrative 'reels you into the world'), and further demonstrates another example of other prevalent reading metaphors: 'reading as transportation' (she discusses the fact that 'the barrier of entry into the world she's created is low') (Stockwell 2009; see also Gerrig 1993; Harrison and Stockwell 2014). The lack of 'complexity' in the writing style, the reviewer argues, creates a more engrossing reader experience ('Tartt's light language ... immerses you fully in her character's experiences'). As argued by Ryan (2001), immersion occurs when readers reorient themselves within a fictional world (see also Zwaan 2004). For Crum, this is created when the world 'barrier' is lowered, allowing readers to have easier access to the protagonist's 'consciousness' and to 'embody his hardships and feelings' more directly.

Most reviewers, however, agree that a particular early scene is one of the most memorable and most immersive in the novel (Crum 2014; Shamsie 2013; Taylor 2013). This passage moves between vagueness and detail, between action and stasis – and despite this contradictory stylistic profile, it is described as 'climactic', 'compelling', 'astonishingly gripping' and 'pivotal' (Shamsie 2013), and has been commented on for its creation of 'fear, disorientation and claustrophobia' (Taylor 2013). The particular extract describes a central moment in the protagonist Theo's life: the death of his mother. Following this event, 'the novel changes gear and, for a while, is primarily involved with showing us, affectingly, the dislocation of Theo's life – a dislocation both emotional and physical' (Shamsie 2013). This division is noted by Theo himself at the beginning of the story: 'the dividing mark: Before and After' (Tartt 2013: 7).

The scene appears early in the novel when Theo and his mother are forced to take shelter in the Metropolitan Museum of Art in New York during the onslaught of a sudden storm. They decide to attend an exhibition on 'Portraiture and Nature Morte', but while they are walking round the exhibition a bomb is detonated in the gallery, killing Theo's mother as well as countless other visitors of the gallery, and knocking Theo unconscious. The scene continues where Theo is regaining consciousness after the detonation, and describes his desperate efforts to escape the collapsing building. The chaos following this 'black flash' (Tartt 2013: 31) – not initially specified as a bomb explosion – makes for an interesting and immersive reading experience, which feels both fast-paced (when I read it, I was conscious of reading more quickly), and, equally, frustratingly ineffectual (I was simultaneously conscious that elements of the scene were left unclear; I felt that I needed to reread particular sentences to make sure I was not missing anything).

The analysis of this chapter examines this felt experience – the immersive yet disorienting quality that is central to the fictional world creation of this pivotal scene – and draws upon ideas from Cognitive Grammar to explore its contradictory stylistic profile and specific literary 'texture' (Stockwell 2009). In particular, this study examines the tension between the atmosphere ('the quality of the world being presented') and the tone ('the quality of the narrative or authorial voice') (Stockwell 2014a; see also Stockwell 2014b) of the text, and consequently how the language generates feelings of 'fear, claustrophobia and disorientation' (Taylor 2013) at pivotal parts of the discourse.

3. Text Analysis (1): Disorientation

Extract 1 below describes the immediate aftermath of the bomb detonation, and details Theo regaining consciousness as he tries to make sense of his surroundings. The scene follows a graphological ellipsis in the text, and so readers are primed to anticipate a shift in time and/or space. Of course, piecing together previous clues in the text (the reference to the 'black flash', the facts that Theo has been knocked unconscious and is disoriented) means that a reader is possibly able to discern what has happened, even if Theo does not immediately. Consequently, the text invites a 'layered construal' process (see Harrison 2017a) in which readers are invited to conceptualise the text-world as Theo construes it, while at the same time guessing or knowing what has taken place.

Extract 1

I didn't know how long I was out. When I came to, it seemed as if I was flat on my stomach in a sandbox, on some dark playground – someplace I didn't know, a deserted neighbourhood. A gang of tough, runty boys was bunched around me, kicking me in the ribs and the back of the head. My neck was twisted to the side and the wind was knocked out of me, but that wasn't the worst of it; I had sand in my mouth, I was breathing sand.

The boys muttered, audibly. *Get up, asshole.*
Look at him, look at him.
He don't know dick.

I rolled over and threw my arms over my head and then – with an airy, surreal jolt – saw nobody was there.

For a moment I lay too stunned to move. Alarm bells clanged in a muffled distance. As strange as it seemed, I was under the impression that I was lying in the walled-up courtyard of some godforsaken housing project.

Somebody had beaten me up pretty good: I ached all over, my ribs were sore and my head felt like someone had hit me with a lead pipe. I was working my jaw back and forth and reaching for my pockets to see if I had train fare home when it came over me abruptly that I had no clue where I was. Stiffly, I lay there, in the growing consciousness that something was badly out of joint. The light was all wrong, and so was the air: acrid and sharp, a chemical fog that burned my throat. The gum in my mouth was gritty, and when – head pounding – I rolled over to spit it out, I found myself blinking through layers of smoke at something so foreign I stared for some moments.

I was in a ragged white cave. Swags and tatters dangled from the ceiling. The ground was tumbled and bucked-up with heaps of grey substance like moon rock, and blown about with broken glass and gravel and a hurricane of random trash, bricks and slag and paper stuff frosted with a thin ash like the first frost. High overhead, a pair of lamps beamed through the dust like off-kilter car lights in fog, cock-eyed, one angled upward and the other rolled to the side and casting skewed shadows. . . .

I looked around, trying to get my bearings, deranged from the crack on the head, with no sense of time or even if it was day or night. The grandeur and desolation of the space baffled me – the high, rare, loft of it, layered with gradations of smoke, and billowing with a tangled, tent-like effect where the ceiling (or the sky) ought to be. But though I had no idea where I was, or why, still there was a half-remembered quality about the wreckage, a cinematic charge in the glare of the emergency lamps. (Tartt 2013: 31–4)

3.1. Spatial Immersion

Ryan (2001) argues that one of the felt experiences of fictional immersion is 'spatial immersion'. This is 'the text's capacity to allow the reader to construct a mental map of the narrative world, and to facilitate recentering by means of strategies such as the deictic shift and second-person narration' (Ryan 2001: 389–90). One of the most disorienting aspects of Extract 1 is the uncertainty regarding Theo's location brought about by the shifting descriptions of the map of the narrative world. In other words, spatial immersion is created through the shifts that readers experience in trying to recentre themselves in this scene.

Readers already know that Theo is in the Metropolitan art museum with his mother, and so this context can be transferred onto the passage as a prior 'reference point' (Langacker 2008); a salient part of the fictional landscape in and around which readers' conceptualisation of the text-world (Gavins 2007; Werth 1999) can be constructed. However, in some ways knowing the location prior to this scene causes more ambiguity: readers can try to compare Theo's current location with their mental model of the Met as presented in the text or from any real-world knowledge about the gallery activated through 'discourse world' information (Gavins 2007; Werth 1999) – but the two scenes do not correspond with each other. The description of the location at first seems unfocused, and the narration moves from clear to ambiguous accounts, and vice versa. Despite the initial lexical 'underspecification' (Emmott et al. 2006), however, it becomes clear that it is the blown-up art gallery that is providing the 'landmark' (Langacker 2008) – the background – for Theo's movements (cf. analysis of Extract 2 in Section 4).

Much of this ambiguity can be traced to the clash of 'scenarios' (Sanford and Emmott 2012) introduced in this passage. The strongest processing assumption of Scenario-Mapping Theory is that a reader automatically seeks out a known situation (scenario) to which a text is referring, what Sanford and Garrod (1981, 1998) termed 'primary processing', which leads to basic comprehension. In reading this scene from *The Goldfinch*, a reader is required to reconstrue the scene through Theo's perspective, and consequently to update their mental map of the fictional world as Theo's description of the location alters.

Theo first describes being situated in 'a sandbox' of some 'deserted neighbourhood', before going on to describe 'a cave', and then, finally, and less specifically, a 'wreckage'. The cohesive chains identified in 1–4 below show how the reference points in the scene undergo continued 'elaboration' and, conversely, 'schematization' (Langacker 2008) in Theo's description of his surroundings. Simply put, Theo provides both increasing and decreasing levels of detail as he describes new locations through which to frame his situation:

1. a sandbox > someplace I didn't know > a deserted neighbourhood
2. > the walled-up courtyard of some godforsaken housing project
3. something so foreign > a ragged white cave
4. the space > the wreckage

NB: in Cognitive Grammar, the symbol '>' represents an elaborative relationship between descriptions, where items increase in level of detail and 'specificity' (Langacker 2008).

In Theo's first string of descriptions (outlined in 1), the 'scope' (Langacker 2008) of the scene is continually adjusted. It begins with a more focused description of 'a sandbox', before zooming out to situate this sandbox within the maximal scope of 'a deserted neighbourhood', and then focusing in again more specifically, and definitely, to 'the walled-up courtyard of some godforsaken housing project', 2.

In terms of primary processing, it seems that this first location fulfils the scenario of an altercation between Theo and a group of boys. The 'deserted neighbourhood' becomes populated with scenario-dependent entities ('A gang of tough, runty boys') who perform scenario-reinforcing actions ('kicking me in the ribs and the back of the head') that fulfil the details of this particular situation. This is continued in the next paragraph, even once Theo has confirmed that 'nobody was there', and reframes the scenario as he assumes he is in 'the walled-up courtyard of some godforsaken housing project'. At this point his construal shifts this event to an action that has already happened ('head beaten'), with a more ambiguous initiator ('Somebody'). Again, Theo fulfils further actions that reinforce this scenario: he searches his pockets to see if he 'had the train fare home', before realising 'that [he] had no clue where [he] was'.

Once this specific scenario has been ruled out and other qualities of the space have been identified ('The light was all wrong, and so was the air'), readers undergo 'secondary processing' – to search for 'alternative scenarios' (Sanford and Garrod 1981; Sanford and Emmott 2012) that help to determine the details of where Theo is and what has happened. Again, however, the alternative scenarios presented are indefinite and ambiguously described. As the extract progresses, the room becomes 'something so foreign'; 'a ragged white cave'. This description is simultaneously coupled with contrasting semantic fields of natural imagery ('white cave', 'moon rock', 'hurricane', 'blown about', 'frosted', 'ash', 'frost', 'dust', 'fog', 'sky') and industrial description ('glass', 'gravel', 'bricks', 'random trash', 'slag', 'paper stuff', 'pair of lamps', 'car lights', 'a cinematic charge in the glare of emergency lamps') that contribute to this scenario clash. Is Theo inside, outside or somewhere in-between? Such ambiguity regarding the location echoes the blurring of boundaries between inside and outside invited by Theo's previous description of the 'walled up courtyard'. All these descriptions, however, are framed through the semantic field of decay and ruin ('swags', 'tatters', 'tumbled', 'bucked-up', 'heaps of grey substance', 'broken', 'gravel', 'trash', 'slag', 'stuff', 'dust', 'off-kilter', 'skewed', 'smoke', 'tangled', 'wreckage'). These lexical sets work in combination to create 'semantic priming', which brings about atmospheric effects in that it invites readers to focus on 'the quality of the world being presented'; to 'feel as if they are experiencing the presented world directly' (Stockwell 2014a: 29).

Further, as Theo takes in his surroundings, the particular reference points within this 'foreign' scene are given equal attentional status through the use of additive conjunctions:

> The ground was tumbled and bucked-up with heaps of grey substance like moon rock, and blown about with broken glass and gravel and a hurricane of random trash, bricks and slag and paper stuff frosted with a thin ash like the first frost. (Tartt 2013: 32; emphasis mine)

The fact that equal attention is paid to these 'world-builders' (Gavins 2007; Werth 1999) means that the various possibilities of scenarios and locations remain activated and, consequently, the 'edges' of 'the space' remain ambivalent and difficult to identify definitively. Since readers are unaware how much time has passed in the narrative since the previous scene, it could be 'day or night', and the space is contained by 'the ceiling (or the sky)' and presents both 'grandeur and desolation' simultaneously. While these lexical choices present contradictory semantic fields, the level of specification included in these references similarly contributes to the sense of narratorial disorientation. The descriptions become less specific ('something so foreign'; 'a ragged white cave'), but also, conversely, more definite ('the space'; 'the wreckage'). Overall, these contradictions and scenario clashes combine to create weaker cohesive ties between the references to the location of this scene (as compared to Extract 2, see analysis in Section 3). This means that the location of the text – and consequently, the atmosphere of the scene – remains particularly foregrounded despite its ambiguous construal.

3.2 Subjectification and Text-World Layers

While the description of the location creates atmospheric effects in how this scene is read, Theo's language choices mean that his tone also remains prominent, however. In Cognitive Grammar, Langacker (1987, 1991, 2008) differentiates between 'objective' and 'subjective' construals of language, where the former places more emphasis on the object of conceptualisation (in this case, the wreckage of the gallery), and the latter places more emphasis on the conceptualiser (Theo).

The language choices mean that, predominantly, a subjective construal is offered, with Theo's disorientation stylistically signposted via features of 'negative shading' (Simpson 2004). Theo is a prototypical disoriented narrator, bewildered and unsure of what is happening; he is attached to mental constructions ('I didn't know' ×2; 'I saw'; 'I looked around'; 'I had no clue') and modalised processes throughout the passage, and repeatedly uses epistemic modality through 'words of estrangement' (Fowler 1986) ('it seemed as if'; 'as strange as it seemed, I was under the impression') as well as approximation ('someplace'; 'Somebody') that further subjectify his account. Additionally, he is acted upon by his surroundings and is a 'patient' or 'energy sink' (Langacker 2008) for many of the actions ('My neck was twisted'; 'the wind was knocked out of me'; 'I lay too stunned to move'), as further expressed through the behavioural process choices ('I was breathing'; 'I ached').

Furthermore, with the exception of 'throwing' his arms overhead, the actions that Theo does initiate are low energy ('I was working . . . reaching'; 'I rolled over' ×2), while grammatical agency and energy is instead assigned elsewhere. The 'gang' of boys, for example, are described as 'kicking [him] in the ribs and the back of the head'. Significantly, this description is given more objectively, with no modalisation. This means that the first scenario is presented more categorically: readers may assume that Theo is in 'a deserted playground', as the construal suggests, until he observes that, in fact, 'nobody was there', and the next scenario is introduced. Similarly, this shift between subjective and objective description appears elsewhere. Theo describes staring at 'something so foreign', until stating through a relational construction that he actually 'was in a ragged white cave'. This movement between categorical and modalised descriptions of the locations means that readers successively undergo conceptualisations of various locations and scenarios, which are then downgraded in text-world status. This in turn creates a list of 'nested locatives' (Langacker 2008), which, within the context of this scene, means that readers' attention runs from one reference point to the next, and that each new location overrides the other in terms of its ontological status. While disrupting the narrative momentum (Simpson 2014), this constant recentring again means that the readers encounter a 'garden-path'-style narrative (Emmott 2003; Sternberg 1978; Tobin 2009); conceptualising each new scenario in turn before being led to acknowledge that the 'half-remembered quality' of the scene confirms that the 'wreckage' is the gallery. That these objective descriptions are included alongside the subjective accounts means that readers encounter – and arguably begin to expect – unstable and fluid text-world parameters. Readers are encouraged to 'focus on the tone of the "voice" in the writing' and the 'quality' of the fictional world (Stockwell 2009: 29) at alternating points. This makes for an unsettling reading experience in that readers cannot entirely be certain what is happening, or how reliable Theo's account is.

4. Text Analysis (2): Claustrophobia

The analysis in Section 3 identified that spatial immersion impacts on how disorientation is displayed in the narrative. It was observed that Extract 1 simultaneously activates atmospheric and tonal effects, and that readers are required to recentre themselves within the world of the text in order to comprehend the narrative. In this second extract, 'temporal immersion' – that is, readers' anticipation of future events (Ryan 2001) – additionally plays a role in how this scene is read. Of course, this type of readerly anticipation of future events affects the creation of suspense in fiction, which is generally defined as delaying a narrative outcome or goal (Hoeken and van Vliet 2000).

It is argued that the stylistic contrast between stillness and action is a fundamental part of the creation of 'narrative urgency' in texts (Simpson 2014). While the gallery scene as a whole fulfils some of the stylistic traits that create narrative urgency (such as the use of free forms of speech and thought, the short duration of the action and the increasing predominance of material action processes [see Simpson 2014 for further discussion of the stylistic profile of narrative urgency]), at the same time there are style choices that stall the pace. Like with the clash of objective/subjective accounts in Extract 1, this stylistic contrast plays an integral role in the felt experience of the latter half of this scene.

Extract 2 describes Theo's attempts to escape the building. He therefore has a clearer goal for his actions than in Extract 1, and the narration is less disoriented and more focused. Certainly, Extract 2 displays a faster pace than Extract 1, but again it is the clash of style choices that creates a feeling of claustrophobia in the reading of this section, as the following analysis details.

Extract 2

Then something snapped. I don't even remember how it happened; I was just in a different place and running, running through rooms that were empty except for a haze of smoke that made the grandeur seem insubstantial and unreal. Earlier, the galleries had seemed fairly straightforward, a meandering but logical sequence where all tributaries flowed into the gift shop. But coming back through them fast, and in the opposite direction, I realized that the path wasn't straight at all; and over and over I turned into blank walls and veered into dead-end rooms. Doors and entrances weren't where I expected them to be; freestanding plinths loomed out of nowhere. Swinging around a corner a little too sharply I almost ran headlong into a gang of Frans Hals guardsmen: big, rough, ruddy-cheeked guys, bleary from too much beer, like New York City cops at a costume party. Coldly, they stared me down, with hard, humorous eyes, as I recovered, backed off, and began to run again. . . .

I tripped; I fell over my feet; I got up again, still hiccupping, and ran down the endless hall. Down at the end of the corridor was a door with a metal bar, like the security doors at my school.

It pushed open with a bark. Down a dark stairwell I ran, twelve steps, a turn at the landing, then twelve steps to the bottom, my fingers skimming on the metal rail, shoes clattering and echoing so crazily that it sounded like half a dozen people were running with me. At the foot of the steps was a gray institutional corridor with another barred door. I threw myself against it, pushed it open with both hands – and was slapped hard in the face by rain and the deafening wail of sirens. (Tartt 2013: 45–7).

4.1. *Ineffective Action and Competing Attractors*

Compared with the first, there are closer cohesive chains in this second extract. In other words, there is a clear semantic field of the 'profiled' (Langacker 2008) – singled out – elements of the art gallery (with descriptions of the 'doors', 'entrances', 'plinths', 'rooms' and 'the gift shop', and so on, acting as reference points to mark Theo's progress through the gallery), which precludes the locative ambiguity of the first extract. This clearer location and the closer chains of cohesion mean that the pace increases in this latter part of the scene.

While the location and reference points in Extract 2 are clearer than in the first, however, readers' attention is again drawn to different parts of the scene at alternating parts in the discourse. Theo has agency in actions, but at the same time the gallery is represented as a competing entity. This is because there is a revision of the archetypal trajector-landmark profile relationship, the 'canonical viewpoint' (Langacker 1991: 123) that prototypically positions a moving trajector against a static landmark. Theo is clearly the main moving figure that readers follow on his way out of the gallery wreckage and the destroyed gallery forms the backdrop for his movements, but it also frequently becomes profiled as Theo gives it greater attention and as it takes on an agent role. That is, the gallery is not represented statically, but rather forcefully and prominently. Consequently, both Theo and the gallery are competing 'attractors' (Stockwell 2009) in this scene and equally vie for readers' attention.

Because of Theo's main goal – to escape the building – Theo holds more superordinate 'agent' (Langacker 2008) roles in the processes in this scene compared to the first extract. Theo is also primarily a 'mover' (Langacker 2008) in the latter half of this extract ('running', 'coming back', 'turned', 'swinging', 'backed off', 'tripped', 'fell over', 'got up', 'began to run', 'ran' [×3], 'skimming', 'threw'). These verb choices are strong purveyors of energy, requiring an agent that exerts a considerable amount of force.

However, one of the strongest reading sensations created through reading the second extract, which arguably creates the feelings of claustrophobia here, is the frustrating sense of stopping and starting; of ineffectual action. This is particularly apparent in the first half of the second passage, where disorientation and repetition are given prominence through the particular lexical choices. For example, the descriptions of how Theo's actions are 'meandering' and repeated 'over and over', and that he continually encounters locations such as an 'endless hall', 'another barred door', additional 'blank walls' and 'dead-end rooms', foreground the futility of his attempted actions. Another stalling feature is that, while holding agency in many processes, Theo also continues to hold an experiencer role with mental and modalised processes attached to his actions ('I don't even remember how it happened'; 'I realized that the path wasn't straight at all'). Like in Extract 1, this is expressed through stylistic choices such as words of estrangement ('seemed'; 'expected'; 'seem'), 'verba sentiendi' (Uspensky 1973) ('remember'; 'realized') and other lexical choices (adverbs such as 'almost', and schematic language such as 'something', 'nowhere'). In Cognitive Linguistics, modality is seen as having a kind of latent or unrealised energy (Langacker 2008) and consequently such style choices are considered a hallmark of a grammar of 'anticipation' rather than 'action' (Stockwell 2014a). The prevalence of modality throughout the scene continuously undermines the representation of action, creating a sense of inertia even in action, a theme that underpins the scene, and as argued by some, the novel, as a whole.

Further, these lexical choices are frequently used in conjunction with abrupt or cut off actions ('tripped'; 'almost ran'; 'almost fell over') which prevent the 'image schema' (Langacker 2008) – the relationships between a trajector and a landmark – from being completed, or from being completed easily. In other words, Theo is an energy source in many of his actions, even if that energy sinks continuously due to his lack of successful direction choices. Since image schemas are said to 'contribute the dynamic scaffolds of a scene' (Kimmel 2011: 237), the fact that there is a disruption of the prototypical image-schematic paths of action here reconfigures these 'dynamic scaffolds' and means that readers' attention is continually pulled away from Theo and back to the gallery as an independent entity. This certainly further emphasises the sense of 'fear' (Shamsie 2013) felt by readers; it seems that, despite his efforts, Theo remains at the mercy of forces outside his control.

Additionally, the gallery maintains its role as attractor through the facts that it is given attentional 'prominence' (Langacker 2008) in particular constructions. It has grammatical agency ('freestanding plinths loomed out of nowhere'), forms the first reference point in particular sentences ('Down a dark stairwell I ran') and also is represented as acting independently to Theo: 'It pushed open with a bark.' The reference to 'bark' of the door in this description instils the gallery with animacy; a description that is further compounded with the description of the Frans Hals guardsmen, who populate a painting that Theo and his mother observed earlier in their visit to the exhibition. Theo's construal assigns these characters with 'experiencer' (Langacker 2008) status: he describes, for example, how 'Coldly, they stared me down, with hard, humorous eyes, as I recovered, backed off, and began to run again.' These descriptions emphasise the construal of the gallery as an animate entity – a force that has energy. Despite Theo being the only character in these two extracts, the description of his location continually makes it seem as though 'half a dozen people' are running with him.

In the final two paragraphs of this second extract, Theo does begin to gain more agency as he nears his destination. The pace increases, as emphasised through the use of short, declarative constructions and the decrease in modalisation: 'I tripped; I fell over my feet; I got up again . . . and ran down the endless hall.' The increase in action is highlighted through the use of the past progressive ('skimming'; 'clattering'; 'echoing'; 'running'), which contrast with the more abrupt, perfective actions of the final sentence ('threw'; 'pushed'; 'slapped'). These action verbs in turn can be contrasted directly with the few attached to Theo in the first extract, which are comparatively much weaker ('came to'; 'lay'; 'working'; 'rolled'). Nevertheless, Theo does not entirely hold a mover role at the end of this passage; even in the final paragraph where he finally escapes the museum, Theo continues to oscillate between agent and patient roles. He 'pushes' the barred door open, but is 'slapped hard in the face by rain and the deafening wail of sirens'. Combined with the semantic field of obstruction and the incomplete actions mentioned before, it could be argued that Theo is the 'agonist', the affected entity, whereas the gallery itself becomes the affecting 'antagonist', who holds contrastively greater force (see Talmy 2000a, 2000b).

In summary, it seems that unlike the contrast of a 'grammar of anticipation' and a 'grammar of action' identified in Stockwell's study of *War of the Worlds*, this scene conflates and complicates features of both stylistic profiles. The descriptions of Theo's movements increase the pace in one instance, to then stall it in another. Equally, the focus of the scene continually shifts between Theo and the gallery, and it is this fact – this tug of war between Theo and his surroundings – that creates the sense of both frustration and futility.

5. Conclusion

Following the reading metaphors identified in the reader reviews at the beginning of this chapter, an additional metaphor can be observed which highlights the relationship between the specific linguistic choices made, and how they combine to form wider patterns in the text that impact on our experience of reading it: that is, the 'novel as a painting' (see Crum 2014; Peretz 2014). Crum (2014), for example, identifies that while some stories are 'pointillist' in that they 'wow on a sentence-level', 'it's debatable whether some of them come together to form a living, moving scene when you step back and view them full-on'. She further describes Tartt's writing as displaying 'some sloppy and apparent brush strokes, but they're arranged so harmoniously that they breathe and move and create a picture that appears very real'. It is arguably the combination of these 'brush strokes' – the contrasting stylistic patterns – that create the 'movie-style' (Perry 2014) experience of reading this scene.

The analysis in this chapter has demonstrated how atmosphere of this particular scene is built upon and established incrementally. As Crum has identified through this latter reading metaphor, consequently, the immersive experience of reading this passage is dependent on a reader's reaction to and comprehension of its various textual components; the 'activation' of particular lexical choices at the 'sentence-level'; the connection of these to the 'construal' of larger clausal units; and the impact this has on 'integration' – how the text guides readers to form an understanding of the discourse as a whole via a comprehension of event sequences (see Zwaan 2004: 40).

In conclusion, this chapter has argued that a combined stylistic application of certain key ideas from Cognitive Grammar and cognitive stylistics, namely, specification and elaboration, scenarios, action chains and attractors, amongst others, successfully account for the text's unsettling atmosphere. It was proposed that the felt experience of reading this scene – that it is memorable, immersive and cinematic – is a direct consequence of these style choices. While other accounts of Cognitive Grammar have focused in greater detail on how these central ideas of construal, reference points and action chains can be used in addition to and in combination with existing stylistic tools (see Giovanelli 2016; Harrison 2017a, 2017b; Harrison et al. 2014; Nuttall 2015, 2018), the cognitive linguistic account of this scene has enabled an exploration of the stylistic contrasts that both draws connection between the specific textual choices and patterns on the one hand, and the felt experience of reading on the other.

References

Burke, M. (2011). *Literary Reading, Cognition and Emotion: An Exploration of the Oceanic Mind*. London: Routledge.

Crum, M. (2014). Why you absolutely should read 'The Goldfinch'. *Huffington Post*, 27 June, <http://www.huffingtonpost.com/2014/06/27/the-goldfinch-book_n_5489272.html> (last accessed 29 November 2018).

Dancygier, B. (2007). Narrative anchors and the processes of story construction: The case of Margaret Atwood's *The Blind Assassin*. *Style* 41 (2): 133–52.

Emmott, C. (2003). Reading for pleasure: A cognitive poetic analysis of 'twists in the tale' and other plot reversals in narrative texts. In J. Gavins and G. Steen (eds), *Cognitive Poetics in Practice*. London: Routledge.

Emmott, C., Sanford, J. A. and Morrow, L. I. (2006). Capturing the attention of readers? Stylistic and psychological perspectives on the use and effect of text fragmentation in narratives. *Journal of Literary Semantics* 35: 1–30.

Fowler, R. (1986). *Linguistic Criticism*. Oxford: Oxford University Press.

Gavins, J. (2007). *Text World Theory: An Introduction*. Edinburgh: Edinburgh University Press.

Gavins, J. and Lahey, E. (2016). *World Building: Discourse in the Mind*. London: Bloomsbury.

Gerrig, R. (1993). *Experiencing Narrative Worlds: on the Psychological Activities of Reading*. New Haven, CT: Yale University Press.

Giovanelli, M. (2016). Construing the child reader: A cognitive stylistic analysis of the opening to Neil Gaiman's *The Graveyard Book*. *Children's Literature in Education*: 1–16.

Harrison, C. (2017a). Finding Elizabeth: Construing memory in *Elizabeth Is Missing* by Emma Healey. *Journal of Literary Semantics* 46 (2): 131–51.

Harrison, C. (2017b). *Cognitive Grammar in Contemporary Fiction*. Amsterdam: John Benjamins.

Harrison, C. and Stockwell, P. (2014). Cognitive poetics. In J. Littlemore and J. R. Taylor (eds), *The Bloomsbury Companion to Cognitive Linguistics*. London: Bloomsbury, pp. 218–33.

Harrison, C., Nuttall, L., Stockwell, P. and Yuan, W. (eds) (2014). *Cognitive Grammar in Literature*. New York: John Benjamins.

Hoeken, H. and van Vliet, M. (2000). Suspense, curiosity, and surprise: How discourse structure influences the affective and cognitive processing of a story. *Poetics* 27(4): 277–86.

Kimmel, M. (2011). From text-linguistics to literary *actants* – the force dynamics of emotional vampirism. *Language and Cognition* 3(2): 235–82.

Langacker, R. (1987). *Foundations of Cognitive Grammar: Volume I: Theoretical Prerequisites*. Stanford: Stanford University Press.

Langacker, R. (1991). *Foundations of Cognitive Grammar: Volume II: Descriptive Application*. Stanford: Stanford University Press.

Langacker, R. (2008). *Cognitive Grammar: A Basic Introduction*. Oxford: Oxford University Press.

Nuttall, L. (2015). Attributing minds to vampires in Richard Matheson's *I Am Legend*. *Language and Literature* 24 (1): 23–39.

Nuttall, L. (2018). *Mind Style and Cognitive Grammar: Language and Worldview in Speculative Fiction*. London: Bloomsbury.

Peretz, E. (2014). It's Tartt – But is it art?. *Vanity Fair*, 11 June, <http://www.vanityfair.com/culture/2014/07/goldfinch-donna-tartt-literary-criticism> (last accessed 29 November 2018).

Perry, D. (2014). Why the backlash against Donna Tartt's *The Goldfinch* was so extreme (2014 Year in Review), 31 December, <http://www.oregonlive.com/books/index.ssf/2014/12/why_the_backlash_against_donna.html> (last accessed 29 November 2018).

Ryan, M.-L. (2001). *Narrative as Virtual Reality: Immersion and Interactivity in Literature and Electronic Media*. Baltimore: Johns Hopkins University Press.

Sanford, A. and Emmott, C. (2012). *Mind, Brain and Narrative*. Cambridge: Cambridge University Press.

Sanford, A. and Garrod, S. (1981). *Understanding Written Language: Explorations in Comprehension beyond the Sentence*. Chichester: John Wiley.

Sanford, A. and Garrod, S. (1998). The role of scenario mapping in text comprehension. *Discourse Processes* 26 (2): 159–90.

Shamsie, K. (2013). *The Goldfinch* by Donna Tartt. *The Guardian*, 17 October, <http://www.theguardian.com/books/2013/oct/17/goldfinch-donna-tartt-review> (last accessed 29 November 2018).

Simpson, P. (2004). *Stylistics: A Resource Book for Students*. London: Routledge.

Simpson, P. (2014). Just what is *narrative urgency*? *Language and Literature* 23 (1): 3–22.

Sternberg, M. (1978). *Expositional Modes and Temporal Ordering in Fiction*. Bloomington: Indiana University Press.

Stockwell, P. (2009). *Texture: A Cognitive Aesthetics of Reading*. Edinburgh: Edinburgh University Press.

Stockwell, P. (2013). The positioned reader. *Language and Literature* 22 (3): 263–77.

Stockwell, P. (2014a). War, worlds and Cognitive Grammar. In C. Harrison, L. Nuttall, P. Stockwell and W. Yuan (eds), *Cognitive Grammar in Literature*. New York: John Benjamins, pp. 19–34.

Stockwell, P. (2014b). Atmosphere and tone. In P. Stockwell and S. Whiteley (eds), *The Cambridge Handbook of Stylistics*. Cambridge: Cambridge University Press, pp. 360–74.

Talmy, L. (2000a). *Towards a Cognitive Semantics (vol. 1): Concept Structuring Systems*. Cambridge: Cambridge University Press.

Talmy, L. (2000b). *Towards a Cognitive Semantics (vol. 2): Typology and Process in Concept Structuring*. Cambridge, MA: The MIT Press.

Tartt, D. (1992). *The Secret History*. London: Penguin Books Ltd.

Tartt, D. (2002). *The Little Friend*. London: Bloomsbury Publishing.

Tartt, D. (2013). *The Goldfinch*. London: Little, Brown.

Taylor, C. (2013). *The Goldfinch* by Donna Tartt, review. *The Telegraph*, 13 October, <http://www.telegraph.co.uk/culture/books/fictionreviews/10372270/The-Goldfinch-by-Donna-Tartt-review.html> (last accessed 29 November 2018).

Tobin, V. (2009). Cognitive bias and the poetics of surprise. *Language and Literature* 18 (2): 155–72.

Tonkin, B. (2013). Book review: *The Goldfinch*, by Donna Tartt. 18 October, <http://www.independent.co.uk/arts-entertainment/books/reviews/book-review-the-goldfinch-by-donna-tartt-8887063.html> (last accessed 29 November 2018).
Uspensky, B. (1973). *A Poetics of Composition* (trans. V. Zavarin and S. Wittig). Berkeley: University of California Press.
Werth, P. (1999). *Text Worlds: Representing Conceptual Space in Discourse*. London: Longman.
Whiteley, S. (2011). Text World Theory, real readers and emotional responses to *The Remains of the Day*. *Language and Literature* 20 (1): 23–42.
Wood, J. (2013). The new curiosity shop: Donna Tartt's *The Goldfinch*. *The New Yorker*, 21 October, <http://www.newyorker.com/magazine/2013/10/21/the-new-curiosity-shop> (last accessed 29 November 2018).
Zwaan, R. (2004). The immersed experiencer: Toward an embodied theory of language comprehension. In B. Ross (ed.), *The Psychology of Learning and Motivation (Vol. 44)*. New York: Academic Press, pp. 35–62.

3

Creativity and Cognition in the Discourse of National Trust Holiday Cottage Guestbooks

Joanna Gavins and Sara Whiteley

1. Introduction

In this chapter, we present some of our recent research into a widespread and unique mode of vernacular communication which has been largely ignored by discourse analysts until now: the discourse used by holidaymakers in the guestbooks of holiday rental cottages. Specifically, the chapter reports some of the initial findings of a research project currently being run between the University of Sheffield and The National Trust in the UK. The project seeks to understand the linguistic means through which holiday cottage guestbooks give permanence to otherwise transient cultural and physical experiences of tourism, reflecting how guestbook inscribers interact with their environment while on holiday. Our key interests lie in the ways in which holidaymakers perform particular identities when making entries into guestbooks, the role linguistic creativity plays in these performances, and the extent to which cognitive-linguistic analysis can help us to understand guestbooks as socially and conceptually complex sites of linguistic interaction. The central argument we present in this chapter is that a cognitive approach to the analysis of this particular type of discourse is essential if a holistic understanding both of the nature of the text produced in the discourse situation and its conceptual consequences is to be reached.

2. The National Trust and Its Holiday Cottage Guestbooks

The National Trust was founded in 1895 with the aim of protecting the UK's cultural heritage and open spaces. The Trust is currently custodian of over 500 historic houses located throughout the British Isles, plus thousands of acres of parkland, coastline and countryside. The Trust has over 4.5 million members and receives over 65 million visits to its properties each year. It is the largest voluntary organisation of its kind in the UK and, with a total income of £592 million in 2016/17 – over £139 million of which was spent on conservation activities in the same year (see The National Trust 2017) – the Trust is a powerful lobbying and campaign body, which occupies an iconic position in the cultural and historical identity of the nation (see Bagehot 2011; Burek 2008; Jenkins and James 1994; Newby 1999; Waterson 2006, 2011; Wright 2009). This establishes a particular relationship between the Trust and the visitors to its properties which, as we show in our discussion below, feeds into the discourse at the heart of our research project in distinct and interesting ways.

Alongside its custodian activities, The National Trust also runs a large holiday business, the income from which helps to support its conservation projects. The Trust currently owns three historical hotels, dozens of campsites and over 400 holiday rental cottages across the UK. Many of these cottages are restored historic houses in their own right, and many are situated in protected countryside owned by the Trust, or within the grounds of other historic properties. National Trust holidays are aimed at an affluent, middle-class market, with the weekly rental prices of their cottages ranging from £350 for the smallest, one-bedroomed properties in low season to over £4,500 for the largest in the peak summer season.[1] All National Trust rental cottages contain guestbooks, which are a prominent feature in the properties and well used by visitors. They are deliberately left by the manager of each property in a highly visible position, often in the middle of a dining or kitchen table, and often with an accompanying pen to encourage holidaymakers to contribute. Many of the Trust's cottages also contain small archives of older, filled guestbooks, and the cottages studied in our project so far contain books dating back as far as the 1960s. As such, The National Trust's guestbooks are important records of tourists' experiences, thoughts, and opinions from the late twentieth century through to the early twenty-first century and contain invaluable examples of language use in a distinctive communicative context: participants interact in a shared physical location of national cultural significance, but at distinct temporal moments.

Working in partnership with The National Trust, we undertook a pilot study in 2014 during which we photographed the guestbooks located in five of its cottages in the Roseland Peninsula in south-eastern Cornwall. The resulting digital images yielded over 300,000 words of data, which were analysed and tagged using NVivo qualitative coding software. NVivo enables the identification of both linguistic and non-linguistic features of the discourse and makes these items searchable. It also allows for emergent coding to be undertaken, facilitating a broad overview of the dataset, the identification of key linguistic patterns across guestbook entries, and a more detailed analysis of individual entries and stylistic choices. We are currently in the process of extending our dataset to include the guestbooks of a further eight National Trust cottages in Cornwall, more than doubling the total number of words collected and analysed over the course of the project to over 800,000.

3. Analysing Guestbook Discourse

Guestbooks more broadly – such as those situated at visitor attractions and other tourist sites – have received academic attention in a number of fields. Within tourism studies, guestbooks are most often approached as a means of evaluating the management practices at tourist attractions, with the inscriptions in visitors' books taken at face value and as an indicator of public opinion (see, for example, Brown et al. 2003; Sullivan 1984). Working from within sociology and cultural studies, Noy (2008) takes a more critical approach to guestbook entries, drawing on the theories of Goffman (1981) and Butler (1988) to view guestbooks as 'stages' for the performance of touristic identities. Noy argues:

> While, as a product, visitor books can be studied as collections of expression and articulation (containers of written discourse), in terms of their function in situ they constitute spaces in which these expressions and articulations materialise and take shape. In precisely this capacity – of supplying public spaces for expression – they can constitute unique sites that elicit tourists' linguistic performance. (Noy 2008: 509)

He goes on to point out that these 'public spaces for expression' have the potential to generate complex and multi-faceted discourses as a result of the involvement of multiple participants in the communicative situation: 'by constructing certain voices and partaking in certain dialogues [inscribers] delineate their voice[s] on the multi-voiced surface of the visitor book, and . . . position themselves rhetorically on the stage' (Noy 2008: 524).

Noy's work is reflective of wider research into tourist behaviour as performance (Adler 1989; Bærenholdt et al. 2004; Edensor 2000, 2001, 2008), and his study of visitor books at an Israeli commemoration site highlights the way identity construction is inherent in guestbook contributions. Similarly, Stamou and Paraskevopoulos (2003, 2004, 2008) conduct one of the few linguistic investigation of guestbooks, applying methods from critical discourse analysis to the language of visitors' books in a Greek national park. They offer insights into the way visitors to the park negotiate what they call 'the duality of ecotourism' in the guestbooks (Stamou and Paraskevopoulos 2004: 105). They find that guestbooks in different locations in the park contain evidence of different social practices which reflect this duality: books situated in a nature reserve contained entries which were more concerned with touristic spectacle, and books situated in an information centre contained entries which were more concerned with environmentalism. The work of Stamou and Paraskevopoulos demonstrates that visitors' inscriptions in guestbooks are situated performances reflective of the physical and cultural spaces in which the books themselves are located.

Historical research has also demonstrated the cultural importance of guestbooks, with visitors' books forming a key primary source in a number of studies of British touristic behaviour in Europe in the nineteenth century (see, for example, Barton 2008; Colley 2010; Heafford 2006; James 2012). James (2012, 2013) draws on the dramaturgical theory used by Noy (2008) to examine the guestbooks in Victorian British and Irish hotels. He notes how guestbooks reveal the complex spatial and social practices involved in visitors' interactions with place. James also notes a shift in the style of guestbook entries between the 1840s and early 1900s, from the 'florid language' of romantic tourism to sparser and more nominal entries in the early 1900s. His work forms a useful counterpoint to our own examination of the style and social practices contained within contemporary guestbooks in a different form of holiday lodging. Furthermore, James (2013) presents evidence to suggest that Victorian guestbooks were widely recognised as sites of stylistic creativity in the period, describing a 'meta-literature' on the genre which appeared in periodicals and newspapers from the 1840s, reproducing excerpts from guestbooks for the purposes of entertainment.

Our own project seeks to address the lack of scholarly attention which has to date been paid specifically to the discourse of holiday cottage guestbooks. It focuses on books located in one of the UK's most popular holiday regions, Cornwall, and dating from the mid-twentieth century to the present day. Our aim is to establish for the first time the typical linguistic features of the discourse of holiday cottage guestbooks within a defined regional and temporal dataset, so that our findings might eventually be comparable with other forms of tourist discourse, such as postcards and visitor attraction guestbooks (e.g. Heller et al. 2014; Jaworski 2010; Jaworski and Thurlow 2011; Thurlow and Jaworski 2010, 2011a, 2011b, 2014, 2015), in both national and international contexts.

The current chapter presents a case-study analysis of the guestbook discourse captured from just one of the cottages in our pilot study, Gwendra Wartha. This two-bedroomed house was once part of a larger farm complex in the hamlet of Gwendra in South East Cornwall. It sits on the very edge of the Roseland Heritage Coast above Carne and Pendower beaches, with spectacular views across the cliffs and over the English Channel. The National Trust uses a 1–5 'acorn' system to grade the comfort and quality of all of its rental cottages and Gwendra Wartha is a 4-acorn cottage (with 5 acorns signifying the highest quality and comfort). Its current rental price ranges from £450 per week in low season up to £1,270 per week in high season.[2] Like all other National Trust rental properties, the cottage contains a current guestbook, as well as a number of older, completed books, dating back to 1968. In what follows, we examine the language of Gwendra Wartha's guestbooks from a fundamentally cognitive perspective, since it is our central contention that it is essential to view the rhetorical 'stage' of guestbooks, as Noy (2008) describes it, as a uniquely complex physical, social and cultural discourse context. Only a cognitive linguistic approach to the language produced and received in this situation can ensure that this complexity is properly recognised and its conceptual underpinnings are fully understood.

4. Understanding the Discourse-World of Holiday Cottage Guestbooks

The 'rhetorical stage' of guestbooks described by Noy can be thought of as a conceptual as well as textual space, co-created by multiple inscribers. The people involved in this co-creation are:

- The National Trust, a large organisation, including all their local employees, who are largely silent in our data;
- the holidaymakers and cottage maintenance staff who write in the guestbooks;
- the holidaymakers, cottage maintenance staff and other visitors (including us, as researchers) who read the guestbooks.

It stands to reason that understanding the cognitive dimensions of such a multi-faceted discourse situation requires a cognitive linguistic approach, and the framework of Text World Theory (see Gavins 2007; Werth 1999) is particularly useful for the analysis of this discourse. This is because Text World Theory considers both the situational context of the discourse, or the 'discourse-world' (see Gavins 2007: 18–33), and the conceptual structures, or 'text-worlds' (see Gavins 2007: 35–72), which result from linguistic interaction in the minds of participants. The unified examination of these two interacting levels of discourse enables a holistic investigation of the pragmatic and conceptual environment which surrounds the production and reception of the discourse; the linguistic and stylistic features of the texts themselves; and the mental representations that arise from them.

All of the interactants listed above are participants in the discourse-world of the guestbook, united by their passage through or ownership of Gwendra Wartha, although they may never meet face to face. The holidaymakers' stays do not overlap, as guests vacate the property before the next visitors arrive, and keys for the cottage are collected from a safe deposit box rather than requiring direct interaction with National Trust staff. Therefore the guestbook of Gwendra Wartha, like those in all the Trust's cottages, provides a unique space for interaction between the discourse participants, and furthermore makes previous interactions visible to new participants in the discourse-world. The discourse-world thus evolves through time, as new participants come and go, contributing to the dynamic and evolving 'rhetorical stage'. The guestbook inscriptions reflect how the participants conceptualise their environment and in turn evoke text-world conceptualisations in the minds of the guestbooks' readers. Part of what is communicated in the discourse of the guestbook is the participants' conceptualisations of the nature of the discourse-world itself: the inscribers' ideas about the people who will be reading their entries, and their relationships to past and future holidaymakers or National Trust staff. These ideas will be partly based on their own past experiences and cultural assumptions, and partly on their encounters with preceding entries in the book.

5. Building Text-Worlds across Time

The guestbooks in Gwendra Wartha, like those in the majority of cottages we have examined in the course of the project so far, are large (B5 landscape size), purpose-made, hard-backed books, the pages of which are lined and ruled into four columns, headed 'Date', 'Name', 'Address' and 'National Trust Member'. Between the first entry in Gwendra Wartha's guestbooks in 1968 and around 1989, the books were mainly used by guests to record their personal details, with the final column 'National Trust Member' normally being filled with a simple 'yes' or 'no'. During this period, the guestbooks served an important function for the Trust, enabling them to build extensive mailing lists and contact non-members with publicity and marketing information following their visit. In these early entries, the discourse-world interaction between holidaymakers and The National Trust was emphasised and controlled through the layout of the books' pages.

Over time, however, there is evidence across our dataset to suggest that the function of The National Trust's cottage guestbooks has shifted, and this is reflected in changes in the style of the language used within them. In Gwendra Wartha's guestbooks, for example, in the late 1970s and early 1980s inscriptions begin to differ in length and detail, and this reflects a different conceptualisation of the discourse-world and the purpose of the discourse itself. For instance, two inscribers – first in 1974 and then in 1979 – deviate from the recording of personal details by also adding short, evaluative comments to the book: 'Wonderful weather and an altogether delightful holiday', and 'A thoroughly enjoyed holiday'. From 1980 onwards, there is a marked increase in the frequency of these kinds of evaluative comments, on

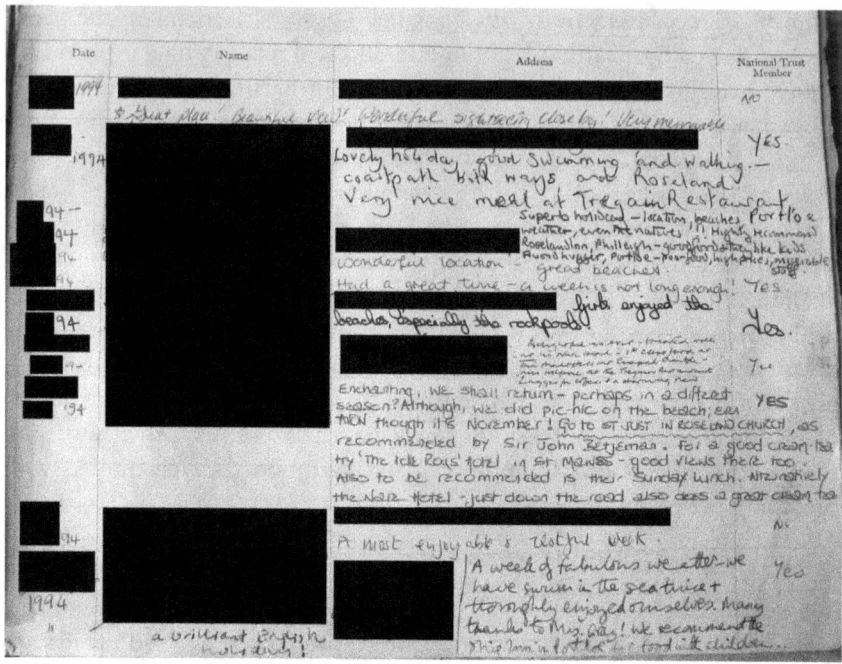

Figure 3.1 Holiday guestbook

average two or three per page. Following renovations to the cottage in 1989–90 (which are recorded in the book by National Trust staff), the 'Address' column is divided – although it is not clear by whom – to form a 'Comments' column too. This formal division lasts for five pages before a more free-form layout is adopted. The majority of entries after 1990 (a typical example of which is shown in anonymised form[3] in Figure 3.1) then feature commentary of some kind, and reflect a clear awareness on the part of the participants of the existence of multiple discourse-world co-participants who might also engage with the book.

Across the earlier entries, which focused on supplying The National Trust with personal contact details, and the later entries which are devoted to more discursive commentary, self-reference is the only guestbook feature which persists – and even this shifts in style and apparent purpose. As noted above, early entries in Gwendra Wartha's books tend to provide full names, full addresses and membership status, which indicates that visitors see the guestbooks primarily as a direct conversation with the Trust, rather than with other holidaymakers. Again, this is a typical pattern across our dataset as, over time, full names and addresses are gradually joined by general family names (such as 'The Smiths', 'The Brown family') and by more general reference to the participants' home locations (such as 'Bristol' or 'Wiltshire'), with some entries combining different levels of detail and specificity. The provision of full addresses eventually wanes to the point where, in the most recent entries to the guestbooks, no visitors supply their complete postal address at all, which might indicate discourse participants' greater awareness of the public nature of the discourse.

However, in the later entries in Gwendra Wartha's guestbooks, inscribers often provide extra information through which they express their identities. Families often specify the ages of their children, or hand the book over to their children so that they can inscribe their own names. Sometimes family members are identified only by their family title rather than their actual name (for example, 'Granny', or 'the oldies'). Holidaymakers also indicate the relationships between the people in their particular group, specifying whether they are friends or family (such as, '4 friends and relations', or 'with our friends from Sweden'). And sometimes animals and fictional creatures are incorporated into the holidaymaker's group. For instance, in one entry from the late 1970s, the names 'Tigger' and 'Piglet' are entered in children's handwriting beside the children's own names and 'Crookus' and 'Clover the frog' are added as family members too.

It is common for inscribers to indicate whether they or their family have visited Gwendra before (for example, 'Lovely holiday again', and '2nd visit') or whether they have any other historical connection with the place, writing things such as: 'Three generations of [our] family enjoyed this lovely place in Cornwall'; 'Five generations to have stayed at Gwendra. My grandparents to my grandchildren'; 'Back to Gwendra after 70 years . . . Happy memories!'; and 'Aged parent was billeted here as a RAF officer [in the 1940s]. Seven shillings and ninepence a day all in. Plus ca change!' Guestbook inscribers may also specify their nationality, particularly if they are not British: for example, 'A memorable English Christmas for a total of 12 "Kiwis" Loved the walks and the pubs!'; and 'US ex-pats camped out in London. (Architects who are going to quit our jobs, relocate to Cornwall and open our own small little office here – or else sell fish and chips)'. Some inscribers go further in elaborating their family identities, for instance entering information about family milestones (such as, 'John (18 months) has learned to say "big birdie"'; and 'started the 2 boys off on walking for "pleasure" – Porthascoe and back aged 5 and 6'). Even within the 'Membership Status' column, there is room for variation in self-presentation. Whilst most inscribers enter 'yes' or 'no', deviations from this norm include emphatic agreement (such as, 'Longstanding'; 'Yes – just'; 'Yes – certainly'; 'Family membership'; and 'I should say!') and apologies (such as, 'No, sorry! I don't think so'; 'No, 'fraid not, I don't think so'), and, with regards to Clover the frog's membership status, 'He might be!'

The shift in the style of Gwendra Wartha's guestbooks over time, through the increase of markers of identity beyond full names and titles, and the increasing appearance of extended commentary, points to holidaymakers' evolving conceptualisations of both themselves as visitors and the purpose of the guestbooks, very much in line with the notion of the guestbook as a site for the performance of identity. This linguistic development also indicates an evolving complexity in the participants' conceptualisations of and communications between each other. The ways in which inscribers refer to past and future visitors, as well as to The National Trust, reveals not only their awareness of the existence of these co-participants in the discourse-world, but also the imaginative and detailed mental representations they construct of who these people are, their likely behaviours and interests, in spite of the fact that it is highly unlikely they will ever meet.

Inscribers refer to other participants, who they assume to be involved in the discourse-world with them, in a variety of ways. In so doing, they nominate these people as present in the text-worlds they create through their entries to the guestbooks. These mental representations of the discourse are constructed in the minds of participants from 'world-building elements' (see Gavins 2007: 36): deictic items in the text which specify the temporal and spatial parameters of the text-world. The text-worlds of guestbook entries are thus structured around descriptions of space (for example, through the use of nouns, pronouns, articles, spatial locatives, spatial adverbs, demonstratives, and verbs of motion) and time (through the use of tense, aspect, temporal adverbs and temporal locatives). References to the self and to others contribute to the building of a text-world in important ways, since this not only creates text-world versions of real or imagined people, but versions which are fleshed out by the discourse participants who read the entries using their background knowledge, cultural assumptions and other discourse-world experiences. In Text World Theory terms, the resulting, often richly detailed entities which populate participants' text-worlds are known as 'enactors' (see Gavins 2007: 41).

In Gwendra Wartha's books, specific people with real-world counterparts are sometimes named or addressed directly in the discourse using proper nouns, such as the caretaker of the cottage during the 1980s, Mrs Gray: for example in, 'Many thanks to Mrs Gray for a beautiful clean flat'; and 'It was our first stay here and now we hope we can come again. Thank you Mrs Gray'. Sometimes a non-specific, imagined caretaker of the house is addressed implicitly through the use of questions, complaints or suggestions for improvements: for instance in, 'Please can we have an anti-slip mat in the bath/shower'; 'One washing machine not enough!'; and 'Kitchen struck us as a little bare (pictures no longer on walls) . . . scourer would be good in kitchen'. The National Trust as an entire organisation is often either directly addressed or nominated in other ways in the text-worlds of visitors' guestbooks entries too: for example in, 'This our second week with NT this year'; 'Pleased to have contributed in a small way to the excellent work of the NT'; and 'Our first NT holiday, hopefully not our last'. Other guests, both past and present, are addressed or nominated as well, most often in non-specific terms, for example in, 'On everyone's recommendation we tried the New Inn and were sorely disappointed'. Gwendra Wartha's guestbooks even contain a direct address to a local brewery – which is notably most unlikely ever to be involved in the discourse-world of the cottage – ('A big TQ to St Austell brewery for supplying us with many a fine beer!'), and also to the house itself: 'You were always so nice to come home to, Gwendra Wartha'.

In each of these instances, the entity explicitly named or implicitly referred to becomes an enactor in the text-world constructed by each guestbook entry, reflecting their presence in the mind of the inscriber responsible. Furthermore, the language that inscribers use to refer to themselves and to others is not only indicative of their rhetorical positioning in the discourse-world, but also serves as part of their performance of social, cultural and familial identity through the pages of the guestbook. The key point here is that, whether they have a real-world counterpart or not, none of the enactors which populate the text-worlds of guestbook discourse, including those of the inscribers themselves, is real; they are the performed personae of the inscribers and their imagined constructions of other visitors, of The National Trust, or of other beings and organisations.

6. Mind-Modelling and Embedded Worlds in Guestbook Discourse

In the later decades of the twentieth century, then, the guestbooks of National Trust holiday rental cottages appear to take on a number of different functions. Their inscriptions may, for instance, thank The National Trust or their staff; evaluate the property and the local area; or provide a summary of visitors' holiday experiences, leaving an enduring trace of the holidaymakers' transient presence in the cottage. The vast majority of entries offer some positive evaluation of their stay and a comment on the weather (for example, 'Lovely 2 weeks. Perfect weather'; 'Another super week in this lovely cottage'; 'Remarkable weather, excellent cottage'; 'A perfect holiday again, looking forward to returning in the spring'; 'A lovely holiday, peaceful spot, lucky with the weather'; 'Not enough wind for wind surfing but had a good holiday anyway'). Our examination of guestbook discourse collected from five different cottages in Cornwall has also revealed that from the 1980s onwards – not just in Gwendra Wartha but across the dataset – visitors' entries become characterised by the repeated occurrence of recommendations to future holidaymakers. This is highly interesting in cognitive terms, since it not only involves inscribers describing imagined entities who will read and/or act upon their recommendations, but the accompanying creation of often richly detailed, embedded text-worlds in which these activities are depicted as taking place.

For example, Gwendra Wartha's books include the following recommendations, which are typical of this sort of guestbook discourse phenomenon: 'Lovely holiday again. Recommend the ice cream from Treburthes Farm just north of Ruan Highlanes. Also the Aero park, Helston, for children in the rain!'; 'Good eating places – with kids. The Captains table, Portscatho, "Secrets" Falmouth, "Milliways" Falmouth. Recommended – the view from Nare Head. Good drinking pub – The Victory Inn, St Mawes'; 'Go to St Just in Roseland church, as recommended by Sir John Betjeman'. In each of these instances, the inscribers address, either directly or indirectly, an imagined future visitor to the cottage, while at the same time building a text-world through which either the recommended place or activity can be conceptualised, or an imagined visit by the reader of the guestbook is described.

In order to understand how these recommendations function in cognitive terms, let us take a more detailed look at the final example in the list above. The full entry is that captured in Figure 3.1 and reads as follows:

> Enchanting, we shall return, perhaps in a different season? Although we did pic-nic on the beach; even though it's November! GO TO ST JUST IN ROSELAND CHURCH, as recommended by Sir John Betjeman. For a good cream-tea try 'The Idle Rocks' hotel in St Mawes – good views there too. Also to be recommended is their Sunday lunch. Alternatively, the Nare Hotel – just down the road also does a great cream-tea.

The inscriber here begins by providing a one-word evaluation of their holiday – 'Enchanting' – before creating a separate text-world in which they 'shall return – perhaps in a different season?' From a Text World Theory perspective, the use of future aspect here causes a switch from the initial, but fleeting text-world of the evaluation to a more remote 'modal-world' (see Gavins 2007: 118), in which a possible, but as-yet-unrealised return visit in a different season is posited. The use of the question mark is interesting here too, as this would could indicate one of two things. The author of the entry could either be posing the modal-world of the return visit to the cottage, and its timing specifically, as a question to an imagined future reader of the guestbook, or it could be read as reflecting the author's own attitude to this proposition. From the latter perspective, this part of the entry bears much in common with the register of a private diary. It implies that the weather at the time the actual visit took place was unpleasant and that a return is something being internally contemplated, but not yet decided.

The entry then switches back to the text-world of the inscriber's holiday, which is further developed through the description of a picnic on the beach. The inscriber then uses an imperative verb, 'go', which also implicitly addresses a future reader, towards whom this instruction is directed. The importance of this part of the entry is additionally emphasised through the use of capital letters and underlining. As Gavins explains,

> Imperatives construct a separate text-world in which a prescribed action, as yet unrealised in the real world, is taking place. The person towards whom the imperative is aimed . . . then has a choice over whether or not to follow the instructions given and realise the action in the real world. (Gavins 2007: 101–2)

The world in which the reader of the entry is invited to imagine themselves going to St Just in Roseland church is thus another modal-world which is positioned more remotely from the initial text-world containing the holiday evaluation and summary. It is a possibility only, and one which the actual reader of the guestbook may or may not choose to recreate in their real world.

In terms of the performance of identity through language, this inscriber's choice to refer to Sir John Betjeman in their entry is particularly noteworthy too. There is another switch in tense in this part of the discourse, as Betjeman's recommendation of the church is positioned as having taken place at a past, but otherwise unspecified moment ('as recommended by . . .'). The nomination of Betjeman as an enactor in the text-world in this way reveals a great deal about how the inscribing participant in the discourse-world of Gwendra Wartha's guestbook conceptualises their potential co-participants who, it is important to remember, do not yet exist at the time of them writing their entry in the book. Not only does the author of this section of the guestbook create enactors of unrealised co-participants through the use of imperative verbs, question marks and remote recommendation worlds, they make clear assumptions about who their future readers are, what they might like to do on holiday and the sorts of cultural knowledge they are likely to share. The mention of the poet, writer and broadcaster Sir John Betjeman indicates that this author assumes an awareness of a real-world figure on the part of their audience and, perhaps further, that no additional detail is needed about where and when Betjeman made his recommendation of the church. In fact, Betjeman referred to St Just in Roseland as 'to many people the most beautiful churchyard on earth' in his 1964 book, *Cornwall: A Shell Guide*, but this information is not supplied. Even more interesting is the way in which a passive construction is used in a later recommendation in the same entry – 'Also to be recommended is their Sunday lunch'. The effect of this syntactic choice is that it avoids assigning responsibility for this suggestion to the inscriber. It is equally possible to read the sentence and assume that Sir John Betjeman is again responsible for making the recommendation as it is to place the inscriber in that agentive role. This aligns these two text-world enactors in a position of equivalency and thus lends additional authority to this visitor's recommendations.

All of the linguistic choices made by inscribers in the guestbooks invite their readers to ascribe particular beliefs, opinions, values and motivations to them. This conceptual process of constructing the mental states of other people, either in the real world or in a text-world, based on textual and other cues has been termed 'mind modelling' (see Stockwell 2009) in cognitive poetics. The inclusion of the name 'Sir John Betjeman' by the author above is likely to signal a number of things to the reader of this entry, whether or not they possess a detailed knowledge of the former Poet Laureate and his connections to the area: it signals their own literary knowledge; their own understanding of the local environment and its cultural history; and also their own mind-modelling assumptions about their co-participants. The language of this entry, like all others in the guestbook, is tailored with a specific audience in mind – an audience that the inscriber clearly believes will be to a great extent just like them. This kind of careful recipient design (see Garfinkel 1967) not only enables holidaymakers to perform certain identities through the language they use in the guestbooks, but also acts to form social and cultural connections across the temporal divide which separates each of the visitors to the cottage. Making assumptions about shared values, knowledge and beliefs, and expressing these linguistically is a highly socially cohesive communicative behaviour, which counteracts the otherwise insurmountably split nature of the discourse situation.

The effect that the recipient design of the guestbook entries has on minimising temporal as well as potentially social differences between the participants is nowhere made more apparent than in the highly creative discourse inscribers often produce. In his study of everyday discourse, Carter (2004) observes that high levels of creativity in language are more likely to occur in certain communicative situations than in others. This is shown in Table 3.1 (adapted from Carter) through a selection of typical types of interaction, separated according to their social contexts, where the more darkly shaded areas indicate an increase in the likelihood that linguistic creativity will be present. What is notable here is that, because the content of the guestbooks' entries is in great part based on the provision of information by participants who are unfamiliar with each other, it might be expected that the style of the language used in this situation would show only low levels of creativity.

However, the essentially collaborative structure of the guestbooks themselves transforms the discourse from something which might otherwise be transactional and professional into a much more playful and creative style. We have already seen how this shift happens gradually over time, as the vehicle for the discourse – the guestbooks provided by one of the participants (The National Trust) for the use of multiple others in a public environment – are first physically altered to allow more room for extended commentary, and then become increasingly free-form and complex sites of self-expression and inter-discursive behaviour.

This transformation also shows itself in the increased occurrence of creative and even poetic forms of language in the pages of the guestbooks over time. In Gwendra Wartha's books, there are numerous instances of linguistic parallelism: for example the syntactic parallelism in 'Wonderful situation, wonderful cottage, wonderful time!'; and 'One week last year, two weeks this year. Next year . . .?'; and phonological parallelism in 'Loved it – we had snow, hail, rain, gales and glorious sun!' and 'The Hale-Bopp comet was spectacular in a sea of stars'. Guests also make creative use of euphemism and metaphor: for example: 'Great place, shame about the weather which has been. . . . . . .!!'; and 'It was like a famous five adventure'. The use of multimodality is also common and ranges from simple emphasis through the use of capitals, emboldened and underlined fonts, through to drawings and cartoons, often but not exclusively added by children.

The participants in the discourse also frequently show self-awareness in the kinds of creativity they engage in, for example when shifting or mixing registers. One entry, for example, starts with a conventional saying and shifts into a more literary register marked by inverted commas: 'super time had by all, etc. etc. . . . . . . "and as we left, the sun broke through the clouds with a triumphant smile"'; whilst other entries play with a military or explorer register in their reference to 'morale' and 'natives' and their syntactic elision: 'Superb holiday – location, beaches, weather, even the natives!' and 'Morale high, despite lashing rain . . .'. Like the reference to John Betjeman above, these manipulations of register are revealing of how the inscribing participant in the discourse-world conceptualises the cultural knowledge of their potential co-participants, and also the decisions they make about their own identity presentation. Across the guestbooks, linguistic creativity appears to function as a way to make the inscriber and their inscription stand out on the rhetorical stage, offering distinctive and playful deviation from the more common inscription styles adopted by other writers.

A more extreme example of such deviation can be seen in the following entry, which appears to be written by a child. Amongst the often repeated positive evaluations and comments on the weather on adjacent pages (such

Context type	Interaction type		
	Information provision	Collaborative task	Collaborative idea
Transactional	commentary by museum guide	choosing and buying a television	chatting with hairdresser
Professional	oral report at group meeting	colleagues window dressing	planning meeting at place of work
Socialising	telling jokes to friends	friends cooking together	reminiscing with friends
Intimate	partner relating the story of a film seen	couple decorating a room	siblings discussing their childhood

Table 3.1 Linguistic creativity and communicative situations (adapted from Carter 2004: 165)

as, 'Always lovely, whatever the weather?!'; 'I wish I lived here'; 'Very comfortable week'; 'Very beautiful spot – time goes far too quickly!'), the inscription reads:

> I think this house is horrid 'yuck'

This deviation creates humour, which arises from this entry's incongruity in relation to the surrounding discourse. The negative comment is quickly followed by 'HA HA April Fools', and is dated 1 April: 'April Fool's Day' in England, when it is permissible to be mischievous and play pranks on other people until midday (the inscriber has also noted the time as 11.10am). The entry is humorous because it sets itself apart linguistically from the 'norm' established throughout the rest of guestbook (of overwhelmingly positive comments). As we have seen above, however, creativity and playfulness in the guestbooks is not restricted to specific days of the year; it arises naturally from the collaborative space created by the discourse situation. Collaboration between the participants is evident in the way that inscriptions either echo each other or deviate from the echoic norms established across the text. It is perhaps most evident on the final page of the most recent guestbook, when the book's lined columns have ended. One guestbook inscriber has written 'The End!!' at the bottom of the final blank page. This inscription is followed, in different handwriting, with '(You've read the book – now go see the film!)'. Two further inscriptions appear below this, in child's handwriting: 'Don't want to!', and in neater, pencil: 'Oh! Like to make the film!' Here we see participants extending the creative inscriptions of others, and adding quips to each other's lines in an inter-discursive and jointly creative manner similar to latrinalia, where visitors to the shared physical space of a public toilet often contribute successively to collaborative, humorous or political graffiti.

7. Conclusion

All of this creative linguistic play, and indeed the rest of the discourse contained in the guestbooks as a whole, is indicative of the assumption made by inscribers of a receptive and to some extent like-minded audience. These discourse-world participants capture their temporary occupation of and interaction with the immediate physical environment of the rental cottage and reflect their conceptualisation of this experience through their inscriptions in the books. However, our data shows that they also create and represent richly detailed text-world identities, both for themselves and of others, through the act of contributing to the guestbook. These textual constructions appear to show extensive acts of mind-modelling at work and an attempt to bridge the temporal as well as any possible social divide through the sharing of remote text-worlds (through recommendations) and the sharing of collaborative or playful creativity. As we have noted, Carter (2004) points out that this sort of linguistic behaviour is more common in intimate relationships and over shared activities than it is in interactions between strangers. For this reason, it is our belief that the creative communicative behaviour exhibited in the discourse of holiday cottage guestbooks acts as an important social unifier in this distinctive discourse situation. It is our further belief that only a cognitive linguistic approach to this discourse, such as that offered by Text World Theory, can account for the conceptual complexity of communication between participants who exist for one another solely through the text of the guestbook and who interact entirely in each other's minds.

Notes

1 <https://www.nationaltrust.org.uk/holidays/> (last accessed 14 January 2019).
2 <https://www.nationaltrust.org.uk/holidays/gwendra-wartha-cornwall> (last accessed 14 January 2019).
3 The data collected throughout our project is anonymised in agreement with The National Trust. No real names are used in this article or in any other publication associated with the project, and we refer only to the year of each inscription, not to the specific dates of inscribers' visits.

References

Adler, J. (1989). Travel as performed art. *American Journal of Sociology* 94 (6): 1366–91.
Bærenholdt, J. O., Haldrup, M., Larsen, J. and Urry, J. (2004). *Performing Tourist Places*. Aldershot: Ashgate.
Bagehot (2011). The National Trust: A big scary opponent for the government. *The Economist*, <http://www.economist.com/blogs/bagehot/2011/09/national-trust> (last accessed 30 November 2018).
Barton, S. (2008). *Healthy Living in the Alps: The Origins of Winter Tourism in Switzerland 1860-1914*. Manchester: Manchester University Press.
Brown, R., Flinders, C., Swartz, J. and Wilkinson, R. (2003). Visitor books – A tool for planning and evaluating visitor management at rock art sites. *Rock Art Research* 20 (1): 23–52.
Burek, C. (2008). The role of the voluntary sector in the evolving geoconservation movement. In C. Burke and C. Prosser (eds), *The History of Geoconservation*. London: Geological Society of London, pp. 61–90.
Butler, J. (1988). Performative acts and gender constitution: An essay in phenomenology and feminist theory. *Theatre Journal* 40 (4): 519–31.
Carter, R. (2004). *Language and Creativity: The Art of Common Talk*. London: Routledge.
Colley, A. C. (2010). *Victorians in the Mountains: Sinking the Sublime*. Farnham: Ashgate.
Edensor, T. (2000). Staging tourism: Tourists as performers. *Annals of Tourism Research* 27 (2): 322–44.
Edensor, T. (2001). Performing tourism, staging tourism: (Re)producing tourist space and practice. *Tourist Studies* 1 (1): 59–81.

Edensor, T. (2008). *Tourists at the Taj: Performance and Meaning at a Symbolic Site*. London: Routledge.
Garfinkel, H. (1967). *Studies in Ethnomethodology*. Upper Saddle River, NJ: Prentice Hall.
Gavins, J. (2007). *Text World Theory: An Introduction*. Edinburgh: Edinburgh University Press.
Goffman, E. (1981). *Forms of Talk*. Philadelphia: University of Pennsylvania Press.
Heafford, M. (2006). Between grand tour and tourism: British travellers to Switzerland in a period of transition, 1814-1860. *Journal of Transport History* 27 (1): 25-47.
Heller, M., Jaworski, A. and Thurlow, C. (2014). Sociolinguistics and tourism: Mobilities, markets, multilingualism. *Journal of Sociolinguistics* 18 (4): 425–58.
James, K. (2012). '[A] British social institution': The visitors' book and hotel culture in Victorian Britain and Ireland. *Journeys* 13 (1): 42–69.
James, K. (2013). The hotel inn and visitors' book in Victorian reading culture: Reading the Pen-y-Gwryd hotel book. Paper presented at the Researching the Reading Experience conference, University of Oslo, Norway, 12 June.
Jaworski, A. (2010). Linguistic landscapes on postcards: Tourist mediation and the sociolinguistic communities of contact. *Sociolinguistic Studies* 4 (3): 569–94.
Jaworski, A. and Thurlow, C. (2011). Tracing place, locating self: Embodiment and remediation in/of tourist spaces. *Visual Communication* 10 (3): 349–66.
Jenkins, J. and James, P. (1994). *From Acorn to Oak Tree: Growth of the National Trust, 1895-1994*. London: Macmillan.
Newby, H. (1999). *The National Trust: The Next Hundred Years*. London: The National Trust.
Noy, C. (2008). Mediation materialized: The semiotics of a visitor book at an Israeli commemoration site. *Critical Studies in Media Communication* 25 (2): 509–28.
Stamou, A. G. and Paraskevopoulos, S. (2003). Ecotourism experiences in visitors' books of a Greek reserve: A critical discourse analysis perspective. *Sociologia Ruralis* 43 (1): 34–55.
Stamou, A. G. and Paraskevopoulos, S. (2004). Images of nature by tourism and environmentalist discourses in visitors' books: A critical discourse analysis of ecotourism. *Discourse & Society* 15 (1): 105–29.
Stamou, A. G. and Paraskevopoulos, S. (2008). Representing protection action in an ecotourism setting: A critical discourse analysis of visitors' books at a Greek reserve. *Critical Discourse Studies* 5 (1): 35–54.
Stockwell, P. (2009). *Texture: A Cognitive Aesthetics of Reading*. Edinburgh: Edinburgh University Press.
Sullivan, K. M. (1984). Monitoring visitor use and site management at three art sites: An experiment with visitor books. In H. Sullivan (ed.), *Visitors to Aboriginal Sites: Access, Control and Management, Proceedings of the 1983 Kakadu Workshop*. Canberra: Australian National Parks and Wildlife Service, pp. 43–53.
The National Trust (2017). *Annual Report 2016-17*, <http://www.nationaltrustannualreport.org.uk> (last accessed 30 November 2018).
Thurlow, C. and Jaworski, A. (2010). *Tourism Discourse: The Language of Global Mobility*. Basingstoke: Palgrave Macmillan.
Thurlow, C. and Jaworski, A. (2011a). Tourism discourse: Languages and banal globalization. *Review of Applied Linguistics* 2: 285–312.

Thurlow, C. and Jaworski, A. (2011b). Banal globalization? Embodied actions and mediated practices in tourists' online photo-sharing. In C. Thurlow and K. Mroczek (eds), *Digital Discourse: Language in the New Media*. New York: Oxford University Press, pp. 220–50.

Thurlow, C. and Jaworski, A. (2014). 'Two hundred ninety-four': Remediation and multimodal performance in tourist placemaking. *Journal of Sociolinguistics* 18 (4): 459–94.

Thurlow, C. and Jaworski, A. (2015). On top of the world: Tourists' spectacular self-locations as multimodal travel writing. In J. Kuehn and P. Smethurst (eds), *New Directions in Travel Writing Studies*. Basingstoke: Palgrave Macmillan, pp. 35–53.

Waterson, M. (2006). *The National Trust: The First Hundred Years*. 2nd edition. London: The National Trust.

Waterson, M. (2011). *The National Trust and its Benefactors*. London: The National Trust.

Werth, P. (1999). *Text Worlds: Representing Conceptual Space in Discourse*. London: Longman.

Wright, P. (2009). *On Living in an Old Country: The National Past in Contemporary Britain*. Oxford: Oxford University Press.

4

Metaphorical Descriptions of Pain on a Trigeminal Neuralgia Forum: Pushing the Boundaries of Cognitive Linguistics

Elena Semino

1. Introduction

The extract below is taken from an online forum dedicated to Trigeminal Neuralgia – a condition that causes disabling and overwhelming episodes of pain in the face:

> I woke this morning to take my bucket full of meds, it feels like I have had a Mike Tyson night![1]

At the time when this extract was posted on the forum, the US heavy-weight boxer Mike Tyson had abandoned his previously illustrious career after being repeatedly beaten. Based on this minimal contextualisation, it should be possible to infer that the simile 'it feels like I have had a Mike Tyson night' is used to suggest that this person woke up with the kind of pain in the face that one might feel if they had been repeatedly and violently punched by a professional boxer the night before. But how does someone writing online about a condition such as Trigeminal Neuralgia come to use an expression such as this?

To answer this question, in this chapter I present an analysis of all similar structures (i.e. 'feels like' similes for pain) on this particular online forum over a period of five and a half years. In line with the goals of this volume, I first consider the ways in which a cognitive linguistic approach to metaphor can account for the use of this kind of expression to describe the pain caused by Trigeminal Neuralgia (henceforth TN). I then point out the challenges that this kind of data poses to current cognitive linguistic accounts of metaphor. Finally, I reflect on the implications of my findings for the systematic analysis of metaphor in discourse and for the potential contribution of such analysis to the understanding of the lived experience of TN, and to the development of better ways of catering for the needs of people with TN.

2. Background: Pain, Metaphor and Trigeminal Neuralgia

Pain is notoriously difficult to communicate (e.g. Scarry 1985). The English language in particularly has relatively few words that specialise in the description of pain: 'hurt' (as a noun and a verb), 'pain(ful)', 'sore' and, less straightforwardly, 'ache' (as a noun and a verb, and in the adjectival form 'achy').[2] As these words cannot do justice to the wide variety of pain sensations that can be experienced, it is well known that pain is often described through figurative language, and particularly similes and metaphors (De Souza and Frank 2000; Schott 2004; Lascaratou 2007; Kövecses 2008; Biro 2010; Semino 2010; Loftus 2011; Deignan et al. 2013; Bourke 2014).

The most prototypical type of pain arguably results from cuts, burns and fractures, and is known as 'nociceptive pain': 'noxious perception resulting from actual tissue damage following surgical, traumatic, or disease-related injuries' (Vadivelu et al. 2011: 46). As the causes of this kind of pain are usually visible, whether to the naked eye or through medical technology, adequate responses to nociceptive pain are less dependent on effective communication than in the case of pain that does not result from obvious physical damage. This includes particularly 'neuropathic pain', that is, pain caused by problems in the nervous system, as in the case of TN. Consider, for example, the expression a 'constant burning pain in her lower abdomen' (from the Oxford English Corpus). In its most basic, literal sense, 'burning' refers to the process of combustion. Here, however, it is used to capture the quality of one of the types of pain that result from problems in the digestive system. This use of 'burning' is part of a conventional tendency in English (and other languages) to describe non-nociceptive pain in terms of properties or processes that would cause tissue damage if applied to the body, and hence result in nociceptive pain (e.g. burning, stabbing, splitting).

From the perspective of Conceptual Metaphor Theory (henceforth CMT), pain is one of the subjective, sensitive and poorly delineated experiences (or target conceptual domains) that tend to be communicated and conceptualised in terms of better delineated, image-rich and intersubjectively accessible experiences (or source conceptual domains). In the case of 'burning pain', for example, a subjective, invisible sensation is described in terms of a concrete, externally perceptible process. This use of 'burning' would be metonymic if it described the nociceptive pain that results from, for example, contact with a flame: in this case, there would be an *association* between the cause of physical damage and the pain experience. In contrast, 'burning' in 'burning pain' is metaphorical when no contact with flames or hot objects is involved: in this case, the use of the expression suggests a *similarity* between a particular pain experience and the kind of nociceptive pain that would result from contact with a flame or a hot object. The conventional tendency to describe pain experiences in terms of causes of prototypical nociceptive pain has been captured by Kövecses (2008) as a series of conceptual metaphors (or cross-domain mappings) with PAIN as target domain, including, for example, PAIN IS FIRE (e.g. 'burning pain') and PAIN IS A SHARP OBJECT (e.g. 'stabbing pain'). I have proposed the more general formulation PAIN IS CAUSE OF PHYSICAL DAMAGE (Semino 2010, 2011; see also Deignan et al. 2013: 267–302). The metaphors suggested by Kövecses (2008) can be seen as specific variants of this general metaphor.

My opening example is a linguistic manifestation of the conventional tendency captured by the conceptual metaphor PAIN IS CAUSE OF PHYSICAL DAMAGE. In the context of the post, 'Mike Tyson night' functions as a metonymic reference to being repeatedly punched by a professional boxer. The resulting physical damage would cause a kind of pain that the forum contributor suggests is similar to his/her own. Even this account, however, does not fully explain the specific choice of 'Mike Tyson night' in the context of the interaction among forum contributors. I will return to this point below.

Trigeminal Neuralgia is a serious but relatively rare condition, in that it affects four or five people per 100,000, with a higher incidence of up to twenty per 100,000 in people over sixty (Frontera et al. 2015: 588). Episodes of pain vary in their frequency and the person is usually pain-free between episodes. However, the intensity of attacks is such that TN has been described as 'the suicide disease' (e.g. Pucci et al. 2017) and as causing 'the world's worst pain' (Zakzrewska 2006). In addition, the relatively low incidence of TN means that diagnosis is often delayed while other more likely diagnostic avenues are pursued (e.g. dental problems). In addition, people with the condition may find it hard to help others understand the severity of their symptoms, and may not easily find other sufferers or support groups locally. While both pharmacological and surgical treatment options exist, TN is usually difficult to cure completely.

Although figurative descriptions of pain have been studied before, including from a cognitive linguistic perspective, no study has, to my knowledge, focused specifically on TN. Given the extreme nature of the symptoms, descriptions of pain associated with TN should therefore provide a challenging testing ground for existing accounts of metaphors for pain. The focus on online forum data means that I will deal with people's own authentic and relatively unconstrained descriptions, in the context of interactions within a community that shares the same, infrequent condition. It is well known that, in spite of occasional issues, such online patient communities can have an important function in terms of exchange of information and mutual support (e.g. Prestin and Chou 2014; Allen et al. 2016).

3. Data and Method

The general definition of metaphor I adopt in this chapter is as follows: metaphor involves talking and, potentially, thinking, about one thing in terms of another where the two 'things' are different, but a similarity can be perceived between them.

This definition encompasses different manifestations of metaphoricity in language, including what Steen et al. (2010) call 'direct' and 'indirect' metaphor. 'Direct' metaphor captures explicit comparisons between unlike things, and particularly similes such as 'it feels like I have had a Mike Tyson night': here a pain sensation that is not caused by damage to bodily tissue is described in terms of a physical attack from a human agent that would cause damage to bodily tissue. 'Indirect' metaphor captures cases where the contextual meaning of a word contrasts with a more basic meaning of the same word (in the sense of more concrete, more precise and more closely related to bodily action), but the contextual meaning can be understood by comparison with the basic meaning. As I explained above, this applies to 'burning' in 'a constant burning pain in the lower abdomen'. The contextual meaning of 'burning' is a particular kind of pain sensation caused by problems in the digestive system. This contrasts with the basic meaning of 'burning', which is the process of combustion, and with the type of nociceptive pain sensation that is metonymically associated with combustion. However, the pain caused by acidity in the stomach can be understood by comparison with the pain that results from being burnt (Pragglejaz Group 2007).

The data for this chapter was obtained from a corpus of contributions to the online forum of a UK-based association for the support of people with TN and their families. More specifically, the corpus contains 2,250,659 words of contributions which were posted between January 2008 and May 2013. The vast majority of contributors self-declare as having TN. The posts cover a wide range of topics, including symptoms, medication and its side effects, surgery, living with TN and so on.

The episodes of pain caused by TN are frequent topics on the forum. The word 'pain' occurs 16,759 times, and is the top third keyword in a comparison between word frequencies in the TN corpus and a general corpus of British English from the same period (the British English 2006 Corpus, compiled by Paul Baker at Lancaster University). To narrow down my analysis, I therefore obtained a concordance of the search string 'feels like' in the corpus. This decision was based on the expectation that, in the kind of data included in the corpus, a substantial number of instances of the expression would be part of descriptions of episodes of TN-related pain.

The search resulted in 254 citations. These citations were manually checked to determine whether (a) they described the pain caused by TN; and (b) they could be classified as similes according to the definition of 'direct' metaphor above. This process resulted in the identification of 152 relevant uses of 'feels like'. In addition, the immediately preceding and following co-text (in the sense of adjacent sentences) was examined for further metaphorical descriptions of pain, whether through direct or indirect metaphor.

4. Main Patterns in the Data: Conceptual Metaphor Theory and Its Developments

In this section I present the main patterns in my data and consider how they can be accounted for within cognitive linguistic approaches to metaphor. I begin by applying Grady's (1997) notion of 'primary metaphor', which is an important addition to Lakoff and Johnson's (1980) original version of CMT. I then focus on examples from the data that require a consideration of the relationship between culture and metaphor, and between conventional and creative metaphors. I show more specifically how the most complex and creative similes in the data can be seen as 'blends' in Fauconnier and Turner's (2002) terms. I finish by pointing out some outstanding issues that, I suggest, cannot be easily accommodated within cognitive linguistic accounts of metaphor.

4.1 Primary Metaphors

Out of 152 relevant similes in the concordance of 'feels like', 101 can be accounted for, at least in general terms, by the metaphor PAIN IS CAUSE OF PHYSICAL DAMAGE, as in the two extracts below (NB: all quotes from the data are reproduced as in the original, including any typographical errors and grammatical infelicities):

(1) Half of my face feels like it's on fire
(2) it feels like I've been rubbing my face in stinging nettles

The metaphor PAIN IS CAUSE OF PHYSICAL DAMAGE differs from conceptual metaphors such as LIFE IS A JOURNEY, which received much attention in early work in CMT (Lakoff and Johnson 1980), in that it does not involve multiple systematic correspondences between source and target domain. Rather, it is best described as a 'primary metaphor' – a particular type of basic conceptual metaphor initially proposed by Grady (1997) and then adopted in Lakoff and Johnson's (1999) version of CMT. Primary metaphors capture correlations between subjective experiences (e.g. intimacy) and sensorimotor experiences (e.g. physical closeness). These connections are experienced in what Grady calls 'primary scenes', that is, repeated situations that tend to occur early in human experience. In infancy, for example, intimacy with other people correlates with being in physical proximity. In later stages of development, the same subjective states can occur in the absence of the sensorimotor experiences (e.g. one can feel intimacy with someone who is not physically close). However, the connection persists as a mapping between what are now separate conceptual domains (as opposed to elements of the same primary scene). The primary metaphor INTIMACY IS CLOSENESS explains conventional metaphorical expressions such as 'close friends' or 'distant acquaintances', where interpersonal relations are described in terms of physical distance.

In the case of pain, the relevant primary scene involves nociceptive pain, that is, a correlation between the subjective sensation of pain and an external process that causes damage to the body. This explanation works well for Examples 1 and 2 above, as they involve basic, natural causes of damage to the body (fire and stinging nettles). Kövecses's (2008) conventional conceptual metaphors for pain, such as PAIN IS A SHARP OBJECT, can be seen as more specific formulations of the same primary metaphor. As I show in the next section, however, the causes of physical damage included in other pain descriptions draw from a much wider range of experiences.

4.2 Culture and the Elaboration of Primary Metaphors

As Grady and Ascoli (2017: 29) put it, primary metaphors involve associations between 'fundamental' concepts which are 'grounded in universal (rather than culturally determined) aspects of human experience', such as HEAVINESS, VERTICAL HEIGHT, BRIGHTNESS and, I argue, PHYSICAL DAMAGE. However, many of the descriptions of pain in my data cannot be explained as straightforwardly as (1) and (2) in terms of the realisation of a primary metaphor. In some cases, the difference lies in the nature of the metaphorical entities and processes involved:

(3) and feels like a thick knitting needle is being twisred round and round it
(4) It feels like a band is tightening round my face
(5) My tongue has been continuesly tingly for years and also it feels like i have put my tongue on a battery

Here the causes of physical damage are artefacts (knitting needles, bands and batteries) that are familiar in the cultural context that forum contributors live in (Kövecses 2005), and the relevant stage of technological development.

In Examples 3 and 4, the choice of metaphorical objects and processes can be described as one of the types of creative exploitations of conventional conceptual metaphor proposed in Lakoff and Turner (1989), that is, the 'elaboration' of a general conventional source concept. The notions of physical damage via, respectively, penetration with a sharp object and tightening, are realised through more specific and less conventional concepts (a knitting needle and a band). Example 5 more specifically relies on the invention of electricity, which, according to Bourke (2014) is a technological development that proved to be a particularly rich and frequent source of metaphors for people in pain (see also Winter and Matlock 2017 on the role of language and culture in reinforcing and enhancing embodied primary metaphors). The description of pain as an electric shock is in fact particularly associated with TN (Zakzrewska 2006). My data includes ten instances of this kind of description, including four instances of 'electric shock' and several extended examples such as the following:

(6) My pain feels like someone has wired my cheek up to the National Grid and flicks the switch off and on at a time of their choosing. When the zaps hit the pain travels up to my forehead and down to my upper jaw and lip.

Here not only is the 'National Grid' a UK-specific term, but the simile also evokes a situation that is far from Grady's basic primary scene. This kind of situation is best captured by the related notion of 'scenario', which has been adopted in some discourse analytic approaches to metaphor as the most appropriate level of conceptual representation for the analysis of metaphorical patters in authentic language use (e.g. Musolff 2006, 2016; Semino 2008; Semino et al. 2018). Scenarios are mental representations of settings that include participants, entities and possible event/action sequences, and that therefore often manifest in language as 'mini-narratives' (Musolff 2006, 2016), as in the case of Example 6. In addition, this example also involves: an explicit reference to a third-person agent causing the physical damage ('someone . . .'), metaphorical movement ('the pain travels up . . . and down') and, overall, a situation that is, at best, implausible. I will discuss these phenomena in the next sections.

4.3 Metaphor Combinations

Example 6 is one of several instances in the data where the pain is explicitly presented as an agent who is causing physical damage to the person. The 'Mike Tyson' extract above is an example of this pattern, but the actual process of causing physical damage is left implicit, or, as I have explained, suggested through metonymy. In other cases, however, there are more explicit references to violent actions performed by a metaphorical agent. This often suggests a sense of vulnerability, helplessness and emotional distress:

(7) Just feels like someone clobbered me with a crowbar on the right side of my head and like someone has tried to gouge my cheekbone out again
(8) I'm also now feeling like I've been repeatedly punched in the cheekbones so it feels like my cheeks are being pulled and tugged in from the inside . . .
(9) Hi folks, well my friend Mr TN is visiting me 24/7 at the moment with what feels like a large hot poker straight from the fire which he has placed in my right eye and I cant get it out aaaaagh!!!!!!!

Several previous studies have captured these kinds of descriptions through generalisations involving the notions of attack and aggression (e.g. Lascaratou 2007; Biro 2010; Frank 2011). In Grady's terms, the conventional representation of pain as a malevolent aggressor can be described as a complex metaphor that results from the combination of PAIN IS CAUSE OF PHYSICAL DAMAGE with other primary metaphors, such as CAUSES ARE PHYSICAL FORCES (Lakoff and Johnson 1999: 53) and, potentially, DIFFICULTIES ARE OPPONENTS. Indeed, in the version of CMT proposed in Lakoff and Johnson (1999), many conventional conceptual metaphors (e.g. LIFE IS A JOURNEY) are described as complex metaphors that involve the combination of several different primary metaphors.

Example 9 above is worthy of further note not just because of the very explicit and potentially humorous personification of TN ('my friend Mr TN'), but also because of an additional way in which it involves the combination of metaphors. Whereas the examples I have quoted so far involve a single metaphorical cause of physical damage, the description in Example 9 combines two, that is, penetration via a sharp object and burning ('a large hot poker straight from the fire'). The tendency for intense pain to be expressed in terms of scenarios that combine different types of physical damage has been noted before (e.g. Deignan et al. 2013), and was observed repeatedly in my data (e.g. 'Mine feels like someone is pulling a red hot barbed fish hook through the bones and tissue'). In Lakoff and Turner's (1989: 70) typology of creative uses of conventional conceptual metaphors, these examples involve 'the formation of composite metaphors', that is, they combine into a single scenario what Kövecses's (2008) calls PAIN IS A SHARP OBJECT and PAIN IS FIRE.

Several contributors to the forum outline even richer metaphorical scenarios that combine multiple and sometimes idiosyncratic causes of physical damage, as in the extract below:

(10) At the moment, it feels like someone of considerable weight (not you [FEMALE NAME] lol) is standing on the side of my face, wearing stilletto's whilst pouring red hot liquid into my ear.

When I get the bolts it feels like someone has decided that I deserve to be cattle prodded!

The first sentence of Example 10 combines three metaphorical causes of physical damage: excessive weight/pressure ('considerable weight'), penetration via a sharp object ('wearing stiletto's') and heat/burning ('pouring red hot liquid'). The following sentence adds electric shocks via a cattle prod. Both sentences explicitly mention an agent ('someone') which, together with the multiple causes of physical damage, can suggest an overall scenario reminiscent of torture. On the other hand, however, the tone of the extract is rather humorous, as suggested by the jokey clarification that 'someone of considerable weight' does not refer to another contributor to the online forum who is likely to be reading the post. I will return to this humorous tone below. As far as metaphoricity is concerned, Example 10 involves two of Lakoff and Turner's (1989) main types of metaphorical creativity: combination of different conventional metaphors, that is, Kövecses's (2008) PAIN IS A BURDEN, PAIN IS A SHARP OBJECT and PAIN IS FIRE; and elaboration, that is, the realisation of the sharp object as stilettos and the source of burning as red hot liquid. The reference to a cattle prod can also be seen as a case of elaboration of the more conventional notion of electric shock.

While this account goes a considerable distance towards explaining both the conventional basis of descriptions such as Example 10 and their creativity, it does not do justice to the way in which the different components combine into a single, dynamic, coherent but counterintuitive whole: while reading the extract, I imagine an overweight person standing in stilettos on an oversize sideways face, pouring some liquid into the person's ear. I expect that something similar applies to readers of the TN forum, and of this chapter. Our ability to imagine something as implausible as this is of course developed from an early age via engagement with different kinds of fantasy, but is not easy to account for in cognitive linguistic terms, and particularly in terms of CMT and its developments. The approach to metaphor proposed within Fauconnier and Turner's (2002) Blending Theory goes some way towards this goal.

4.4. Creative Similes as Blends

The theory of Blending, or Conceptual Integration (Fauconnier and Turner 2002), accounts for much of human thinking in terms of the ability to combine different mental representations formed during online cognitive activities ('input spaces') into more complex mental spaces ('blends'), in which new meanings can develop dynamically as a result of the interaction of elements from the input spaces ('emergent structure'). A 'conceptual integration network' minimally includes two input spaces, a 'generic space' that contains structures shared by the input spaces and a blended space.

When applied to metaphor, Blending Theory can account for aspects of metaphorical meaning that cannot be straightforwardly explained in terms of the unidirectional mappings of CMT and its developments. For example, the metaphorical statement 'That surgeon is a butcher' (Grady et al. 1999) is likely to be interpreted as suggesting that the surgeon is incompetent, and therefore a threat to patients. However, the notion of incompetence is not a conventional element of the concept of butcher, which, in CMT terms, functions as the source domain. In Blending Theory terms, the interpretation of the statement involves the blending of elements from two input spaces: Butcher (the source input space) and Surgeon (the target input space). These spaces share some structure (captured by the notion of generic space): they both involve a human being using a sharp instrument to make cuts on bodies. However, there is a contrast in terms of instruments (cleaver vs scalpel), kinds of bodies involved (dead animals vs live humans) and goal of cutting (severing flesh vs healing). When elements from the two input spaces are merged in the blended space, the combination of the means of butchery with the goals of surgery results in incompetent, and dangerous, professional behaviour. This is the emergent structure that arises from the imaginative development or 'running' of the blend, and that corresponds to the meaning of the metaphorical statement.

This approach has been used in the analysis of humour (e.g. Coulson 2005; Coulson and Pascual 2006) and can potentially be applied to examples such as 10 above. Let me just take this part of the example: 'it feels like someone of considerable weight . . . is standing on the side of my face, wearing stilletto's whilst pouring red hot liquid into my ear'. A possible Blending Theory account of this extract is as follows. The target input space contains the face of the writer of the post. The source input space contains an overweight person in stilettos standing on something and holding a container with red hot liquid in it. This source space is itself a blend between a space with a person in it and three spaces each containing different conventional causes of physical damage (excessive weight, sharp objects, hot fluid). The source and target input spaces are merged into a blended space, where the person from the source space stands on the face from the target space. Note that the relative sizes of the person and the face need to be such that the person can actually stand on the face but still cause discomfort through their weight. When the blend is run, the person from the source space is in a position to both pierce the face with the stilettos and simultaneously pour the liquid into the ear of the owner of the head from the target space. This constitutes a scenario in which considerable nociceptive pain would be experienced. And that is what the writer of the post says that the pain feels like.

While this approach provides a more satisfactory account of how this kind of lengthy simile can be interpreted, it is also rather problematic. Like similar applications of Blending Theory, it can be accused of post hoc rationalisation: one starts from an interpretation of a linguistic example and works backwards to derive a conceptual integration network that explains that interpretation. The accusation of ad-hocness can definitely be levelled at my account in the previous paragraph.

In the next section I will move on to the challenges that my data poses to cognitive linguistic accounts of metaphor. I start with a closer look at 'impossibility' in the scenarios outlined in the similes I analysed and then move on to how specific expressions such as 'Mike Tyson night' arise in the interactive context of the online forum.

5. The Challenge of Unfamiliar Metaphorical Scenarios

Example 10 is a particularly clear case of a pattern that is common throughout my data, and in descriptions of pain more generally: the metaphorical processes and/or scenarios that are used to communicate pain are often unlikely to have been experienced directly by the pain sufferer and their audience. This in fact applies to most of the extracts I have presented throughout this chapter, which include having half of one's face on fire, being pierced in the ear with thick knitting needles, being wired up to the National Grid and so on. Such descriptions arguably involve both metaphor and hyperbole, although invoking the latter concept should not be interpreted as dismissing the credibility of the accounts of pain in the data. On the contrary, it should be recognised that going beyond realistic familiar experiences is necessary to do justice to the nature of TN-related pain. In fact, as has been noted before, even conventional metaphorical descriptions of pain as 'stabbing' or headaches as 'splitting' tend to involve experiences that are (thankfully) rare (De Souza and Frank 2000; Pither 2002; Semino 2010; Deignan et al. 2013). Crucially, the successful use of these descriptions does not seem to depend on an assumption that the people involved in communication have direct experience of the metaphorical scenarios.

A more systematic analysis of the data from this particular perspective reveals different degrees to which metaphorical scenarios may be described as implausible or unfamiliar, at least as far as direct experience is concerned. Some instances involve possible but rare or unlikely experiences, such as one's face being on fire, or being stabbed. The more specific the metaphorical scenario is (e.g. being pierced in the ear with thick knitting needles), the more unlikely it is to have been experienced by the participants in communication, or anyone else. Instances such as Example 10 are not just very specific but also involve details that make the whole scenario unrealistic: as I mentioned earlier, we have to imagine that someone can stand on someone else's face in stilettos and pour liquid in their ear at the same time. Other cases from the data are more clearly impossible, whether physically (Example 11) or technically (Example 12):

(11) The burning feels like acid has been poured behind my eyes
(12) I'd like to see him eat when it feels like you have an electric sub-station wired up to your face.

All of this emphasises the extreme nature of the pain associated with TN, but also poses a potential challenge to cognitive linguistic accounts of metaphor. Within CMT in its various forms, the relationship between source and target domains is often described in terms of a contrast in concreteness, that is, the source domain (e.g. MOVEMENT) is more concrete and grounded in physical experience than the target domain (e.g. TIME) (e.g. Lakoff and Johnson 1980; Kövecses 2010, 2017). It is also recognised in some studies, however, that a contrast in concreteness does not apply all the time, and, even when it does, it may not be the only or main contrast between source and target domains (e.g. Dancygier and Sweetser 2014: 64–7). Other relevant contrasts are expressed in terms of degrees of delineation and image-richness: source domains tend to be more clearly delineated and image-rich than target domains (e.g. Lakoff and Johnson 1980; Grady 1997). Dancygier and Sweetser (2014) make a cogent argument for degrees of intersubjective accessibility being a more appropriate and accurate description of the contrast between source and target domains: source domains tend to be more intersubjectively accessible than target domains, especially in the case of primary metaphors such as MORE IS UP (e.g. 'prices are going up') (see also Grady and Ascoli 2017).

So far, one might argue, so good. Pain, and non-nociceptive pain in particular, is not an abstract experience, but it is certainly subjective, poorly delineated and image-poor. This 'invisibility' is what makes it a challenge for communication in the first place. In contrast, the various scenarios involving causes of physical damage to the body are concrete, clearly delineated and image rich, whether or not they are realistic or plausible. However, there is an additional assumption that lies behind the use of the concepts of concreteness, image-richness, intersubjective accessibility and so on to explain the understanding of one conceptual domain in terms of another in CMT: that source domains are more familiar than target domains, or, minimally, familiar enough to be used to make sense of and communicate about target domains. This does not of course necessarily require direct embodied experience. For example, using and understanding WAR metaphors (e.g. 'She lost her battle against cancer') does not rely on first-hand experience of war: what matters is knowledge about war, and that knowledge may be acquired indirectly via reading, watching films and so on. This works well for WAR metaphors because they primarily rely on factual knowledge about participants, actions and outcomes (e.g. 'losing a battle' is an unsuccessful outcome, and therefore suggests that the person has died).

In the case of pain descriptions, in contrast, what is being conveyed is a physical sensation. The goal, therefore, is to express what it is like to have that kind of pain, so that others know or even feel what that pain is like, through a process that can be described as embodied simulation (Semino 2010). However, as I have shown, this is often done by outlining scenarios that are not familiar or accessible from previous direct experience (although some aspects of those scenarios may be familiar from scenes of crime or torture from news reports, books, films, etc.).

The ability to relate to and potentially simulate those scenarios can be explained in terms of analogy with less extreme but more familiar experiences: for example, being pierced with a thick knitting needle is an extreme case of being cut; having one's face on fire is an extreme case of being burnt; being attached to an electric sub-station is an extreme case of a minor electric shock and so on. Nonetheless, the frequency of these metaphorical descriptions, not just in my data but in accounts of pain generally, requires some refinement to some central notions in cognitive linguistic accounts of metaphor, and particularly the assumption of differences in familiarity that lies behind different accounts of the contrasts between source and target domains. This kind of data also raises some questions concerning whether and how is possible to achieve some degree of intersubjective accessibility via metaphors that are not based in shared experiences, or, more fundamentally, whether intersubjective accessibility actually matters to successful communication about pain, in the sense of, for example, eliciting empathetic responses or accurate diagnoses.

6. The Challenge of Emergent Metaphor Patterns in Discourse

In this final section of the data analysis, let me return to my opening example: 'I woke this morning to take my bucket full of meds, it feels like I have had a Mike Tyson night!'

I have already explained how the simile in this extract conveys the person's pain through a combination of metonymy and metaphorical comparison. The implied scenario of physical aggression is also consistent with the broader pattern I have described, whereby the pain of TN is described in terms of causes of nociceptive pain, including violent attacks from another agent. While this can be explained in terms of a combination of primary metaphors, the reference to Mike Tyson is a culture-specific elaboration of the source of physical harm, and of course assumes that others on the forum know that Mike Tyson is a former heavyweight boxing champion, and that he ended his career after being repeatedly defeated. However, all of this still does not fully answer the question I started with: How does someone writing online about a condition such as Trigeminal Neuralgia come to use an expression such as this? For example, the simile is potentially humorous, and, unusually, it only makes an implicit reference to a cause of nociceptive pain (i.e. through metonymy, as I mentioned earlier). To explain these aspects of the extract, I need to turn to the context in which it was posted on the online forum.

The post in which this example occurs is part of a series of responses to the post below, which includes Example 10:

> On a lighter note gang, how many times during our suffering has someone asked you 'what does it feel like?'
>
> Pain is probably the worst thing to put into words, sometimes when I describe it to someone I get the 'wish I never asked' look from them, how about we 'share' our pain descriptions.
>
> At the moment, it feels like someone of considerable weight (not you [FEMALE NAME] lol) is standing on the side of my face, wearing stilletto's whilst pouring red hot liquid into my ear.
>
> When I get the bolts it feels like someone has decided that I deserve to be cattle prodded!
>
> Come on guys, add your descriptions, let the only pill we take at this moment be a 'Chill Pill' lots of love, crazy but gorgeous (gosh these meds make me type crazy things)

This post makes explicit the individual and social consequences of TN-related pain and exploits the affordances of the forum to set up a space within which contributors can safely describe exactly what their pain feels like, without having to face negative reactions from people who do not share that experience. This is done within a 'humorous frame' (Kotthoff 2006; Coates 2007) that is explicitly set up at the beginning of the post ('on a lighter note gang') and then realised through the poster's own description, as I mentioned earlier, and through the references to 'Chill Pill' and 'crazy but gorgeous' in the final paragraph. Humour is well known to be a way of dealing with adversity, defusing difficult situations, empowering oneself and strengthening social bonds with others, including in the context of illness (Demjén 2016).

A number of other forum contributors respond to this post with their own descriptions of pain. Several of these descriptions are humorous, and pick up on some aspects of the original description, for example via variations on the topic of shoes and stilettos. More specifically, one description of the aftermath of an episode of pain includes the expression 'having been 12 rounds with Ricky Hatton'. Ricky Hatton is a former British boxing champion, and this particular forum contributor explicitly refers to a match with him as the kind of cause of physical damage and pain that best resembles his own experience.

The 'Mike Tyson' simile occurs in the following post, by the contributor who initiated the whole thread. Having provided its context, it is now possible to explain the characteristics of this simile that are not accounted for by a cognitive linguistic account. The reference to a famous boxer champion builds on the previous reference to Ricky Hatton. The fact that the previous post includes a reference to '12 rounds' makes it possible to use Tyson's name as a metonymy for a whole boxing match, and particularly an uneven boxing match, rather than having to be more explicit for the sake of clarity. And the potentially humorous tone (see also the informal 'bucket full of meds') is consistent with and reinforces the humorous frame set up at the beginning of the thread and subsequently adopted by other respondents. In this way, this post also both reflects and reinforces a sense of intimacy, solidary and complicity among forum contributors, who do not only share the experience of TN but also ways of talking (humorously) about it.

In other words, the combination of cognitive linguistic concepts and a detailed consideration of the dynamics of the interaction on the forum provides a full answer to my original question as to how the 'Mike Tyson' simile came to be used on the forum to describe TN-related pain. While different aspects of 'context' are increasingly taken into account within a CMT approach (Kövecses 2015), the richness and complexity of 'metaphor performance' in discourse are best accounted for within a Dynamic Systems approach to metaphor (e.g. Gibbs and Cameron 2008; Gibbs 2017a, 2017b; Semino and Demjén 2017). From this perspective, the choices of metaphor made by participants in communication are seen as resulting from the interaction of multiple interrelated cognitive, cultural, pragmatic and linguistic factors, which operate at different timescales. In my specific case, these include: cultural knowledge about violent sports such as boxing and specific knowledge about Mike Tyson in 2008; conventional linguistic and conceptual metaphors for pain in English; the nature of the particular online forum; previous contributions by members of the online forum; relationships between contributors; the specifics of individual experiences of TN; and so on. Within this approach to metaphor, cognitive linguistic accounts make an important contribution as part of a larger framework for making sense of communicative behaviour in context.

7. Conclusions

The systematic analysis of pain descriptions through 'feels like' similes on an online forum dedicated to Trigeminal Neuralgia has highlighted both the strengths and weaknesses of cognitive linguistic approaches to metaphor, and specifically Conceptual Metaphor Theory and its developments.

As I have shown, a cognitive linguistic approach accounts for the tendency to describe TN-related pain in terms of a variety of causes of damage to the body, including both conventional patterns, culture-specific applications and different types of creativity. On the other hand, this approach does not fully explain at least two aspects of the data: the fact that many of the similes evoke scenarios that are unlikely or impossible to be familiar through direct experience; and the specific formal, affective and pragmatic aspects of individual similes in context. I have suggested that the former challenge requires a reconsideration of the notions of contrasts in concreteness, familiarity and intersubjective accessibility between source and target domains in CMT, while that the latter challenge can be met through a Dynamics Systems approach to metaphor, in which conventional conceptual metaphors are one of a variety of interacting factors that influence metaphor use in discourse.

A more general and important point lies behind both my application of cognitive linguistic approaches to metaphor and my claim that Dynamics Systems provides a more satisfactory and exhaustive account of choices and patterns in my data. The point is that the forms and functions of metaphor in discourse are so varied, rich and complex that they can only be satisfactorily accounted for by bringing together different levels of analysis and different theoretical perspectives. This applies both within and beyond Cognitive Linguistics, as I have shown, and is consistent with much current thinking in metaphor research. For example, from a cognitive linguistic perspective, Dancygier and Sweetser (2014) advocate a multi-level approach to metaphor, including image schemas, primary metaphors, different kinds of metaphor hierarchies, and blends (see also Semino et al. 2018). Beyond Cognitive Linguistics, Gibbs (2017a, 2017b) explains his adoption of a Dynamics Systems approach to metaphor as stemming from the realisation that different theories and methods account for different factors, aspects or dimensions in 'metaphor performance', and therefore ideally need to be brought together, rather than applied and developed separately and in competition with one another.

To conclude, let me return to the data. In many respects, in this chapter I have treated the 'feels like' pain descriptions on the TN online forum as the test bed for what cognitive linguistic approaches to metaphor in discourse can and cannot do. However, my choice of this specific data is motivated by a broader concern for first-person accounts of the experience of illness, and particularly chronic and intense pain such as that experienced by people with TN. The growth of online peer-to-peer communication about illness provides unprecedented opportunities for individual experiences to be shared, and also studied. The kind of analysis I have carried out treats the forum contributors as experts by experience with regards to pain and TN, and identifies patterns in their accounts that can be relevant to the provision of better support and medical care. On the one hand, the associations of vulnerability and emotional distress of many of the descriptions I have presented highlight the need for psychological support, and the role of online fora in the provision of such support. On the other hand, the descriptions of pain on online patient fora can be systematically compared with the linguistic structures used in diagnostic questionnaires (e.g. the McGill Pain Questionnaire; Melzack 1975), and the findings of such comparisons can then be used to develop diagnostic tools that better reflect the ways in which people actually talk about their pain. In this sense, an eclectic and augmented cognitive linguistic approach to metaphor in discourse about pain can help to understand and improve communication about pain in both clinical and non-clinical settings.

Acknowledgment

The research reported in this chapter was supported by the UK's Economic and Social Research Council; grant no: ES/R008906/1.

Notes

1 I am grateful to the Trigeminal Neuralgia Association UK for permission to study the language that is used on their patient online forum. Any information that might lead to the identification of individuals has been omitted from the quotes included in this chapter.
2 The experience captured by 'ache' is sometimes seen as different from that captured by 'pain' (as in the expression 'aches and pains'), or as a type of pain, as in the McGill Pain Questionnaire (Melzack 1975), where 'aching' is included as one of many possible descriptors of pain.

References

Allen, C., Vassilev, I., Kennedy, A. and Rogers, A. (2016). Long-term condition self-management support in online communities: A meta-synthesis of qualitative papers. Journal of Medical Internet Research 18 (3): e61
Biro, D. (2010). *The Language of Pain: Finding Words, Compassion and Relief.* New York and London; Norton.
Bourke, J. (2014). *The Story of Pain.* Oxford: Oxford University Press.
Coates, J. (2007). Talk in a play frame: More on laughter and intimacy. *Journal of Pragmatics* 39 (1): 29–49.
Coulson, S. (2005). What's so funny? Cognitive semantics and jokes. *Cognitive Psychopathology/Psicopatologia Cognitive* 2 (3): 67–78.

Coulson, S. and Pascual, E. (2006). For the sake of argument: Mourning the unborn and reviving the dead through conceptual blending. *Annual Review of Cognitive Linguistics* 4: 153–81.

Dancygier, B. and Sweetser, E. (2014). *Figurative Language*. Cambridge: Cambridge University Press.

De Souza, L. H. and Frank, A. O. (2000). Subjective pain experience of people with chronic back pain. *Physiotherapy Research International* 5 (4): 207–19.

Deignan, A., Littlemore, J. and Semino, E. (2013). *Figurative Language, Genre and Register*. Cambridge: Cambridge University Press.

Demjén, Z. (2016) Laughing at cancer: Humour, empowerment, solidarity and coping online. *Journal of Pragmatics* 101: 18–30.

Fauconnier, G. and Turner, M. (2002). *The Way We Think: Conceptual Blending and the Mind's Hidden Complexities*. New York: Basic Books.

Frank, A. W. (2011). Metaphors of pain. *Literature and Medicine* 29 (1): 182–96

Frontera, W. R., Silver, J. K. and Rizzo, T. D. (2015). *Essentials of Physical Medicine and Rehabilitation*. Philadelphia: Elsevier Saunders.

Gibbs, R. W. Jr. (2017a). Metaphor, language and dynamical systems. In E. Semino and Z. Demjén (eds), *The Routledge Handbook of Metaphor and Language*. London and New York: Routledge, pp. 56–70.

Gibbs, R. W. Jr. (2017b). The embodied and discourse views of metaphor: Why these are not so different and how they can be brought closer together. In B. Hampe (ed.), *Metaphor: Embodied Cognition and Discourse*. Cambridge: Cambridge University Press, pp. 319–34.

Gibbs R. and Cameron, L. (2008). The social-cognitive dynamics of metaphor performance. *Journal of Cognitive Systems Research* 9 (1–2): 64–75.

Grady, J. (1997) *Foundations of Meaning: Primary Metaphors and Primary Scenes*. Unpublished PhD thesis. Berkeley: University of California.

Grady, J. E. and Ascoli, G. A. (2017). Sources and targets in primary metaphor theory: Looking back and thinking ahead. In B. Hampe (ed.), *Metaphor: Embodied Cognition and Discourse*. Cambridge: Cambridge University Press, pp. 27–45.

Grady, J., Oakley, T. and Coulson, S. (1999). Blending and metaphor. In G. Steen and R. W. Gibbs, Jr (eds), *Metaphor in Cognitive Linguistics*. Philadelphia: John Benjamins.

Kotthoff, H. (2006). Pragmatics of performance and the analysis of conversational humor. *Humor* 19: 271–304.

Kövecses, Z. (2005). *Metaphor in Culture: Universality and Variation*. Cambridge: Cambridge University Press.

Kövecses, Z. (2008). The conceptual structure of happiness and pain. In C. Lascaratou, A. Despotopoulou, and E. Ifantidou (eds), *Reconstructing Pain and Joy: Linguistic, Literary and Cultural Perspectives*. Cambridge: Cambridge Scholars Publishing, pp. 17–33.

Kövecses, Z. (2010) *Metaphor: A Practical Introduction*, 2nd edition. Cambridge: Cambridge University Press.

Kövecses, Z. (2015). *Where Metaphors Come From: Reconsidering Context in Metaphor*. Oxford: Oxford University Press.

Kövecses, Z. (2017). Conceptual Metaphor Theory. In E. Semino and Z. Demjén (eds), *The Routledge Handbook of Metaphor and Language*. London and New York: Routledge, pp. 13–27.

Lakoff, G. and Johnson, M. (1980). *Metaphors We Live By*. Chicago: The University of Chicago Press.
Lakoff, G. and Johnson, M. (1999). *Philosophy in the Flesh: The Embodied Mind and Its Challenge to Western Thought*. New York: Basic Books.
Lakoff, G. and Turner, M. (1989). *More than Cool Reason: A Field Guide to Poetic Metaphor*. Chicago: The University of Chicago Press.
Lascaratou, C. (2007). *The Language of Pain: Expression or Description*. Amsterdam: John Benjamins.
Loftus, S. (2011). Pain and its metaphors: A dialogical approach. *Journal of Medical Humanities* 32: 213–30
Melzack, R. (1975). The McGill Pain Questionnaire: Major properties and scoring method. *Pain* 1: 277–99.
Musolff, A. (2006). Metaphor scenarios in public discourse. *Metaphor and Symbol* 21 (1): 23–38.
Musolff, A. (2016). *Political Metaphor Analysis: Discourse and Scenarios*. London: Bloomsbury.
Pither, C. (2002). Finding a visual language for pain. *Clinical Medicine* 2 (6), 570–1.
Pragglejaz Group (2007). MIP: A method for identifying metaphorically used words in discourse. *Metaphor and Symbol* 22 (1): 1–39.
Prestin, A. and Chou, W. S. (2014). Web 2.0 and the changing health communication environment. In H. Hamilton and W. S. Chou (eds), The Routledge Handbook of Language and Health Communication. London and New York: Routledge, pp. 184–97.
Pucci, F. G., Asaad, W. F. and Doberstein, C. E. (2017). Trigeminal neuralgia in the rehabilitation patient. In A. Carayannopoulos (ed.), *Comprehensive Pain Management in the Rehabilitation Patient*. Cham: Springer, pp. 851–72.
Scarry, E. (1985). *The Body in Pain: The Making and Unmaking of the World*. Oxford: Oxford University Press.
Schott, G. D. (2004). Communicating the experience of pain: The role of analogy. *Pain* 108: 209–12.
Semino, E. (2008). *Metaphor in Discourse*. Cambridge: Cambridge University Press.
Semino, E. (2010). Descriptions of pain, metaphor and embodied simulation. *Metaphor and Symbol* 25 (4): 205–26.
Semino, E. (2011). Metaphor, creativity, and the experience of pain across genres. In J. Swann R. Pope and R. Carter (eds), *Creativity, Language, Literature: The State of the Art*. Basingstoke: Palgrave, pp. 138–71.
Semino, E. and Demjén, Z. (2017). The Cancer Card: Metaphor, intimacy and humour in online interactions about the experience of cancer. In B. Hampe (ed.), *Metaphor: Embodied Cognition and Discourse*. Cambridge: Cambridge University Press, pp. 181–99.
Semino, E., Demjén, Z. and Demmen, J. (2018). An integrated approach to metaphor and framing in cognition, discourse and practice, with an application to metaphors for cancer. *Applied Linguistics* 39 (5): 625–45.
Steen, G. J., Dorst, A. G., Herrmann, B. J., Kaal, A. A., Krennmayr, T. and Pasma, T. (2010). *A Method for Linguistic Metaphor Identification: From MIP to MIPVU*. Amsterdam: John Benjamins.
Vadivelu, N., Urman, R. D. and Hines, R. L. (2011). *Essentials of Pain Management*. New York: Springer.

Winter, B. and Matlock, T. (2017). Primary metaphors are both cultural and embodied. In B. Hampe (ed.), *Metaphor: Embodied Cognition and Discourse*. Cambridge: Cambridge University Press, pp. 99–116.

Zakzrewska, J. M. (2006). *Insights: Facts and Stories behind Trigeminal Neuralgia*. London: Trigeminal Neuralgia Association.

5

Simulation in Deictic Space: Scenes and Episodes in the Lord's Prayer

Jeremy Holland

1. Introduction

In cognitive psychology, mental models are posed as theoretical entities necessary to explain how both explicit and implicit inference is possible. Since mental models are much richer in information than the discourses that are based on them, it is plausible to assume that mental models 'play a central and unifying role in representing objects, states of affairs, sequences of events, the way the world is, and the social and psychological actions of daily life' (Johnson-Laird 1983: 397). Following the field of cognitive psychology, socio-cognitive discourse analysis conceives of mental models as 'cognitive representations of our experiences' (Van Dijk 2008: 61).

In order to examine how mental models are constructed, Van Dijk (1987: 174) points to common 'semantic categories' humans use to comprehend each situation as encountered in text, and argues these categories are 'more or less invariant'. The fundamental categorical elements of the situation, potentially active in the building of every single mental model, include both scenic (time, location, conditions and participants) and episodic (evaluations, actions and goals) components. Having pinpointed the key categorical ingredients that may be present in each model, Van Dijk does not suggest any other format for their arrangement other than a hierarchical structure. Moving beyond hierarchical structures suggested for mental models in cognitive psychological approaches, my intention is to explore how mental modes are constructed while consulting cognitive linguistic approaches to text analysis.

Cognitive Linguistics is a research field concerned to incorporate language studies into cognitive science generally. Common concerns holding the paradigm together are concept formation, categorisation, metaphorical blending and conceptual space construction. Cognition is claimed to be 'embodied', which means that our bodies provide the basis for structuring devices that work their way up into our abstract reasoning processes (Grady 2005). A central claim of any embodied perspective to language structure is that conceptualisation is not an innate logic, but emerges from the logical entailments of schematic structures that arise as the result of sensorimotor experience (Johnson 1987). In Cognitive Linguistics these structures are known as image schemas and are claimed to be integral to the conceptualisation process because they consist of irreducible gestalt structures. Lakoff and Johnson (1999) theorise that 'image schemas plus a metaphorical projection' are the primary devices for structuring conceptual relations. Thus, attending to the way metaphorical projection is employed in mental model construction, the cognitive analyst is provided a way to describe how discourse contents are structured in conceptual space.

In this embodied approach to language, it is claimed that certain lexical and grammatical constructions cue image-schematic structures, which provide constraints to reasoning. This structural interaction within mental models is governed by the 'invariance principle' (Lakoff 1993). The 'invariance principle' is the claim that 'image schemas project a topological structure, and that this structure is always preserved by metaphor' (Lakoff 1993: 229). Taking into account the topological nature of image schemas, abstract inferences are thought to be metaphorical versions of spatial inferences. In other words, 'propositional inferences arise from the inherent topological structure of the image schemas projected by metaphor onto concepts like times, states, changes, actions, causes, purposes, means, quantity and categories' (ibid.). This means that abstract reasoning is a special kind of imagistic reasoning, where schema topologies are metaphorically projected onto abstract domains.

In cognitive discourse studies, Chilton's (2005, 2010, 2014) work with political texts has progressively become more concerned with exploring the structure of conceptual space. Inspired by geometric investigation in language studies, Chilton (2014: 1) has developed his own representational format for discourse processing by employing a 'three-dimensional geometry in order to model meaning in a cognitive embodied framework'. Chilton's model is meant to capture configurations of image schemas that bring about set conceptual arrangements necessary for discourse comprehension. Chilton's aim is to propose a 'deictic space model' that consists of a 'rather simple vector geometry in variable coordinate systems' in order to explore some fundamental properties of human discourse (ibid.).

Building on socio-cognitive and cognitive linguistic approaches to text analysis, I trace the topological construal of discourse contents within a geometric backdrop in order to highlight unconscious inference relations. In this chapter I intend to refine the basis of a *cognitive discourse grammar* for mental models, which is a grammar responsible for simulating image-schematic arrangements of discourse contents. Taking Matthew 6: 9–13 as data, I discuss which lexical and grammatical constructions prompt the reader to simulate fundamental image schemas. Additionally, I provide a way to model the basic scene and episode structure being simulated within a three-dimensional backdrop during text processing. In sum, the purpose of this analysis is to consider the interconnection of fundamental ontological domains (e.g. space, time and evaluation), semantic model categories (e.g. participants, values, cultural mindsets, actions and goals) and image schematic gestalt structures (e.g. CONTAINER, SURFACE, PATH and GOAL) within deictic space in order to better elucidate the processes involved in the conceptualisation of Matthew's version of the Lord's Prayer.

2. Lord's Prayer (Matthew 6: 9–13)

In the Christian tradition, Catholicism recognises the model prayer Jesus provides to his disciples by its Latin title 'Pater Noster' (Our Father), while in Protestantism it is known as the Lord's Prayer. During the first century, the Jewish people observed many prayers. According to religious law, everyone was to pray at least twice daily at the third and ninth hours, roughly at sunrise and sunset (Green et al. 1992: 617). An Aramaic prayer used in the liturgy of the synagogue, known as the Kiddish, may have provided Jesus some of the original source material for the prayer (Gundry 1982: 104). The Kiddish reads in part, 'Exalted and hallowed be his great name in the world which he created according to his will. May he let his kingdom rule.' The novelty to Jesus' variation of this prayer is that he releases his disciples from having to make a special effort to gain access to god (i.e. temple rituals or exacting legal codes) by 'turning prayer into a conversation with a concerned father' (Schweizer 1975: 146).

Mark is thought to be the earliest written gospel account, designed to make the teachings of Jesus intelligible to a gentile audience. Within biblical scholarship it is widely acknowledged that Mark is the principle source for Matthew, containing up to 80 per cent of the same material (Beare 1981). The author(s) of Matthew followed Mark's narrative outline, yet relied on other source materials when inserting five lengthy teaching passages at opportune points within the overall narrative structure (Matt. chapters 5–7, 10, 13, 18, 23–5). The Lord's Prayer also appears in the gospel of Luke 11: 2–4 in a much shorter form, which is probably more true to the original source material. Consulting the Greek versions (Aland et al. 1993), both prayers can be seen to rely on a common collection of Jesus' teachings known as the 'Q source' (Luz 1995: 7).

The most obvious difference between the two versions of the prayer is that Matthew's account includes two extra petitions not found in Luke. The concluding doxology is also unique to Matthew, 'yours is the kingdom and the power and the glory forever'. The doxology is a later addition, not appearing in any manuscripts until the beginning of the second century. For this reason, I do not take the doxology of the prayer into consideration in the analysis below. In Matthew's version, the prayer consists of an address and seven petitions. The primary way Matthew's prayer varies from Luke's is stylistic in nature, being structured according to a strict parallelism. By adding a more formalised address and two extra petitions, the author is able to arrange the prayer according to three couplets (Gundry 1982: 105). Here I show Matthew's additions to the prayer in italics:

1. *Our* Father *who are in heaven*, hallowed be your name.
2. Your kingdom come,
3. *your will be done on earth as it is in heaven.*
4. Give us this day our daily bread,
5. and forgive us our debts as we also have forgiven our debtors.
6. And do not lead us into temptation,
7. *but deliver us from evil.*

In the next section, I focus on image schemas as simulation devices, lexical and grammatical cues for schematic simulation (i.e. Cognitive Grammar) and the topology of schemas within a three-dimensional conceptual space. Coming at discourse analysis from a cognitive perspective, I utilise Chilton's (2014) extended theory of deixis in order to explore the inner structures of mental models. In the analysis section, I present a scenes-and-episodes approach to deictic space modelling in order to account for the imagistic construction of the Lord's Prayer.

3. Image Schemas as Simulation Devices

To begin, let us take a moment to consider some of the cognitive theories underpinning this modelling effort. In infant cognition research, Mandler (2012) suggests that meaningful interaction begins at birth, arriving prior to any language learning. Early meaning-giving patterns do not come as a result of lexical or propositional learning, but from emerging forms of reasoning that are grounded in early perceptual patterns via bodily activity. Mandler (2005) claims that infants perform a 'perceptual meaning analysis', where conceptualisation is grounded in bodily orientations, manipulations and movements. She discusses the format of this perceptual analysis in terms of image schemas (Mandler and Cánovas 2014). Building on Mandler's view of the role of image schemas as early meaning making patterns, Vandervert (1997) conceives of them as viable candidates for being simulation structures. Vandervert (1997: 114) claims that image schemas have developed evolutionarily as 'feedforward templates, where simulation-structured schematic information storages optimize an organism's survival'. Fundamental image schemas have been identified (Johnson 1987: 126), and can be categorised into the domains of space, motion and force. The spatial domain includes, but is not limited to, CONTAINER, PART-WHOLE, CENTRE-PERIPHERY, SURFACE, CONTACT, NEAR-FAR and FULL-EMPTY schemas. Schemas in the motion domain consist of SOURCE-PATH-GOAL, SCALE, LINK, PROCESS, CYCLE, while commonly encountered schemas in the force domain include ENABLEMENT, COMPULSION, ATTRACTION, BLOCKAGE, COUNTERFORCE, EQUILIBRIUM and POINT BALANCE.

A key claim in cognitive discourse studies is that these early imagistic structuring abilities of infants continue to develop and are used in adulthood in order to conceptualise highly abstract political texts (Chilton 2014). As we learn language, these image schematic structures become linked with certain lexical and grammatical constructions. In embodied grammatical approaches, the claim is that function words work to combine textual contents together and constrains their representations within a mental simulation (Bergen and Chang 2013). However, there is little empirical evidence on exactly what components of an utterance drive what aspects of simulation. In fact, one of the main gaps in theories of language understanding is explaining the exact ways in which language triggers simulation and which aspects of simulation it triggers. In order for this embodied grammatical approach to progress, at least two questions must be answered:

1. Which linguistic elements trigger the spatial backdrop for and schematic movements of discourse entities within mental simulations?
2. How do these linguistic triggers work together conceptually when building scenes and episodes in mental models as a series of congruent simulations?

In attempts to model the conceptual relations linguistic items evoke, cognitive language theorists have suggested various representational formats. 'Mental spaces' (Fauconnier and Turner 2002), 'text worlds' (Werth 1999), 'deictic spaces' (Chilton 2014) and 'event models' (Hart 2014) are all contemporary approaches seeking to describe the phenomenon of conceptualisation. To remedy the proliferation of terms, I follow Chilton in referring to online discourse processing in working memory as the creation of deictic spaces. Thus, I move forward using the term deictic space suggested by

Chilton to indicate a conceptual space that enables a schematic simulation of discourse elements.

To systematise how lexical and grammatical constructions cue imagistic simulations, I follow Fauconnier (1985: 16) in defining 'space builders' as 'expressions that may establish a new space or refer back to one already introduced in the discourse'. Up to this point, identified space builders include prepositions, identity references, adverbials, demonstratives and verb tenses (Fauconnier 1997: 40). While intending to account for the building of conceptual space, I also want to explore how schemas facilitate the movement of contents and how they are involved in directing the reader's attention within conceptual space. In so doing, I mean to distinguish between linguistic constructions that build the setting from those that are responsible for simulating episodes and from those involved in connecting particular locations within conceptual space. To this end, I intend to show which image schemas, cued by lexical and grammatical constructions, act as:

- Space builders: image schemas that create new scenes in conceptual space. These schemas form the setting and provide the conceptual background for discourse contents.
- Content movers: image schemas that create new episodes in conceptual space. These schemas drive the action sequences by determining the direction and magnitude of travelling discourse contents and their final locations.
- Attention pointers: image schemas that direct the reader's attention within conceptual space. These schemas modify existing discourse contents and attract observation to certain locations within the constructed space.

To date, the linguistic triggers known as 'space builders' have been the most widely examined in cognitive linguistic literature (Werth 1999). Yet, the lexical and grammatical constructions that cue the movement of contents or direct the conceptualiser's attention have not yet been attended to in an inclusive, formalised manner. Thus, I am offering the categories of content movers and attention pointers as a way of clearly distinguishing between the functionality of different schematic elements. To get a better grasp of these linguistic triggers, I will focus specifically on four key schemas in the analysis. Two schemas attended to, fall within the spatial domain (CONTAINER and SURFACE), while the other two stem from the motion domain (PATH and GOAL).

4. A Cognitive Grammar of Scenes and Episodes

Beginning with the space builders, the CONTAINER schema is first conceptualised around two and a half months of age, specifically the distinction between in and out (Aguiar and Baillargeon 1999). Based on the fact that containment is the first spatial schema acquired during infancy, I infer that it goes on to be the most productive schema used for setting the scene in mental representations. The CONTAINER schema possesses three main gestalt elements, an interior, boundary and exterior, from which emerges the basic logic that any particular discourse entity can be either inside or outside (Lakoff and Johnson 1999). Because of these unchanging gestalt elements, the CONTAINER schema is able to consistently project a number of entailments during discourse processing. For instance, in political discourse the topological character of the CONTAINER schema, usually triggered by some variation of the preposition 'in', is typically used to draw boundaries around geographical areas (e.g. in the West) or social groups (e.g. in the Progressive Party). This construal of a land mass or political party as a CONTAINER enables the reader to apply the inference constraints of the schema (Núñez-Perucha 2011). Also, more abstract ideas like internal states-of-being can be construed with a CONTAINER schema such as 'in answering questions' or 'in defining religious matters'.

As for schemas considered content movers, I attend to both PATH and GOAL schemas. From birth infants follow moving objects with their eyes and prefer to look at animate over inanimate motion (Haith 1980). Experimental evidence indicates that animate motion along a PATH is the first image schema active in infancy (Simion et al. 2008). Since PATH is likely the first schema that is used for conceptualisation, I assume PATHS are the most productive content movers in representing episodes. Lakoff and Johnson (1999) record that participants (or objects) in motion are structured by four main gestalt elements. These are a starting point (SOURCE) where discourse entities move in a specific direction (MOMENTUM) along a series of locations (PATH) toward a destination (GOAL). Thus, when modelling the topological properties of the PATH and GOAL schemas, discourse contents are shown as being in motion, possessing a distinct direction and coming to rest in a particular location. In discourse, PATHS are cued by verbs and may represent verbal actions (e.g. asking, praying) material actions (e.g. pushing, dividing) or internal actions (e.g. thinking, feeling). Lexis filling the GOALS slot is highly flexible as well, able to be construed in terms of humans (e.g. Take them away.), institutions (e.g. Let's improve the education system.) or utopian solutions (e.g. We must fight for complete redistribution of wealth.)

In contrast to space builders and content movers, attention pointers are considered secondary schemas in that they are superimposed over more fundamental spatial and motion schemas. These schemas are active in augmenting conceptual spaces established by space builders and driven by content movers. During conceptualisation, these more primary schemas (e.g. CONTAINER and PATH) provide the conceptual background upon which all other schemas are added in order to modify the established space. Image schemas that act as attention pointers help to construe the situation by directing the reader's mental gaze within conceptual space (Hart 2015). The SURFACE schema arrives at five months of age, existing as a combination of multiple other conceptual primitives including CONTAINER, CONTACT, OVER and ON. I consider the SURFACE schema as an attention pointer because it draws the reader's attention to a particular location within the conceptual space under construction. Usually, it is some variation of the preposition 'on' that serves as the lexical prompt for the SURFACE schema. The topology of the schema can be fused with geographical areas (e.g. on the sea), ideological worldviews (e.g. dependent upon Christianity) and many other abstractions (e.g. on time).

To be clear, in the analysis below I assume that CONTAINERS are explicitly evoked by prepositional phrases in order to set the scene. Spatially, setting the scene involves placing participant categories within a particular time and location, which entails a specific set of circumstances. Verb phrases cue PATH schemas that initiate new episodes as temporal causal sequences, while GOALS are represented by noun phrases. Individual and group identities are construed as AGENTS moving along PATHS indicating action toward specified GOALS. Also, prepositions prompt for the SURFACE schema in order to guide the reader's attention to particular locations within the conceptual space. Within abstract religious discourse, image schemas provide the reader with crucial spatial and motion relations existing conceptually between elements encoded in the text. I now move from considering individual image schemas, to the way scenes and episodes are topologically projected into a conceptual space during conceptualisation. As noted earlier, 'image schemas project a topological structure, and that this structure is always preserved by metaphor' (Lakoff 1993: 229). I am claiming that these projected topological properties are active in discourse processing during the construction of situations in mental models.

5. Topological Projection in Geometric Conceptual Space

Deictic space theory is currently being developed to deal with text above the sentence level within cognitive discourse studies (Cap 2014; Hart 2015; Kaal 2017). The deictic space approach is well suited to discovering how essential model categories active in socio-cognitive discourse analysis (e.g. participants, evaluations, cultural mindsets, strategic actions and future goals) fit within an

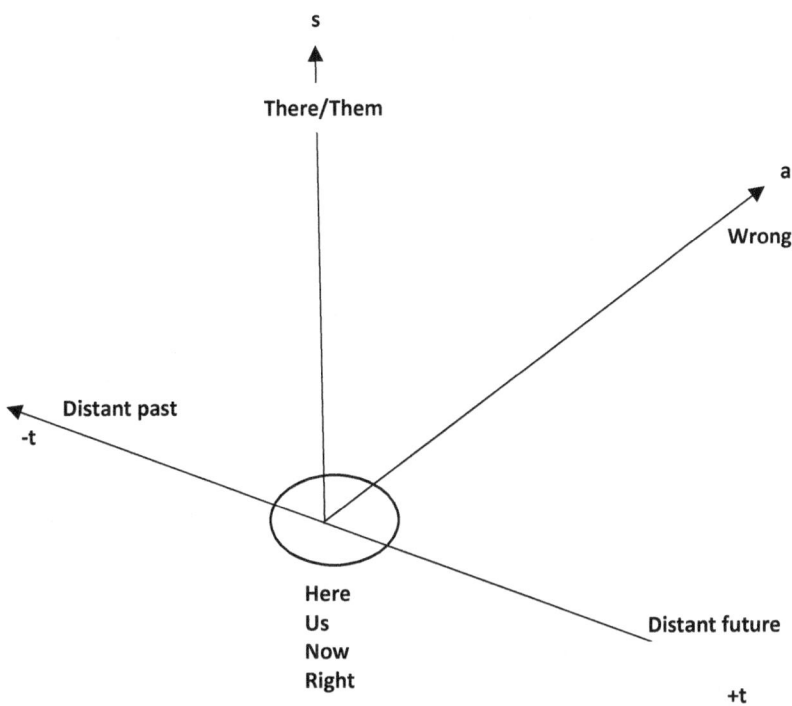

Figure 5.1 Basic deictic space model

embodied approach for mapping out construal operations. In deictic space theory, spatial, temporal and evaluative deixis are fundamental. The underlying assumption is that human minds set up a three-dimensional conceptual space as we process linguistic utterances, a conceptual space that is inevitably tied to a point of view attributed to the writer. From this geometric starting point, Chilton's (2010: 193) model posits reference frames as 'simple three-dimensional axis systems with the origin usually located at the point of text producer'.

The fundamental axis system of the deictic space model (Figure 5.1) consists of three unbroken lines, s, t and a, converging at the self. In brief, the s-axis is socio-spatial in that discourse entities (participants, places or objects) can be located at relative social distances from the reader. The t-axis is temporal representing time in a bidirectional manner, where past and future events are represented as coordinate points along an internal timeline as being closer or more distant to the current temporal location of the reader. More recently, Chilton (2014) uses the third axis as a way of viewing the epistemic certainty and deontic force of statements. However, since I am primarily interested here in discourse level meaning making, I am following the path of

Chilton's early work (and later discourse analysts) in limiting the third axis to an axiological one. This means evaluative concepts in the text are claimed to be metaphorically spatialised as well, where normative values are located at relative distances from the reader. In the deictic space model, every utterance always has the potential to connect simultaneously to all three dimensions as discourse contents are recognised as being set at specific coordinate locations within the axis system.

Intersection of the three geometric axes is indicative of the origin point (i.e. deictic centre), which defines the viewpoint of the speaker (e.g. us, here, now, real and right vs there, then, suspect and wrong). In this three-dimensional axis system, vectors represent movements of discourse entities within conceptual space. Vectors, positioned along the axes, possess both a magnitude and direction. They serve to relate contents to one another within conceptual space by depicting movements of discourse elements relative to the deictic centre. Dashed lines appearing in the model are conceived as connectors which depict various kinds of relation including 'attribution and possession' (Hart 2014: 167). With this geometric model of conceptual space, Chilton proposes that linguistically encoded conceptualisation can be represented in terms of a deictic centre point relative to the writer's point of view, three axes with a series of coordinate locations and vectors which record relations of distance, direction and magnitude. The elementary geometry of coordinate systems, vectors and transformations act as a heuristic for exploring linguistic-conceptual space. My goal in using the tools of deictic space modelling is to chart how lexical and grammatical constructions locate the reader at a deictic origin, and simulates scenes and episodes within a three-dimensional conceptual space. Thus, Chilton's geometric formalism of the mental model is applied in order to depict topological and deictic relations from the reader's perspective when processing the Lord's Prayer.

6. Deictic Space of the Lord's Prayer

Building on contemporary cognitive discourse approaches (Filardo-Llamas et al. 2015), I trace imagistic arrangements of discourse contents within a geometric backdrop in order to highlight unconscious inference relations. The goal of this analysis is to utilise the deictic space model to consider how image schemas interact in conceptual space. I am claiming that this topological and deictic interaction of concepts is necessary to create coherent representations of scenes and episodes encountered in texts. In the analysis, I intend to show how image schemas are involved in providing spatial boundaries, setting discourse contents in motion and directing the reader's attention within conceptual space. To clarify the purpose of each particular schema's function, I

DEICTIC SPACES IN THE LORD'S PRAYER | 103

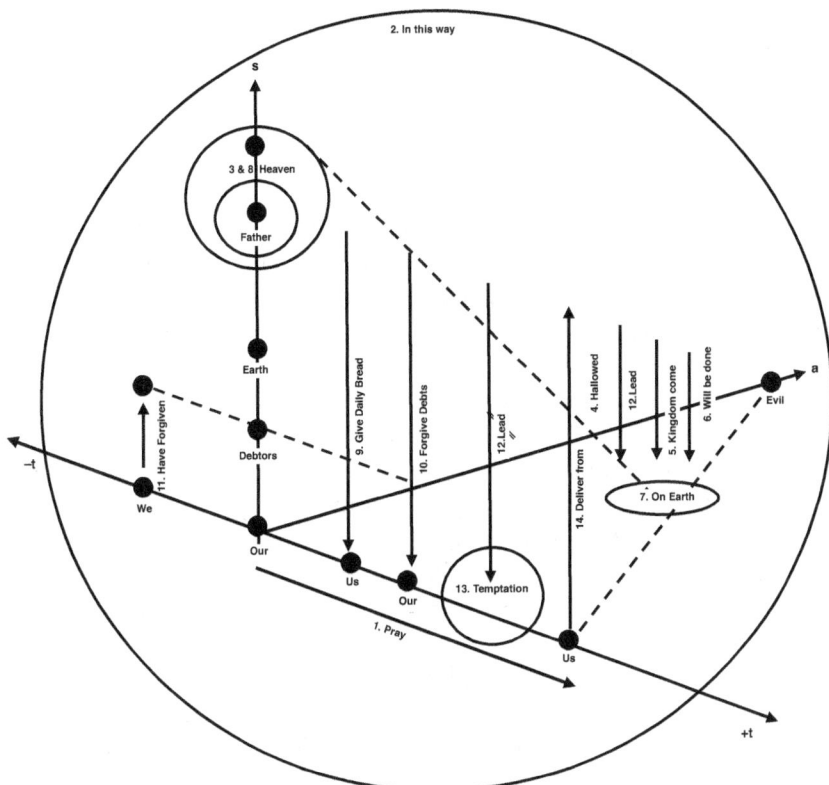

Figure 5.2 Deictic space of Matthew 6: 9–13

make a distinction between schemas that are active in setting scenes and those enacting episodes. In the analysis, I claim the spatial schemas of CONTAINER and SURFACE are involved in scene setting, while the motion schemas of PATH and GOAL are crucial for constructing episodes.

6.1. Matthew 6: 9–13

The Lord's Prayer consists of an address and seven petitions total. The first half of the prayer covers three petitions for the fulfilment of God's divine plans, while the second half is made up of four petitions concerning human needs. In regards to temporal orientation, the first three petitions have a far future emphasis, while the remaining four petitions are based in the near future. Figure 5.2 represents one complete deictic space, capturing the entirety of the prayer. For clarity in the modelling process, the numbers in the textual coding of schemas correspond with their depiction in the deictic space model.

Verse 9
1. Pray <PATH>, then,
2. in this way <CONTAINER>:
3. Our Father who is in heaven <CONTAINER>,
4. hallowed <PATH> be your name <GOAL>.

At the beginning of the Lord's Prayer the author, through the mouth of Jesus, determines to construe the first episode. The present tense verb 'pray' cues a PATH schema moving from the temporal centre forward into the future along the +t-axis. In the mental simulation, the disciples are placed at the deictic centre, and the verbal movement of praying supplies the reader with the first episodic movement.In the deictic model, I have depicted the vector evoked by 'pray', as extending the entirety of this conceptual space. The prepositional phrase 'in this way' prompts the CONTAINER schema, which topologically encircles a way of performing prayer. Notice that I have drawn this CONTAINER as encompassing the remainder of the following schematic relations. In this case, the CONTAINER schema explicitly signals to the reader what is and is not to be included inside this type of religious speech act.

Anticipating later first-person plural pronouns, 'our' immediately brings into focus the communal nature of the prayer. Divine agency can be inferred throughout the prayer because of this initial address to the 'father' during the opening scene. The CONTAINER, cued by the prepositional phrase 'in heaven', surrounds this divine identity. In contrast to other gospel accounts, Matthew often adds 'in heaven' when addressing the 'father', providing spatial distinctions not found elsewhere. Heaven, in Matthew's account, often represents the upper reaches of the created order, including the dwelling place of god. Since the s-axis indicates social distance relative to the in-group deictic centre, the identity 'father' is placed at a distal location. So the second CONTAINER simulates a location for god, which is a divine realm separate from earth.

Moving to the second episode of the prayer, the community asks for god's 'name' to be honoured. This first petition is rooted in prophecies found in Hebrew Scriptures (cf. Isaiah 40: 25; 43: 15), and reflects the significance of a person's name in the ancient world. Honouring someone's name meant recognising that person's power and authority (Green et al. 1992: 621). Notice that while PATH ('hallowed') and GOAL ('your name') elements are present in the gestalt structure, the AGENT is left implied. This speaks to the commonly known eschatological nature of the prayer, where petitioners infer god to be the AGENT in a coming future where he will usher in an earthly kingdom. Nolland (2005: 286) remarks how the 'eschatological orientation' of the prayer connects with the thought of earlier Jewish prophets where god is the only being able to bring honour to his name (Ezk. 36: 23). Matthew's pairing of the prayer in three couplets helps the reader to infer that 'your name' at the end of the first petition is a reference back to 'father'.

Verse 10
5. Your kingdom <GOAL> come <PATH>.
6. Your will <GOAL> be done <PATH>,
7. on earth <SURFACE>
8. as it is in heaven <CONTAINER>.

The next two petitions continue from the first, being a triple request for the father to usher in a new eschatological age. In the deictic space model, the first three requests are placed at the most distal temporal location along the +t-axis, as they are to be fulfilled at some point in the undetermined future. When the completion of these actions will occur is unknown, and every generation of Jews hope and expect this kingdom to arrive in their lifetimes (e.g. 1 Ch. 16: 33, Is. 13: 6, Joel 2: 1, Mi. 1: 3, Zc. 14: 1 Mal. 4:5). The three PATH vectors, evoked by the verbs 'hallowed', 'come' and 'will be' all move from a distal ('heaven') to a medial location ('earth') along the s-axis.

The preposition 'on' cues the SURFACE schema, where the reader is invited to construe the planet topologically as such. In this passage, all god's fulfilments of ancient prophecies move from inside the heaven CONTAINER down to the SURFACE of the earth. This speaks to the fact that the Jews were not looking for a purely spiritual reign, but an actual kingdom being set up in Jerusalem (cf. Psalms 72: 8). Immediately after arriving at the earth-SURFACE construal, the author rounds out the ending of the prayer's first couplet by directing the reader's attention back into the previously encountered CONTAINER ('in heaven'). This usage of repetition is a poetic way to move from three petitions making future oriented requests to the remaining four petitions dealing with daily concerns.

In verses nine and ten, the reader encounters the first three petitions of the prayer. Within these initial requests, the author opens the first scene in deictic space, which includes locations ('heaven' and 'earth'), times (now and undetermined future) and main actors ('father', 'our'). Simulating multiple episodes, the scene contains three movements toward the protagonist ('hallowed', 'come' and 'be done') from a distal ('in heaven') to a medial location ('on earth'). The first couplet encourages the Christian community to be looking forward to the prophetic fulfilment of God's kingdom. This will be a time when all people on earth honour his name, desire his kingdom and do his will.

Verse 11
9. Give <PATH> us this day our daily bread <GOAL>.

The narrative structure of the Lord's Prayer moves in reductive sequence, from the large concerns of god to the everyday needs and problems of humanity (Schweizer 1975: 153). The remaining four petitions move away from the long-term fulfilment of an earthly kingdom that mirrors the one 'in heaven' to asking for everyday essential provisions. In verse eleven, the action along the temporal axis is now located proximally to the praying community stationed at the deictic centre. Notice the petitioner does not pray for his/herself alone but for the entire community ('us'), coming back to the first-person plural originally encountered in verse nine.

The verb 'give' cues a PATH schema where, consistent with the first three petitions, an entity is moving from a distal location on the s-axis toward the petitioners. In the Greek text, the adjective ('daily') appears as an infinitive ('to come'), pointing to bread for the coming day. This implies the prayer could have been spoken in both the evening and the morning asking god to supply each day's bread, which is positioned as the GOAL. In verse eleven, the vector is indicative of an object ('bread') being transferred from a remote location into the possession of the petitioners, which is to occur in the near future along the +t-axis.

Verse 12
10. And forgive <PATH> us our debts <GOAL>,
11. as we <AGENT> also have forgiven <PATH> our debtors <GOAL>.

In verse twelve, the reader finds the fifth petition following the same schematic arrangement, where a PATH schema is cued by the present tense verb ('forgive'). The PATH schema simulates movement toward the disciples from an unnamed AGENT, which the reader can infer from verse nine is the 'father'. Here, the GOAL is for god to forgive the petitioners' moral debts. These debts are held proximally, presumably being shared by the entire community of disciples.

In order to round out the second couplet, the author temporarily shifts the deictic centre to the −t-axis, where Jesus' followers are portrayed as AGENTS following a PATH of releasing others from moral transgressions. In the deictic space model, I use a connecter to point out the analogical link between the forgiveness given by disciples in the near past with the present request for god to do likewise in the near future. This is the only point in the mental simulation where the action is moving proximally from the ingroup to a more distal location along the s-axis. In this case, the past tense verb 'forgiven' cues a vector moving to the identity category located most proximally on the s-axis.

'Debtors' are located as the most proximal social group, as the concept of the earth's SURFACE indicates a much larger scale of people, and the identity 'father' is located far away in the CONTAINER of heaven.

Verse 13
12. And do not <NEGATION> lead <PATH> us
13. into temptation <CONTAINER>,
14. but deliver <PATH> us from evil <GOAL>.

Coming to the last of the three couplets, the reader finds two petitions remaining. The purpose of the remaining requests are to implore god to be merciful in his guidance. The two petitions of this verse are linked through their usage of verbal imagery. The first petition envisages God bringing the disciples into a potentially dangerous situation, whereas the second portrays him as rescuing the community from danger (Nolland 2005: 291). To accomplish this, the author projects a hypothetical space through use of negation ('not') (Jeffries 2010: 107). The verb 'lead' cues the PATH schema with the implication that god is out in front of the disciples directing them into upcoming locations along the +t-axis. The preposition 'into' prompts for the CONTAINER schema and creates a logical entailment of a bounded area surrounding a state entitled 'temptation'. The disciples are asking not to be led into this potentially hazardous CONTAINER, and have their faith tested. With this last couplet, the author finishes the prayer by explicitly mentioning an axiological category for the first time ('evil'). In the deictic space model, I place a connector between the most distal location on the a-axis and the origin point of the action sequence on the +t-axis. In the last request of the prayer, a PATH schema is cued by the verb 'deliver', where the GOAL is for god to move the petitioners away from an 'evil' location.

Reviewing the entirety of the imagistic simulation of the Lord's Prayer, the reader encounters nine episodes simulated by PATH and GOAL schemas, all set within a series of complementary scenes cued by CONTAINER and SURFACE schemas. To review, the prayer's deictic mental space opens by setting the scene as an internal consideration space ('in this way'), which comes to hold various other scenes and episodes. After the major scenes are set ('heaven' and 'earth'), the author simulates a series of three episodes asking god to fulfil eschatological prophecy ('hallowed', 'come', 'be done') at some unknown point in the future. Afterwards, the next five episodes are simulated as occurring near to the temporal centre. The first two of these latter episodes represent movements of objects from god to the disciples ('bread' and 'forgiveness'). The final two episodes are requests not to be led into a hostile CONTAINER ('temptation'), but to be taken in a direction away from a negatively evaluated ('evil') location. In sum, I have concentrated on four fundamental image schemas that are explicitly invoked by lexical and grammatical constructions in the text. As for space builders, the reader encounters three CONTAINER schemas contributing to setting the scene. In the division of content movers, the PATH schema is cued nine times and the GOAL schema eight, while the AGENT is mentioned only once and implied throughout. One attention pointer was present in the form of a SURFACE schema, directing the reader to construe the earth as such throughout the prayer.

In this chapter, we have discussed how language utilises both image schemas and deictic spaces in order to construe discourse contents during text processing. We have seen how mental models not only share invariant categorical elements (i.e. identities, values, cultural mindsets, actions and goals), but image schematic designs as well (i.e. space builders, content movers and attention pointers). We have also discussed how readers pull from the syntactic surface structure of the text in order to create an imagistic simulation of situations. In this cognitive discourse analysis of the Lord's Prayer we have witnessed how lexical and grammatical constructions cue topological projections that act as fundamental gestalt structures in creating the scenes and episodes in conceptual space.

What Chilton's (2014) format for conceptual structure takes into consideration that other proposed formats neglect is that discourse elements exist as a series of interconnected deictic relations within geometric space. The embodied simulation produced by image schemas is built upon spatial cognition active during infancy and goes on to play a key role in conceptualisation of abstract texts (Mandler 2012). By offering a deictic space model, Chilton formalises the metaphorical projection of topological and deictic structures working together to provide local coherence relations during text processing. With this scenes-and-episodes approach to deictic space modelling, I have explored how meanings being constructed in religious discourse are richly imaginative with schematisations, categorisations and metaphorical projections being fundamental.

References

Aguiar, A. and Baillargeon, R. (1999). 2.5 month old infants' reasoning about when objects should and should not be occluded. *Cognitive Psychology* 39 (2): 116–57.

Aland, B., Aland, K., Karavidopoulos, J., Martini, C. M. and Metzger, B. M. (eds) (1993). *The Greek New Testament*, 4th edition. Stuttgart, Germany: Deutsche Bibelgesellschaft.

Beare, F. W. (1981). *The Gospel According to Matthew*. Oxford: Basil Blackwell.

Bergen, B. and Chang, N. (2013). Embodied construction grammar. In T. Hoffmann and G. Trousdale (eds), *The Oxford Handbook of Construction Grammar*. Oxford: Oxford University Press, pp. 168–90.

Cap, P. (2014). Applying cognitive pragmatics to critical discourse studies: A proximization analysis of three public space discourses. *Journal of Pragmatics* 70: 16–30.
Chilton, P. (2005). Vectors, viewpoint and viewpoint shift: Toward a Discourse Space Theory. *Annual Review of Cognitive Linguistics* 3: 78–116.
Chilton, P. (2010). The conceptual structure of deontic meaning: A model based on geometrical principles. *Language and Cognition* 2 (2): 191–220.
Chilton, P. (2014). *Language, Space and Mind: The Conceptual Geometry of Linguistic Meaning.* Cambridge: Cambridge University Press.
Fauconnier, G. (1985). *Mental Spaces: Aspects of Meaning Construction in Natural Language.* Cambridge: The MIT Press.
Fauconnier, G. (1997). *Mappings in Thought and Language.* Cambridge: Cambridge University Press.
Fauconnier, G. and Turner, M. (2002). *The Way We Think: Conceptual Blending and the Mind's Hidden Complexities.* New York: Basic Books.
Filardo-Llamas, L., Hart, C. and Kaal, B. (2015). Introduction for the special issue on space, time and evaluation in ideological discourse. *Critical Discourse Studies* 12 (3): 235–7.
Grady, J. E. (2005). Image schemas and perception: Refining a definition. In B. Hampe and J. E. Grady (eds), *From Perception to Meaning.* New York: Mouton de Gruyter, pp. 35–56.
Green, J. B, McKnight, S. and Marshall, I. H. (1992). *Dictionary of Jesus and the Gospels.* Downers Grove, IL: Intervarsity Press.
Gundry, R. H. (1982). *Matthew: A Commentary on His Literary and Theological Art.* Grand Rapids, MI: William B. Eerdmans Publishing Company.
Haith, M. (1980). Ontogenetic development during the first years of life. *Enfance* 33 (4): 25–7.
Hart, C. (2014). *Discourse, Grammar and Ideology: Functional and Cognitive Perspectives.* London: Bloomsbury.
Hart, C. (2015). Viewpoint in linguistic discourse: Space and evaluation in news reports of political protests. *Critical Discourse Studies* 12 (3): 238–60.
Jeffries, L. (2010). *Critical Stylistics: The Power of English.* Basingstoke: Palgrave Macmillan.
Johnson, M. (1987). *The Body in the Mind: The Bodily Basis of Meaning, Imagination and Reason.* Chicago: The University of Chicago Press.
Johnson-Laird, P. N. (1983). *Mental Models: Towards a Cognitive Science of Language, Inference, and Consciousness.* Cambridge: Cambridge University Press.
Kaal, B. (2017). *Worldview and Social Practice: A Discourse-Space Approach to Political Text Analysis.* Unpublished PhD dissertation. Amsterdam: Vrije University.
Lakoff, G. (1993). Contemporary theory of metaphor. In A. Ortony (ed.), *Metaphor and Thought*, 2nd edition. Cambridge: Cambridge University Press, pp. 202–51.
Lakoff, G. and Johnson, M. (1999). *Philosophy in the Flesh: The Embodied Mind and its Challenge to Western Thought.* New York: Basic Books.
Luz, U. (1995). *The Theology of the Gospel of Matthew.* Cambridge: Cambridge University Press.
Mandler, J. M. (2005). How to build a baby: III. Image schemas and the transition to verbal thought. In B. Hampe and J. E. Grady (eds), *From Perception to Meaning.* New York: Mouton de Gruyter, pp. 137–56.

Mandler, J. M. (2012). On the spatial foundations of the conceptual system and its enrichment. *Cognitive Science* 36: 421–51.

Mandler, J. M. and Cánovas, C. P. (2014). On defining image schemas. *Language and Cognition* 6 (4): 510–32.

Nolland, J. (2005). *The Gospel of Matthew: A Commentary on the Greek Text*. Grand Rapids, MI: W. B. Eerdmans Publishing Company.

Núñez-Perucha, B. (2011). Critical discourse analysis and Cognitive Linguistics as tools for ideological research: A diachronic analysis of feminism. In C. Hart (ed.), *Critical Discourse Studies in Context and Cognition*. Amsterdam: John Benjamins, pp. 97–118.

Schweizer, E. (1975). *The Good News According to Matthew* (trans. D. E. Green). Atlanta, GA: John Knox Press.

Simion, F., Regolin, L. and Bulf, H. (2008). A predisposition for biological motion in the newborn baby. *Proceedings of the National Academy of Sciences in the United States of America* 105 (2): 809–13.

Van Dijk, T. A. (1987). Episodic models in discourse processing. In R. Horowitz and S. Jay Samuels (eds), *Comprehending Oral and Written Language*. San Diego: Academic Press, pp. 161–96.

Van Dijk, T. A. (2008). *Discourse and Context: A Socio-cognitive Approach*. Cambridge: Cambridge University Press.

Vandervert, L. R. (1997). The evolution of Mandler's conceptual primitives (image schemas) as neural mechanisms for space-time simulation structures. *New Ideas in Psychology* 15 (2), 105–23.

Werth, P. (1999). *Text Worlds: Representing Conceptual Space in Discourse*. Harlow: Pearson Education Limited.

6

Cultural Responses to 9/11 and the Healing Power of Songs: A Text-World-Theory Analysis of Bruce Springsteen's 'The Rising'

Laura Filardo-Llamas

1. Introduction

Songs can be considered socio-cultural discourses with both a ludic and a communicative function: through lyrics (and music), singers can establish a power/solidarity interpersonal relationship with audiences (Halliday 2004; Van Leeuwen, 2012: 322), while, at the same time, promoting a given view of reality. The emotional impact – or cognitive effect (Steen and Gavins 2003: 6) – of artistic responses to socio-political events is partly caused by the mental representation built within the lyrics, and partly by the relationship established between such mental representation and the audience's experience of the world. This implies that a song's meaning cannot only change in different contexts (cf. Hidalgo-Downing and Filardo-Llamas 2019), but it can also vary depending on the amount, and type, of knowledge shared between the singer and the audience. This implies that there is an inextricable link between the mental representations triggered by a song and the existence of a common ground (Gavins 2007) – or shared knowledge – between the participants taking part in a communicative event. This may eventually result in the reinforcement or blurring of boundaries between socio-political groups (McKerrell, 2012), in the creation of shared identities (Filardo-Llamas 2017a), or, as I will argue in this chapter, in inducing emotion (Juslin and Sloboda 2010; Lozon and Bensimon 2014).

Following this, and previous research, songs are understood as multimodal instances of discourse which may react to given socio-political events (Filardo-Llamas 2015, 2017b; Way and McKerrell 2017). This is the case of Bruce Springsteen's 'The Rising' (2002), which was written as a response to the 9/11 attacks in New York City. Unlike some other songs that were popular at the time, in 'The Rising' we find a celebration of the heroes that were involved in this tragedy (Yates 2010). This focus on the human aspect, together with the linguistic strategies used to create physical and metaphorical worlds (Gavins 2007), are of key importance to explain the healing effect of this song.

With this in mind, I hypothesise that the song is effective because it relies on a multiple layering of meaning. Text-World Theory (TWT) (Gavins 2007; Werth 1999) will prove to be a useful tool for analysing and explaining how this multiple accretion of layers of meaning works (Lugea 2016). This is possible because the decontextualised text-worlds triggered by the song become meaningful discourse-worlds when used in context. Van Dijk's (2005, 2008) identification of multiple types of knowledge and how they are dependent on different contexts will become useful here. Besides, it will be proved that it is through the proximal/distal relationship (Cap 2010, 2013; Chilton 2005) established between the participants and values represented in the uncovered text-worlds that cognitive effect – related to evaluation and emotion – is achieved. To prove this hypothesis, Springsteen's 'The Rising' will be analysed following the postulates of TWT and Discourse Space Theory (Chilton 2004, 2005). This analysis has a triple objective: (i) identify the text-worlds (or mental representations) evoked by the song, (ii) explain how these mental representations result from contextual interpretation of the text-worlds evoked by the song thus becoming discourse-worlds, and (iii) reflect on how these discourse-worlds are the combination of multiple layers of meaning which result from the activation of different mental frames and therefore of different types of knowledge.

2. Bruce Springsteen and 9/11

On 11 September 2001, a terrorist attack against New York's Twin Towers took place. That day al-Qaeda-affiliated terrorist hijackers flew two planes into these towers. Images of the collapsing towers rapidly spread on television, and the official number of death victims was 2,977 (CNN 2016). The United States government quickly reacted to this attack by passing new laws to prevent terrorism, focusing particularly on the Islamist one. Although these new laws, and subsequent wars in Afghanistan and Iraq, are the main political consequences, the social effect of 9/11 is an increase of the American fear of their national identity and unity being under attack (Harf and Lombardi 2005; Lakoff 2007).

In the aftermath of the attack, society tried to cope with the new situation, which resulted in different tributes to the victims or the erection of memorials. It could be thus argued that not only the change in policies – particularly those related to immigration and security – has had an effect in shaping the new American cultural mind, but significant changes can be also seen in more popular manifestations of culture, including books, films, songs and visual images. Analysing how popular culture reflects the 9/11 attacks can help us to understand how 'the attacks were processed by ordinary people' (Quay and Damico 2010: xi).

Although there is a significant number of songs in which we can see different interpretations of 9/11, Bruce Springsteen's 'The Rising' (2002) is significant because it was a collection of songs produced about New York's attacks. This album, which includes a number of songs recalling the attacks from a variety of individual perspectives, has been 'hailed as the first significant cultural response to the events that took place on September 11' (Quay and Damico 2010: 221). These songs are not only interesting for the way in which Springsteen manages to capture the sad feeling of the nation while offering redemption and hope (Tyrangiel 2002: 40), but also because they are stripped of their narrative. Springsteen relies on a language that is generic and which may result in universal meanings (Sawyer 2004). Thus, we do not find Springsteen's usual references to individual and specific characters, but a string of words and images that are repeated in the different songs of the album and that eventually reduce the attacks to an 'anonymous domestic fragment' which becomes an allegory of a broader social condition and which manages to capture the mood of the whole nation. It is this use of language, which seems to strive for universality, that renders TWT as a useful tool for analysing how meaning is contextually triggered. As will be explained below, TWT relies on the deictic construction of reality (Werth 1999). Since deictics and referential entities necessarily rely on context in order to be interpreted (Lugea 2016: 30–4), a number of frames – and types of knowledge – are activated and result in a given discursive representation of a state of affairs (Werth 1999: 69).

'The Rising,' as the track whose title is adopted for the album, offers an account of the sacrifice done by a fire-fighter who dies after entering the Twin Towers and trying to save those who were trapped inside. Its core themes are those of faith and hope, which are also combined with the ideas of strength and force (Yates 2010). Even if the song recalls the physical action done by a fire-fighter, some people have interpreted it as referring to the resurrection as well. This interpretation has not been denied by Springsteen, who explains how his Catholic education has had an impact on the way that he sees and understands life (Yates 2010: 40–1). Although 'The Rising' as an album has been characterised as missing references to politics (Tyrangiel 2002: 46), 'The Rising' was used on a number of political campaigns during the 2008 US presidential election, including those of John Edwards, Hillary Clinton and Barack Obama (Bosman 2008; Miller 2008; Nabourney 2007). As we will see below, these multiple uses of the song and the different meanings it triggers can be explained by doing a TWT analysis of its lyrics.

3. Method of Analysis

To understand how Springsteen's use of universal language in 'The Rising' may acquire multiple meanings in such a way that different feelings, including sadness and hope, are evoked, I have followed a combination of three theoretical schools: Text-World Theory (TWT) (Gavins 2007; Lugea 2016; Werth 1999), Van Dijk's (2005, 2008) socio-cognitive approach to the study of context and its relationship with knowledge, and Discourse Space Theory (DST) (Chilton 2004, 2005, 2014).

TWT has already been proved to be a useful tool for clarifying which entities can be included in an ideologically motivated instance on discourse (Filardo-Llamas 2013), and how these entities can be re-contextualised across different modes of discourse (Filardo-Llamas 2015) or different contexts (Hidalgo-Downing and Filardo-Llamas 2019). The main objective of TWT is to identify mental representations of the world – or 'text-worlds' (Gavins 2007: 10) – which are discursively spread. Two main elements determine the existence of these worlds: world-building elements (including participants, locations and times), and function-advancing propositions (or the actions done by participants). As will be seen below, a textual analysis based on Cognitive Linguistics helps in identifying both of these categories.

What Werth (1999) originally tries to do while proposing this theory is explain how our understanding of the real – or fictional – world is a 'product of our mental processes' (Lugea 2016: 63). This implies acknowledging that the representation of a state of affairs is the outcome of two sources of information: (i) the text itself and the elements – or linguistic cues – which accumulate to build up a given representation; and (ii) the knowledge of the participants in the communicative situation (Werth 1999: 69). This connection between these two sources of information stems from the text-drivenness phenomenon, that is, 'the text is responsible . . . not only for defining its own parameters, but also for stipulating which areas of the knowledge are to be activated' (Werth 1999: 358).

This double source of information lies at the core of the two types of worlds which can be identified: text-worlds, which are the decontextualised mental representations we construct when we first encounter a piece of language (Gavins 2007: 3), and discourse-worlds which are the contextually determined interpretations construed at the moment of discourse production and discourse reception (Gavins 2007: 9, 18–31).[1] This second stage is particularly significant to understand how the different layers of meanings are produced, and how these may result in different types of discourse-worlds.

This chapter tries, in this way, to fill in a gap: doing more research at the discourse-world level which can help us understand how Werth's (1999: 48–51) notion of common ground is influenced and determined by participant knowledge (Lugea 2016: 71).[2]

Werth (1999: 120) identifies the text-world as being a combination of textual information and background knowledge. Van Dijk's (2005, 2008) socio-cognitive approach to the study of context and knowledge proves to be a useful addition for understanding the 'background knowledge', and its being a component of the common ground. Both authors take the notion of frames – or related notions such as 'schemas' or 'scenarios' – as their point of departure. These are understood as a 'cognitive space, mapping out an experiential category' (Werth 1999: 108). These cognitive – or mental – spaces can be equated to what Van Dijk (2008: 76) calls a 'context model schema', and which includes the following categories: (i) setting, including aspects related to the time, and space where a given situation takes place; (ii) participants, and descriptions of them, such as their communicative and social roles and associated identities; and (iii) communicative and other actions or events. A close look at this description of the context model schema shows that its inherent categorisation is somehow equivalent to the components which can be identified in a text-world: (i) world-building elements, or the basic parameters within which entities in the text-world may operate including aspects such as time, space and participants; and (ii) function-advancing, or those items which propel an instance of discourse forward (Gavins 2007: 56). This equivalence is summarised Figure 6.1.

Although Werth (1999: 94–103) tries to provide a description of the different types of shared knowledge one may find, this does not seem to be specific enough in order to explain how one text-world may have multiple – and combined – interpretations. Both Werth and Van Dijk rely on the 'overall epistemic strategy' (Van Dijk 2008: 83) in discourse production, which assumes that shared knowledge need not be expressed, and thus may remain implicit. Van Dijk (2008: 83) proposes the term K-Device to account for any explicit and implicit expression of knowledge in discourse. This K-Device activates existing knowledge on the part of the recipient, and it is of key importance for communication to be successful. This existing knowledge may be of different types, namely (i) personal knowledge, or 'autobiographical knowledge about personal experiences', (ii) interpersonal knowledge, or 'personal knowledge that is shared by two or more individuals on the basis of previous interpersonal communication or common experiences', (iii) group knowledge, or 'socially shared knowledge, either of group experiences, or of general, abstract knowledge acquired by the members of a group', (iv) institutional or organisational knowledge, or 'social knowledge shared by members

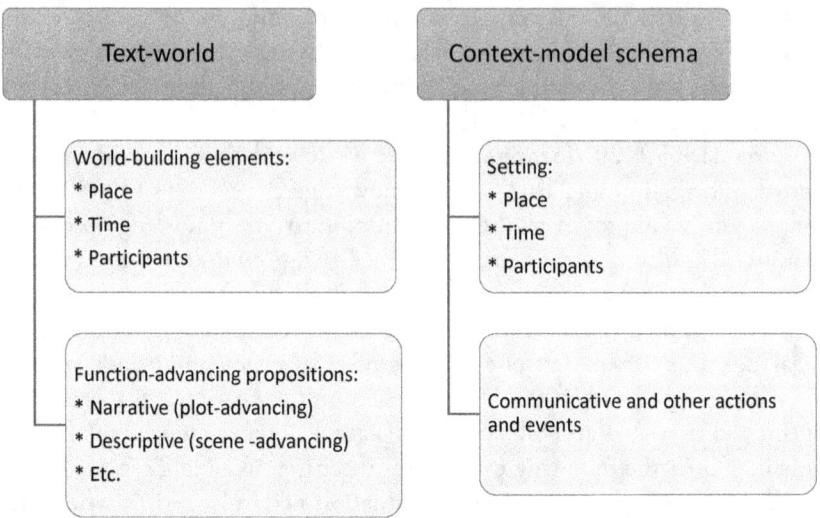

Figure 6.1 Components of text-worlds and context models as mental spaces

of an institution or organization', (v) national knowledge, or 'knowledge shared by the citizens of a country' and (vi) cultural knowledge, or 'the general knowledge shared by the members of the same "culture"' (Van Dijk 2005: 77–9). Given the text-drivenness phenomenon explained above, it can be argued that all these types of knowledge may be separately or simultaneously activated by different textual cues. This may eventually explain how and why every time a recipient encounters an instance of discourse, a 'new text-world is formed in accordance with the experience and knowledge they bring to it' (Lugea 2016: 73).

If we go back to the research hypothesis set out above, I argued that the analysis of linguistic strategies is important to understand the healing effect of 'The Rising.' DST (Chilton 2004, 2005) is a useful tool to explain the relationship between linguistic strategies and evaluation. As claimed by Simpson (1993: 46), much of the emotions evoked by an instance of discourse can be 'attributable to the point of view it exhibits'. Previous studies (Filardo-Llamas et al. 2016) have shown the need of connecting point of view to the notion of construal, since the former can be understood as one of the operations of the latter (Hart 2014: 111). One of the basic tenets of Cognitive Linguistics is that language encodes construal, that is, 'the same situation, event, entity or relation can be conceptualized in different ways and alternative linguistic forms impose upon the scene described alternative conceptualizations' (Hart 2014: 110). How point of view is achieved in a text can be thus explained as a manifestation of positioning, which can be understood as the strategy that guides discourse recipients towards adopting a given perspective in relation to the described reality (Filardo-Llamas et al. 2016). The notion of perspective, and its conceptual relation to space, can be explained through DST (Chilton 2004, 2005).

DST becomes a useful incorporation to TWT in order to understand how a given instance of discourse can acquire evaluative meaning by placing entities in a proximal–distal relationship to the deictic centre. Some of world building entities in the text-world are deictic in nature, that is they are clustered 'around a notional zero-point' (Werth 1999: 52), or deictic centre. By relying on DST, the identified mental representations can be recast and placed 'across spaces as coordinate correspondences on three fundamental dimensions' (Chilton 2005: 81): space, time and axiology (Cap 2010). It is this last dimension which is particularly significant to explain how emotion may arise, as if words are not sufficiently anchored geographically or temporally, they tend to emphasise that the discursively portrayed axiological values are close – or distant – to the deictic centre.

Both TWT and DST are theories of discourse which rely on the idea of deicticity. Given that deictics encode the speaker's relation to the situational context at the moment of utterance (Hart 2014: 164), they are of key importance to explain the new meanings that are contextually acquired. Deictics, combined with other linguistic cues as we will see in the analysis below, are thus a key linguistic element which can help us to explain how 'all participants in the discourse actively construct a working relationship between their use of language and their shared, or individual, context' (Lugea 2016: 33). Likewise, both TWT and DST account for an axiological construal of reality, which can be explained either in terms of proximal/distal positions in the modality/axiology axis (Chilton 2004) or as a world-shift (Gavins 2007) or sub-world (Werth 1999).

In short, a text analysis of 'The Rising' can help us to uncover its underlying text-world(s) – or mental representations – and their discursive construal. As we will see below, this construal is not only the result of the conceptualisation that is evoked by the linguistic choices made by the singer. This conceptualisation also reflects the different types of shared knowledge that are activated by those textual cues, and the proximal-distal evaluation that is related to them. This activation of multiple types of knowledges is possible because of the schematic (Langacker 1991: 7) and universal use of language, which only becomes specific – or content-full – when the said knowledge is activated. Once text-worlds are construed, the song may have a cognitive and emotional effect, which stems from the proximal–distal relationship that is established between mental categories and their contextual counterparts.

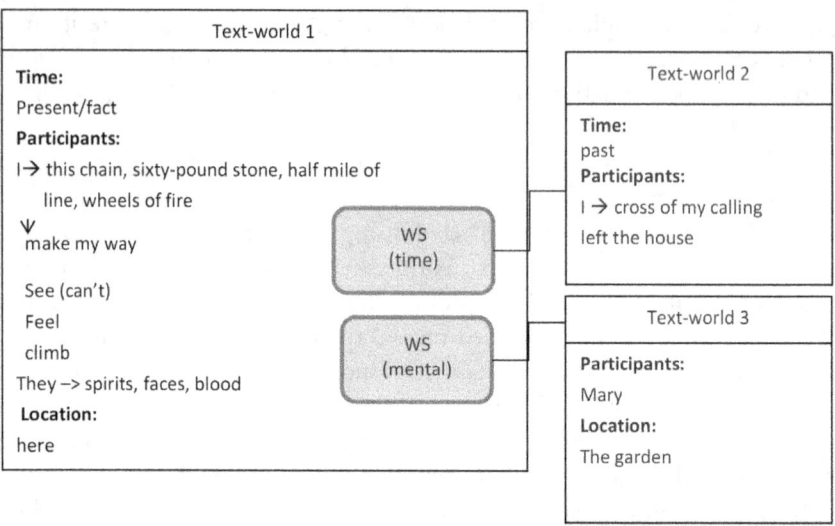

Figure 6.2 Summarised text-worlds in Springsteen's 'The Rising'

4. Analysis

In Figure 6.2, we can see a summarised version of the text-worlds in Springsteen's 'The Rising' which includes the main features of this mental representation. There is only one main discourse participant, 'I', a pronoun which, in the communicative situation, indexes the singer. There are no clear spatio-temporal anchoring devices, as we only have a reference to the present tense, and the use of the deictic adverb 'here'. There is a temporal world-switch (text-world 2) that is caused by a change in tense, and which recalls the actions done in the past. Besides, there is a mental projection triggered by the lexical verb 'see' (Halliday 2004; Nuyts 2000: 29) that results in an epistemic sub-world (text-world 3), which reflects the speaker's memories.

The main stylistic feature of Springsteen's 'The Rising' has already been identified as a use of a language that is generic and which results in universal meanings (Sawyer 2004). This is also reflected in the text-worlds included in Figure 6.2, as a vagueness can clearly be observed when pointing and referring to the main world-building elements (Werth 1999): participants, time and space. This vague discursive construction of deictic entities allows the text-world to acquire multiple meanings, as the main elements of the context-model schema (Van Dijk 2008) which is triggered are arguably 'empty' of meaning and could activate different knowledge schemata.

The first possible interpretation relies on national knowledge (Van Dijk 2005: 77) about what happened in the US on 11 September 2001. It could be argued that this triggers an 'event-bound' discourse-world. Following Springsteen's explanation of the song being about a fire-fighter trying to rescue the people who were at the Twin Towers in New York (Yates 2010), the deictic world-defining elements (Werth 1999: 52) are anchored to that situation and, thus, become contextually meaningful. The main discourse participant, 'I', is equated to a fire-fighter. As shown in the matrix text-world in Figure 6.2, there are a number features that characterise this fire-fighter and which serve as textual cues that activate this knowledge schema.[3] Amongst them, the 'chain that binds' the fire-fighter and the 'half mile of line' could be understood as being a hose, the 'sixty-pound stone' is the oxygen tank, the 'wheels of fire' on which the discourse participant rides is the fire-fighter truck, and the 'cross' that he[4] wears refers to the St Florian cross that can be seen on most fire-fighters' uniforms, as he is their patron saint.

Once that knowledge about the fire-fighter in 9/11 is activated, the only space deictic in the song, 'here', acquires contextual meaning: the Twin Towers in New York immediately after the attack. This interpretation is also related to other textual cues, such as 'through the darkness', which is caused by the chaos and the collapsing of the building, or the function-advancing proposition triggered by the material verb process 'climb' (Halliday 2004). A close analysis of the function-advancing propositions shows that the narrative they create is based on the idea of movement, exemplified in the verbs 'go', 'leave' or 'come'. These verbs of motion do not only contribute to constructing a narrative, but they also index space by relying on the proximity or distance that is established between the speaker and the deictic centre. 'The rising', or the upwards part of the building, is what one should 'come up to', and therefore occupies the deictic centre.

Besides the idea of moving up, two key evaluative aspects can be found in the lexical term 'the rising' combined with the verb 'come'. On the one hand, the choice of the verbal process 'come' triggers a MOTION event which results in the emphasis of an inanimate landmark towards which discourse participants, both the utterer–fire-fighter and the audience, should move (Hart 2014: 116–7). This highlights (Langacker 2008) the idea of moving away from the destruction and chaos caused by the terrorist attacks towards a place which is meant to be more positive. This contrast can be seen in the final verses of the song where an opposition is presented between the negative space that is occupied by the speaker and the one that is sought, and which is presented as occupying a mental space triggered by the word 'dream': 'Sky of blackness and sorrow (a dream of life), Sky of love, sky of tears (a dream of life) . . .'.

On the other hand, the idea of 'rising' also recalls the orientational metaphor GOOD IS UP (and BAD IS DOWN) (Lakoff and Johnson 1980). Since the deictic centre discourse participants are coming to is placed in the upwards position, it becomes positively evaluated, and it is thus presented as the desired destination that should be reached.[5] As we will see below, the evaluative connotation of this metaphor is also matched by the religious interpretation that can be made of this song. Likewise, this positive evaluation is also co-textually subordinated to the deontic command (Gavins 2007: 110) issued by the singer and which can be seen in the imperative form of the verb 'come' with which most of the verses in the chorus start. This requirement implies a linguistic grounding not only of the deictic centre in terms of space, but also in terms of values and axiology (Cap 2010; Chilton 2004).

The text-worlds identified in Figure 6.2 could have another interpretation that relies on the activation of religious knowledge, which can be considered a specific type of cultural knowledge (Van Dijk 2005). As mentioned above, some people have argued that the word 'rising' does not only evoke the going up of a fire-fighter in the Twin Towers, but it could also recall Jesus Christ's resurrection (Yates 2010: 40–1). Since the world-building elements of the text-world are mostly deictic in nature – with personal pronouns, the present verb tense and the adverbial 'here' as the main anchoring devices – it is possible for them to acquire new referential meaning when a different knowledge schema is recalled. A number of textual cues evoke (Werth 1999: 151) this area of knowledge, and characterise Jesus Christ.[6] Thus, the action of 'climb[ing]' done by the first-person discourse participant has both a physical and a metaphorical meaning and does not only refer to the metaphorical going up to heaven done by Jesus Christ in the resurrection (Luke 24: 51), but it also refers to the physical upwards journey done by Jesus Christ on the way to the Calvary, the mountain where he was crucified (Luke 23: 33). Likewise, the weight that lies on the back of this person could be physically understood as the cross which Jesus Christ carries, which is also textually recalled as 'wearing the cross of my calling', or the metaphorical burden of being the Saviour of humanity (John 4: 42).

This interpretation of the main discourse participant as the Saviour of humanity is also textually triggered by the reference to those who are going to be saved by him: 'There's spirits above and behind me, faces gone black, eyes burning bright, may their precious blood bind me.' In this quote, we can see how those who are going to be saved are deictically indexed through the third-person plural pronoun 'their', which stresses the deictic distance between the people – humanity – and the Jesus Christ speaker. However, a link is established between these two main discourse participants through the verb 'bind', which contributes to proximising (Cap 2010) the people to the deictic centre. This proximisation arguably occurs on two levels. First, in the physical space, as they both occupy the same location identified by the event-bound text-world interpretation: the Twin Towers in New York; and second, in the metaphorical space. Since space is one of the basic conceptualisations underlying cognitive interpretations of ideology (Cap 2010; Filardo-Llamas et al. 2016), and it lies at the core of many metaphorical interpretations (Lakoff and Johnson 1980), it could be argued that the physical action of binding and creating proximity equates the metaphorical binding, and relationship (Goatly 2007: 242), that is established between Jesus Christ and humanity, whom he is meant to save. The interpretation of the people in the Twin Towers as metonymically representing the whole of humanity is justified because they are referentially built as entities in the text-world through a genericisation process (Van Leeuwen 1996). This can be seen in the plural nouns 'faces', 'eyes' and 'blood', which can be all understood as a part-for-whole metonymy indexing a group of unidentified persons (Goatly 2007: 93).

There are two other textual cues in the song which evoke Jesus Christ's passion and resurrection. In the third stanza, the first-person discourse participant seems to directly talk to the 'Lord', before whom he 'stand[s]' before dying. The use of the word 'lord', whose connotation as referring to God is taken from the Latin Vulgate translation of the Bible (OED 2009), together with the second-person pronoun 'you' evoke a dialogue with God similar to the one Jesus Christ had with God before expiring (Matthew 27: 46). In the fourth stanza, we have a reference to 'Mary', whom the first-person discourse participant sees 'in the garden'. In the event-bound construal of the text-world, this could be understood as a reference to the fire-fighter remembering his partner. However, when the religious schema associated with the resurrection is activated, the reference to Mary could be understood as indicating the first encounter Jesus Christ has after coming back from his death, when he appears to Mary Magdalene in an unidentified garden (John 20: 11–15).

Why and how it is possible for us to construe two different discourse-worlds out of the text-worlds identified in Figure 6.2 can be explained by relying on how the song is structured. If we look at the activity schema (Machin 2010: 78–80) of the song, we can identify three levels, as shown in Table 6.1: the textual activity schema, and two other schemata that are activated by the textual clues explained above, and which correspond to two different discourse-worlds – the fire-fighter knowledge schema and the resurrection knowledge schema. In the case of the latter, both the physically determined interpretation of Jesus Christ's Passion and the metaphorical meaning associated with the resurrection have been included. As we can see below, a clear parallelism can be established between the three.

Conceptual Blending Theory (Fauconnier 1997; Fauconnier and Turner 2002) is useful to explain how the text-worlds identified in Figure 6.2, and

Textual activity schema	Fire-fighter knowledge schema	Resurrection knowledge schema	
		Physical passion	Metaphorical resurrection
Person starts climbing	Firefighter starts climbing Twin Towers	Jesus climbs towards the Calvary	Jesus metaphorically rises to heaven
⇩	⇩	⇩	⇩
Person sees faces and talks to the Lord	Firefighter sees victims of attacks and addresses God	Jesus sees people and addresses God	Jesus remembers his role as saviour
⇩	⇩	⇩	⇩
Person sees women [Mary] in the garden	Firefighter sees [remembers] his partner and kids	Jesus appears to Mary Magdalene in the garden	Mary Magdalene as first person Jesus appears to

Table 6.1 Textual and knowledge-determined activity schemata in 'The Rising'

the two distinct discourse-world explained above, become a single blended discourse-world. This, combined with the notion of layering (Gavins 2007: 73–90; Werth 1999: 336–54), can help to explain how the multiple mental representations triggered by the song are construed by the audience, and eventually how hearers can implicate themselves in the text-world (Gavins 2007: 86). When explaining how the mind works, the property of layering proposes that we process discourse by moving from a more general and broadly sketched meaning to a more specific, fine-tuned one (Werth 1999: 339). As mentioned above, this means that a text can activate different types of knowledge schemata (Van Dijk 2008) depending on the linguistic cues, as I have summarised in Table 6.1. This idea seems to also underline the notion of conceptual blending, which explains how 'knowledge of background frames, cognitive and cultural models' are combined into a larger meaning structure that is called a 'blend' (Fauconnier 1997: 150).

We can consider that any text-world is a mental space, that is, a 'small conceptual packet' (Fauconnier and Turner 2002: 40). Similarities can be observed in the construction of text-worlds and mental spaces, as the former relies on the existence of world-building elements while the latter relies on space-builders. Both text-world and mental spaces are abstract and mental entities which may result in different representations dependent on the knowledge frames activated. Mental spaces lies at the core of conceptual blending, which is the result of a combination of a generic space that 'reflects

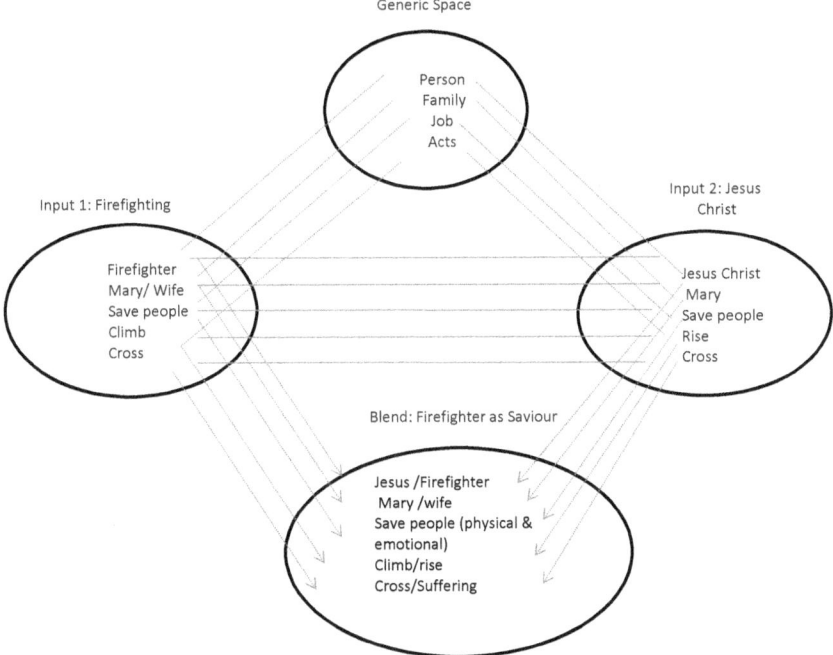

Figure 6.3 Conceptual blending in 'The Rising'

some common, usually more abstract, structure and organization' that is shared by two input spaces, or knowledge schemata, which may be totally or partially 'projected onto a fourth space, the blend' (Fauconnier 1997: 150). In the case of 'The Rising', the generic space would correspond to the text-world identified in Figure 6.2 and the schematic and basic activity schema summarised in Table 6.1, while the input spaces would be each of the knowledge schemata evoked: the fire-fighter going up the Twin Towers on 9/11 and Jesus Christ's passion and resurrection. As we can see in Figure 6.3, the generic space and the input spaces share some features which result in a blend of the fire-fighter with Jesus Christ. The fire-fighter is thus not only the physical and event-bound saviour of the victims after the 9/11 attacks, but also a metaphorical saviour which is associated with religious connotations.

The role of the first-person singular pronoun, together with the present simple and the adverbial here as the key deictic world-building elements is of key significance to explain the healing power of Springsteen's song. Like TWT and Mental Space Theory, DST understands mental representations as conceptual spaces which are deictic in nature. Discourse meaning is thus the conceptualisation of 'the integrated representation of the

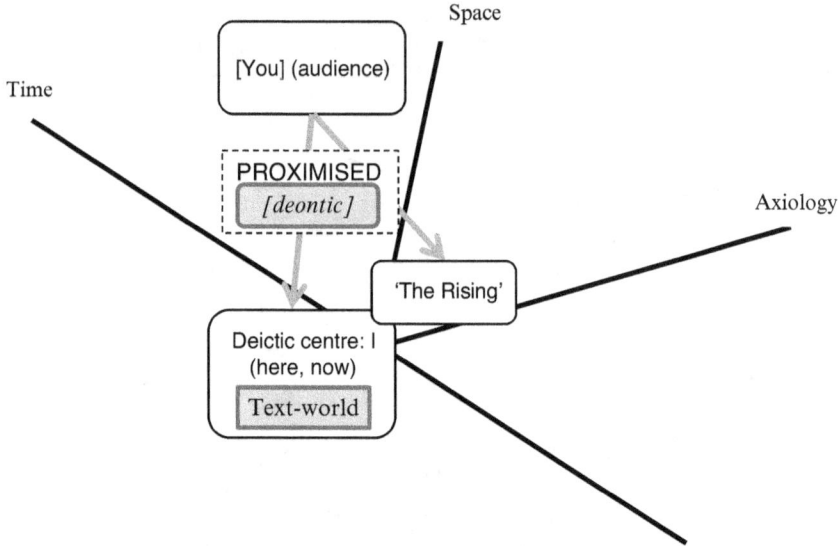

Figure 6.4 Proximity and distance in Springsteen's 'The Rising'

speaker's consciousness of his/her own position in space' (Chilton 2005: 86). Originating from Chilton's (2004) first development of DST, Cap's (2010, 2013) notion of proximisation may help in explaining how emotions may arise out of the relationship that is established between the (ideally egocentric) deictic centre and the other entities present in the discourse-world: the closer entities are located in terms of space, time and axiology to the speaker – and those who share knowledge and beliefs with him/her – the more effective discourse is in creating a shared identity, characterised by a shared notion of space, time, values and beliefs, and shared feelings between the speaker/singer and the audience.

As we can see in Figure 6.4, the deictic centre is occupied by the matrix text-world that was depicted in Figure 6.2. In that, we find the construction of the main discourse participants: the first-person singular fire-fighter–saviour, the audience (you) and those who have to be saved. A clear proximising relationship is established between the three of them: in the case of the 'I' and 'they' through the word 'bind', as it was explained above, and in the case of 'I' and 'you' through the deontic command issued with the verb 'come' in the imperative. Both of them contribute to widening the scope of the participants which occupy the deictic centre, with it reflecting not only the first-person singular position, but also including in it the position of the second- and third-person participants. Since all the discourse participants are included within the scope of the deictic centre, those values which occupy a deictically central position in the discourse space are not only positively evaluated by the speaker, but also by the audience with whom the central position is shared. Given that there are hardly any referential elements (Werth 1999) in the matrix text-world, and that deictics only acquire meaning in context, axiology acquires a more important role (Cap 2010). Besides, conceptual metaphors also play a key role in explaining how and why the song is effective.

'The Rising', as the title and main phrase in the song, plays a key role in explaining how evaluation is achieved. As it has been explained above, a multiplicity of knowledge schemata are evoked by it, thus resulting in a blended discourse meaning which presents the main discourse participant not only as a fire-fighter, but also as a physical and metaphorical saviour. The deictic trigger of this discourse participant, 'I', manages to transfer those saving traits to Bruce Springsteen, or any other person singing the song, who is indexed by the first-person pronoun whenever the song is sung, that is, in the immediate communicative situation. Besides, the phrase 'the rising' is deictically combined with a metaphorical use of the verb 'come'. There are no referential world-building elements which can help the listener to identify a concrete location, but the verb 'come' is a pure space deictic which necessarily indexes some location. As we can see in Figure 6.4, 'come' metaphorically indexes the deictic centre – both spatially and axiologically – of the discourse space (Chilton 2005) that is occupied by the matrix text-world. Given that perspective and evaluation are associated with the beliefs of the speaker (Filardo-Llamas et al. 2016; Hart 2014), those entities which are located in the deictic centre are thus positively evaluated.

Two conceptual metaphors stress that evaluation. As it has been explained above, the action of 'rising' necessarily implies going up, a location which according to Lakoff and Johnson (1980) is positively evaluated. Besides, the word 'comes' triggers the need of reaching a destination –'the rising', in this case – and the importance of moving forward if we want to reach it. That is closely related to the metaphor LIFE IS A JOURNEY, and its mapping SUCCESS IS MOVEMENT FORWARD (Goatly 2007; Kövecses 2002). As explained above, 'the rising' is also the desired destination both for the speaker–singer and the audience, given that this verb appears in the imperative form. The use of this verbal form evokes a deontic world-shift (Gavins 2007: 110) which is tied to the speaker's desire for the audience to carry out that action, as shown in Figure 6.4. Thus, 'the rising' does not only occupy the space and axiological deictic centre in the matrix text-world, but it would also occupy the central deictic position in another layer of meaning which is associated with the speaker's (and audience's) desires. Since the word 'come' implies movement, 'the rising' is proximised to the speaker and audience, and is thus transferred to the central spatial and axiological position.

5. Conclusion

Two distinguishing features shall be highlighted when describing the text-worlds in Bruce Springsteen's 'The Rising' and explaining the healing power of this song. On the one hand, the song is characterised by the deictic vagueness of the world-building elements in the song, which are combined with a lack of clear referential indexation. This deictic vagueness combined with metaphorical conceptualisations evokes a number of knowledge schemata which eventually result in three main mental representations: (i) the event-bound interpretation of a fire-fighter going up the Twin Towers after the 9/11 attacks; (ii) the religious understanding of the main discourse participant being Jesus Christ going up the Calvary mount and resurrecting to save humanity; and (iii) a performative interpretation of the song metaphorically acquiring an energising and healing value which results from the textual conceptual blending between the fire-fighter and Jesus Christ, and from the discursive, communicative and contextual blending between the singer and the fire-fighter/Jesus Christ first-person discourse participant.

On the other hand, the song is characterised by the proximity relationship established between the first-person discourse participant and the title phrase 'the rising', which is presented as the desired goal of both the speaker–singer and the audience. This is the result of a double proximisation: (i) a spatial proximisation that locates 'the rising' at the deictic centre of the text-world and (ii) an axiological proximisation that results from the deontic world-shift triggered by the imperative, and its resulting modalised text-world, in which 'the rising' is constructed as the key 'moral' value.

The analysis of 'The Rising' shows how a single text-world can result in several discursive construals that are the result of the activation of the audience's K-Device. The textual analysis has proved the text-drivenness phenomenon identified by Werth (1999), which emphasises the role of linguistic cues in activating different areas of knowledge. TWT thus proves useful in identifying the core mental representations triggered by a text, and in explaining how these are construed in context. As show in the analysis, 'The Rising' requires multiple mental representations to be constructed in the minds of discourse participants, and the notion of layering (Gavins 2007; Werth 1999), and therefore addition of meanings, becomes useful to explain this.

Van Dijk's (2008) identification of different types of knowledge and their relation to the context model has proved to be a useful addition to TWT in as much as it helps to explain how multiple representations are cognitively processed. Given that not all discourse participants necessarily share the same schematic knowledge, acknowledging the different types of knowledge that are activated by a text-world is useful to explain how an instance of discourse is interpreted. This interpretation does not only include the objective mental representation of the content of the text, but also the subjective stance of the discourse participants towards the information presented in the text-world. As shown in the analysis, TWT already includes elements for the analysis of evaluation, namely modality and conceptual metaphor. However, the proximity/distance relationship that lies at the core of DST (Chilton 2005) and proximisation theory (Cap 2013) are significant additions to being able to explain how the different entities which are part of a text-world are related not only between them, but also with the speaker's and audience's point of view. In this sense, the analysis done of 'The Rising' proves that proximisation does not necessarily involve a threat or something negative for the audience, but can be a useful concept to account for positive evaluation. By relying on the analysis of 'The Rising', this chapter has tried to explain how the discourse-world level of a text is construed, both by accounting for the activation of participants' knowledge and for the evaluation that textual choices may evoke.

Acknowledgement

Research funded by the Spanish Ministry of Economy and Competition and the Fodor Funds in the framework of the projects RECDID (Retórica Constructivista: Discursos de la Identidad (FFI2013-40934R)) and CONDISCO (Construcción discursiva del conflicto (FFI2017-85227-R)).

Notes

1 Given the emphasis that is placed on the text-drivenness phenomenon in this chapter, I will only focus on how those discourse-worlds are textually triggered. However, we cannot forget that songs are multimodal instances of discourse, and that further layers of meaning are added through the other modes of communication, such as music (see Filardo-Llamas, 2015, 2017a, 2017b; Filardo-Llamas and Perales García, 2017 for examples of analysis).
2 Werth's (1999) notion of common ground is combined here with Van Dijk's (2008: 83) definition of it as the knowledge shared between speaker(s) and recipient(s).
3 Although Werth (1999: 191) identifies verbs which recall a state as function-advancing in the text-world because they contribute to describing a state, I have decided to mark them as establishing a relational relationship (Halliday 2004) with the first-person singular discourse participant. Since all the examples mentioned above serve to characterise the discourse participant, and contribute to activating a specific knowledge schema, it could be argued that they are in fact helping in representing the fire-fighter as a social actor whose description is generalised through a 'categorisation' (Van Leeuwen 1996: 52–3) process which stresses the social identity of that actor as being a fire-fighter at work.
4 The use of the masculine pronoun to refer to the fire-fighter who is the main discourse participant in the song does not intend to neglect the possibility of it being a female actor, but rather reflects the masculine voice of the singer.

5 It is not the aim of this chapter to include a musical analysis of this song, but this metaphor can be also observed in the music. The word 'rising' appears in the final position of the verses of the chorus which is also characterised by a rising melody.
6 This interpretation of 'the rising' being the resurrection is also reflected in the music of the song. In the second part of the song, both the stanzas and the chorus are sometimes preceded by a number of voices singing 'lilillili lililili' accompanied with a rising tone and a more prominent use of instruments. All these elements together seek the active role of the audience who is meant to accompany Jesus Chris on his resurrection. The prominent role of instruments together with the use of multiple voices stresses the idea of the social unity which is desired in the United States after the 9/11 attacks, with it being a united nation. See Machin (2010) and Van Leeuwen (2012) for an explanation of the analysis of musical devices and their associated meaning.

References

Bosman, J. (2008). Bruce for Barack: Ohhhh he's the one. *The New York Times*, <https://thecaucus.blogs.nytimes.com/2008/04/16/bruce-for-barack-ohhhh-hes-the-one/> (last accessed 30 November 2018).

Cap, P. (2010). Proximizing objects, proximizing values. Towards an axiological contribution to the discourse of legitimisation. In U. Okulska and P. Cap (eds), *Perspectives in Politics and Discourse*. Amsterdam: John Benjamins, p. 119–42.

Cap, P. (2013). *Proximization. The Pragmatics of Symbolic Distance Crossing*. Amsterdam: John Benjamins.

Chilton, P. (2004). *Analysing Political Discourse. Theory and Practice*. London: Routledge.

Chilton, P. (2005). Vectors, viewpoint and viewpoint shift: Toward a Discourse Space Theory. *Annual Review of Cognitive Linguistics* 3: 78–116.

Chilton, P. (2014). *Language, Space and Mind. The Conceptual Geometry of Linguistic Meaning*. Cambridge: Cambridge University Press.

CNN (2016). September 11 terror attacks fast facts. CNN News, <http://edition.cnn.com/2013/07/27/us/september-11-anniversary-fast-facts/> (last accessed 30 November 2018).

Fauconnier, G. (1997). *Mappings in Thought and Language*. Cambridge: Cambridge University Press.

Fauconnier, G. and Turner, M. (2002). *The Way We Think. Conceptual Blending and the Mind's Hidden Complexities*. New York: Basic Books.

Filardo-Llamas, L. (2013). Committed to the ideals of 1916. The language of paramilitary groups: The case of the Irish Republican Army. *Critical Discourse Studies* 10 (1): 1–17.

Filardo-Llamas, L. (2015). Re-contextualizing political discourse. *Critical Discourse Studies* 12 (3): 279–96, https://doi.org/10.1080/17405904.2015.1013478.

Filardo-Llamas, L. (2017a). The (re)construction of gender roles in the genre of song: In search of female empowerment. In E. Morales-López and A. Floyd (eds), *Developing New Identities in Social Conflicts. Constructivist Perspectives* Amsterdam: John Benjamins, pp. 181–202.

Filardo-Llamas, L. (2017b). When the fairy tale is over: An analysis of songs and institutional discourse against domestic violence in Spain. In L. C. S. Way and S. McKerrell (eds), *Music as Multimodal Discourse. Semiotics, Power and Protest.* London: Bloomsbury, pp. 159–78.

Filardo-Llamas, L. and Perales García, C. (2017). ¿Se acabaron las lágrimas? Estudio de las respuestas culturales a la violencia de género. *Athenea Digital* 17 (1): 291–315, https://doi.org/http://dx.doi.org/10.5565/rev/athenea.1828.

Filardo-Llamas, L., Hart, C. and Kaal, B. (eds) (2016). *Space, Time and Evaluation in Ideological Discourse.* London: Routledge.

Gavins, J. (2007). *Text-world Theory. An Introduction.* Edinburgh: Edinburgh University Press.

Goatly, A. (2007). *Washing the Brain. Metaphor and Hidden Ideology.* Amsterdam: John Benjamins.

Halliday, M. A. K. (2004). *An Introduction to Functional Grammar*, 3rd edition. London: Edward Arnold.

Harf, J. E. and Lombardi, M. O. (2005). Introduction: The unfolding legacy of 9/11. In J. E. Harf and M. O. Lombardi (eds), *The Unfolding Legacy of 9/11.* Lanham, MD: University Press of America, pp. 1–10.

Hart, C. (2014). *Discourse, Grammar and Ideology. Functional and Cognitive Perspectives.* London: Bloomsbury.

Hidalgo-Downing, L. and Filardo-Llamas, L. (2019, in press) Singing for peace: Metaphor and creativity in the lyrics and performances of three songs by U2. In L. Hidalgo-Downing and B. Kraljevic-Mujic (eds), *Performing Metaphorical Creativity in Context: Exploring Modes and Cultures.* Amsterdam: John Benjamins.

Juslin, P. N. and Sloboda, J. A. (2010). Introduction: Aims, organization, and terminology. In P. N. Juslin and J. Sloboda (eds), *Handbook of Music and Emotion. Theory and Research.* Oxford: Oxford University Press, pp. 3–19.

Kövecses, Z. (2002). *Metaphor. A Practical Introduction.* Oxford: Oxford University Press.

Lakoff, G. (2007). *No Pienses en un Elefante. Lenguaje y Debate Político.* Madrid: Editorial Complutense.

Lakoff, G. and Johnson, M. (1980). *Metaphors We Live By.* Chicago and London: The University of Chicago Press.

Langacker, R. (1991). *Concept, Image, and Symbol. The Cognitive Basis of Grammar.* Berlin, New York: Mouton de Gruyter.

Langacker, R. W. (2008). *Cognitive Grammar. A Basic Introduction.* Oxford: Oxford University Press.

Lozon, J. and Bensimon, M. (2014). Music misuse: A review of the personal and collective roles of 'problem music.' *Aggression and Violent Behavior* 19 (3): 207–18, https://doi.org/10.1016/j.avb.2014.04.003

Lugea, J. (2016). *World Building in Spanish and English Spoken Narratives.* London: Bloomsbury.

Machin, D. (2010). *Analysing Popular Music: Image, Sound and Text.* London: Sage.

McKerrell, S. (2012). Hearing sectarianism: Understanding Scottish sectarianism as song. *Critical Discourse Studies* 9 (4): 363–374.

Miller, S. (2008). Springsteen songs slip into Obama's play list post endorsement. *ABC News*, <http://blogs.abcnews.com/politicalradar/2008/04/springsteen-son.html> (last accessed July 2017).

Nabourney, A. (2007). Do you know the words to the Edwards fight song? *The New York Times*, <https://thecaucus.blogs.nytimes.com/2007/12/19/do-you-know-the-words-to-the-edwards-fight-song/> (last accessed 30 November 2018).
Nuyts, J. (2000). *Epistemic Modality, Language, and Conceptualization*. Amsterdam: John Benjamins.
OED (2009) *Oxford English Dictionary*. Oxford: Oxford University Press, 2nd edition. CD-version.
Quay, S. E. and Damico, A. M. (2010). *September 11 in Popular Culture. A Guide*. Santa Barbara: Greenwood.
Sawyer, J. S. (2004). *Racing in the Street. The Bruce Springsteen Reader*. New York: Penguin.
Simpson, P. (1993). *Language, Ideology, and Point of View*. London: Routledge.
Steen, G. and Gavins, J. (2003). Contextualising cognitive poetics. In J. Gavins and G. Steen (eds), *Cognitive Poetics in Practice*. London: Routledge, pp. 1–12.
Tyrangiel, J. (2002). Bruce rising. An intimate look at how Springsteen turned 9/11 into a message of hope. *Time*, 5 August, pp. 40–7.
Van Dijk, T. A. (2005). Contextual knowledge management in discourse production: A CDA perspective. In R. Wodak and P. A. Chilton (eds), *A New Agenda in (Critical) Discourse Analysis*. Amsterdam: John Benjamins, pp. 71–100.
Van Dijk, T. A. (2008). *Discourse and Context: A Sociocognitive Approach*. Cambridge: Cambridge University Press.
Van Leeuwen, T. (1996). The representation of social actors. In C. R. Caldas-Coulthard and M. Coulthard (eds), *Text and Practices. Readings in Critical Discourse Analysis*. London and New York: Routledge, pp. 32–70.
Van Leeuwen, T. (2012). The critical analysis of musical discourse. *Critical Discourse Studies* 9 (4): 319–28. https://doi.org/http://dx.doi.org/10.1080/17405904.2012.713204.
Way, L. C. S. and McKerrell, S. (2017). *Music as Multimodal Discourse. Semiotics, Power and Protest*. London: Bloomsbury.
Werth, P. (1999). *Text Worlds: Representing Conceptual Space in Discourse*. Harlow: Pearson Education.
Yates, B. L. (2010). Healing a nation: An analysis of Bruce Springsteen's The Rising. *Journal of Popular Music Studies* 22 (1): 32–49. https://doi.org/10.1111/j.1533-1598.2010.01218.x.

7

'A Nation Divided': Metaphors and Scenarios in Media Coverage of the 2016 British EU Referendum

Veronika Koller and Josie Ryan

1. Introduction

In this chapter, we will demonstrate how Conceptual Metaphor Theory (CMT; see Lakoff and Johnson 1980; Gibbs 2017) can enrich, and be enriched by, the analysis of discourse, here specifically news reports and opinion pieces. In so doing we highlight some of the issues and opportunities that arise when CMT is applied to language in use, particularly in a complex discourse such as that surrounding the vote in the British European Union (EU) referendum of 2016. We suggest that discourse analysis can help to add conceptual complexity to the notion of metaphor scenarios (Musolff 2004, 2006) while at the same time testing CMT against empirical data.

We address the following specific research questions:

> RQ1: What embodied metaphors are used in news reports and opinion pieces about the 2016 British EU referendum on popular British news websites?
> RQ2: What relationship can be found between embodied metaphors, images schemas and source domains?
> RQ3: What scenarios do the source domains motivate?
> RQ4: How can Conceptual Metaphor Theory and metaphor scenarios be employed in the analysis of discourse?

In order to answer our research questions, the chapter is structured as follows: in the next section, we outline the political context to our study and review the literature on media discourse, including the use of metaphor, concerning the EU. Following that, we give an overview of the theoretical background to conceptual metaphors and metaphor scenarios and how they can enhance the analysis of discourse. The subsequent section describes our data and the methods used to analyse it. We then report what metaphors for the UK electorate and political establishment were most prevalent and how they were lexicalised. This section also presents an analysis of how spatial and ontological metaphors are perspectivised by image schemas and specified by source domains. The latter also motivate scenarios. We conclude with a discussion of how discourse analysis enriches Conceptual Metaphor Theory while our study in particular also adds conceptual complexity to the notion of metaphor scenarios.

2. Context and Literature Review: Media Discourse on the EU

The political background to our study is the British EU referendum in June 2016, in which the British electorate defied expectations when a slight majority voted to leave the European Union.[1] In the aftermath of the vote, politicians, pundits and the public have been trying to make sense of the motivation behind such a momentous and unexpected decision. The result of the referendum is even more surprising when we consider that referenda tend to favour the status quo and that the campaign for leaving the EU was somewhat fractured and did not appear to present any coherent plan in the event of a 'Brexit' vote (Fitzgibbon 2016). Reasons include the possibility that, for sections of the electorate, the EU came to represent an out-of-touch elite that favoured globalisation and immigration over national sovereignty, coupled with an absence of factual knowledge about how the EU works or what it achieves. It is also possible that the EU referendum was treated by the electorate as an opportunity to vent their frustration at not only the EU but also, and perhaps foremost, the British political establishment (Farrell 2016; Gifford 2016).

There is also a great deal of speculation about the influence of the media in the Brexit vote; the extent to which news, websites and social media contribute to the outcome of such polls is always an open question. However, there is evidence to suggest that at times of intense political activity, such as during the EU referendum campaign, people rely more heavily than usual on the media for information; 90,000 more daily newspapers were sold in Britain during June 2016 (Newsworks 2016). A post-mortem of media behaviour prior to the EU referendum (Wring 2016), whilst unable to determine in how far the media influenced the referendum outcome, indicates ways in which the media contributed to the campaign. The British media has a long tradition of Euroscepticism (Berry 2016; Wring 2016) which could not be undone over the course of a few months. Many areas of the media have been consistent in their anti-EU and Eurosceptic views (Hardt-Mautner 1995; Henkel 2018), so it is unsurprising that the national press was found to have been heavily biased in favour of Brexit during the referendum campaign (Levy et al. 2016). Furthermore, the newspaper editorials supporting the Leave campaign were found to be more tenacious and given greater salience in the immediate run-up to the vote (Firmstone 2016).

The specific question of how the European project and relations within the EU are represented in discourse has been the subject of much analysis. While Hardt-Mautner (1995) and Sowińska (2009) investigate the representation of EU/UK relations in newspapers from a more general critical discourse analytical viewpoint, Chilton and Ilyin (1993), Semino (2002) and Musolff (2004, 2006, 2016, 2017) have focused particularly on what metaphors are used in media discourse on EU relations and policies. Chilton and Ilyin (1993) problematised the metaphor of the 'common European House' in Russian, French and German political discourse by demonstrating that it had contextually dependent interpretations which arose from culturally different frames for House: the metaphor was 'processed in accordance with local languages, local discourse formations, local political interests' (Chilton and Ilyin 1993: 27). Semino (2002) also engaged in a cross-linguistic analysis of discourse relating to a later stage in the development of the EU, namely the advent of the single currency. She concluded that, although the frequently used source domains of Humans (personification), Journeys and Containers were common to both the Eurosceptic British press and the more pro-EU Italian press (where the euro was adopted), they were instantiated differently according to the stance and, to some extent, the culture of the discourse producer, particularly in the case of novel metaphors.

Musolff's work in particular has led to the development of metaphor scenario analysis because straightforward CMT is found not sufficient to explain how the metaphors used in complex texts and discourses are appropriated and adapted to represent different positions in the same debate. Building on his considerable work on metaphors for the EU and the UK, Musolff (2017) revisited the 'discourse career' of the metaphoric phrase 'Britain at the heart of Europe' in the context of the Brexit vote. His analysis charts how a scenario that was originally intended as a positive metaphor for Britain's involvement at the centre of the European Union in the early 1990s has been exploited over the years in political and media discourse to the point where 'it appears, in references to a sick, non-functioning or rotten organ of a dying body' (2017: 648; emphasis omitted). This demonstrates how metaphor scenarios can be appropriated and operationalised by opposing positions in a given debate. Durović and Silaški (2018) use Musolff's approach to bring his work on *marriage* and *divorce* scenarios for the UK/EU relationship (Musolff, 2004) up to date in the context of Brexit. Continuing this line of research, the present chapter focuses on media coverage of the referendum vote for 'Brexit', that is, the process of the UK leaving the EU. The different referendum campaigns, the analysis of the vote, the political consequences and the negotiations around leaving the EU all provide a rich discourse with implications for national identity, attitudes towards immigration, inter-European relations and the rise of populism in various countries, see chapters in Koller et al. 2019. As Britain's relationship with the EU is about to change significantly, we ask how the UK electorate, the UK political establishment and the relationship between them was represented metaphorically on news websites in the immediate aftermath of the vote. The next section elaborates the theoretical model which arose from our study.

3. Theoretical Framework: Conceptual Metaphor Theory and Metaphor Scenarios

CMT (Lakoff and Johnson 1980) incorporates the central ideas upon which Cognitive Linguistics is based; namely, that the linguistic system represents our conceptual system, which is, in turn, derived from our embodied perception of the world. Conceptual metaphors map concrete conceptual domains that relate to our embodied experience onto more abstract conceptual domains (Lakoff and Johnson 1980: 57).

Spatial cognition, as a primary form of embodied experience, plays a particularly important role in language (Levinson 2003), and Lakoff and Johnson go so far as to say that 'most of our fundamental concepts are organised in terms of one or more spatialisation metaphors' (1980: 17). For example, the human experience of moving in three-dimensional space as concurrent with different affective states gives rise to primary metaphors (Grady 1997), such as PHYSICAL PROXIMITY IS EMOTIONAL PROXIMITY, which can then be realised by metaphoric expressions that describe lack of empathy as spatial distance, as in our data (e.g. 'evidence of how out of touch [London] has become').

Lakoff and Johnson's work on metaphor and cognition has had a profound influence on Cognitive Linguistics in general and metaphor research in particular. However, there are a number of criticisms of the theory that need to be considered, particularly when analysing metaphor in discourse. One is that the two-domain model, whereby features of a source domain are mapped onto features of the target domain, is too simplistic a structure, and that the domains in question are often too broad to account for the complexity of actual metaphor use (Musolff 2006; Kövecses 2017). In addition, Lakoff and Johnson focus on the conceptual aspect of metaphor rather than its linguistic instantiation (1999: 123) and rely on native-speaker intuition when looking for systematic and regular patterns of metaphor in English, drawing conclusions from these about the structure of human cognition in general. Discourse analysts have raised a number of issues with this approach. First, the examples selected to illustrate conceptual metaphors are decontextualised and artificial (Musolff 2004): they are expressions and idioms that would be familiar to many speakers of English in Britain and the USA, but there are no criteria on which the authors' selection of linguistic examples is based (Semino 2002). The effect of this is that Lakoff and Johnson risk misrepresenting English speakers' use of metaphoric language, ignore the pragmatic effects of metaphor use in discourse, and fail to account for the richness and creativity of metaphor use in authentic language data (Chilton and Ilyin 1993; Semino 2002, 2008; Musolff 2004, 2016).

A range of complementary theories of metaphor have been proposed to account for the limitations of CMT, including metaphor scenario analysis (Musolff 2006). Kövecses (2017) and Dancygier and Sweetser (2014) have developed taxonomies of metaphor that attempt to incorporate a range of metaphor theories and terminologies, for example image schemas, domains, frames and mental spaces. Kövecses (2017: 340) proposes a 'multi-level view of conceptual metaphor' in which metaphor is organised according to four levels of schematicity. In his model, image schemas are the most general level, including concepts such as Container, Object or Force. The equivalent in our analysis is spatial and ontological metaphors, where ontological metaphors are defined as the figurative construal of an abstract notion in terms of a concrete object (Kövecses 2010: 39). We further posit that embodied metaphors of space, objects, force and movement – and combinations thereof – can be perspectivised by image schemas; for example, the clause 'people of our country rise up against [the] political class' realises space and movement metaphors that are perspectivised by an UP-DOWN image schema.

Kövecses' (2017) next level, domains, is somewhat more detailed in that knowledge of a domain comprises a number of image schematic concepts. For example, Musolff (2004) identifies the metaphor THE EU IS A HUMAN BODY in his corpus of newspaper articles about the EU, whereby the source domain of Human Body frames our understanding of the EU (the target domain). In our data-driven model, we see such source domains as specifying embodied metaphors of space and objects, for example by construing the electorate with its differences in opinion not only as an object that has been divided, but specifically as a scarred body (e.g. 'a scar that has never been properly treated'). The construal of an idea is thus affected by how a basic metaphor is specified.

The least schematic level in Kövecses' model is that of mental spaces, which account for contextualised, novel, blended and mixed metaphors (2017: 341). Mental spaces correspond to Musolff's scenarios (2004, 2006, 2016), which are described as 'figurative mini-narratives that carry with them an evaluative stance' (Musolff 2017: 643). In our understanding, only specific

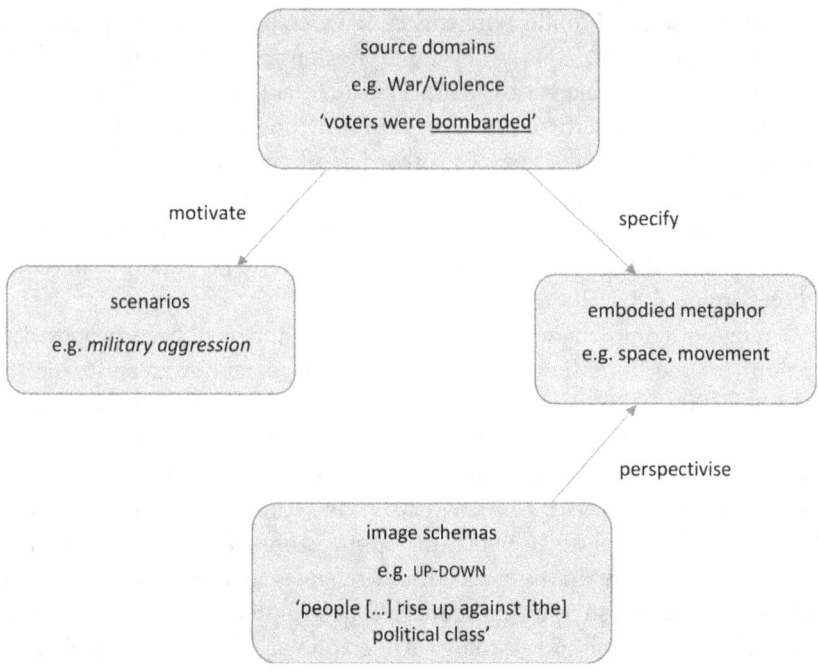

Figure 7.1 A model of metaphor and scenarios in discourse

source domains motivate scenarios, which include – at least implicitly – actors, actions and evaluations. We can conceive of the relation between specific source domains and metaphor scenarios by understanding the former as something like a 'stage' before the 'play' starts: the props are there, allowing for certain actions and relations between characters to be played out. In the action unfolding on the stage, certain actions and relations are more likely and more desirable than others. To illustrate, take the example of the War/Violence source domain: the scenario it gives rise to needs to include at least two opposing groups who exert violence to defeat the respective other, but some actions and relations (e.g. victory) are more positively evaluated than others (e.g. war crimes). While Kövecses' taxonomy has four levels – image schemas, domains, frames and mental spaces – in a vertical relation, we omit frames and model the relationships as seen in Figure 7.1.

Scenario analysis aims to rectify a number of the issues identified with CMT in order to provide a more thorough and nuanced account of metaphor in discourse. Firstly, it is text-based: scenarios are found and analysed in authentic texts and corpora to make available 'an interface to text-linguistic and discourse-analytical dimensions of the linguistic investigation of figurative language' (Musolff 2016: 138). By analysing metaphors and scenarios that are found in authentic language, insights and conclusions can be drawn about how metaphorical language is actually used. In this way, scenario analysis enriches CMT by testing it against empirical data, and demonstrates the flexible and dynamic nature of metaphor use in discourse (Musolff 2016: 31), rather than attempting to fit it into a fixed, two-domain structure. At the same time, drawing on CMT helps to add conceptual complexity to the notion of metaphor scenarios.

In the following section, we will translate our model into methods to analyse a specific set of texts.

4. Data and Methods

Our data capture a snapshot of the immediate reaction to the EU referendum result in the British media. As such, they consist of six articles from the three most popular UK news websites, all published on the day after the EU referendum, that is, on 24 June 2016. The three most popular news websites in the UK are BBC News, the Mail Online and the online version of *The Guardian* (Statista 2017), with the Mail Online representing the Leave and the Guardian the Remain campaign, while BBC News ostensibly aims for an impartial middle ground. News websites have overtaken newspapers as most people's source of news, as demonstrated by the fact that the Mail Online and Guardian websites got 15 million and 10 million visits per day respectively in June 2016, whilst their print circulations in the same month were 1.75 and 1.5 million (Press Gazette 2016).

We analysed one news report and one opinion piece from each of the websites. These two genres fulfil different functions in a news publication: the purpose of news reporting is 'to convey salient facts about a set of circumstances in a way that is easily comprehended' (Sheridan Burns 2013: 107), whilst opinion pieces can include more analysis and background, and present the views of the columnist. As part of our overarching question about how metaphor is used to represent the electorate and the British political establishment, we also wanted to analyse how metaphors and scenarios construe social groups and the relations between them, even in ostensibly non-argumentative texts such as news reports. Table 7.1 provides an overview of our data.

After stripping out figures, photos, embedded videos and hyperlinks, we saved the raw texts and uploaded them into the collaborative online annotation tool eMargin (https://emargin.bcu.ac.uk/), which allows for highlighting, colour-coding and tagging parts of text, including metaphoric expressions, and searching for annotations. We coded the data individually, comparing and adjusting our results in discussion.

The first stage of our analysis followed the Metaphor Identification Procedure, or MIP (Pragglejaz 2007), which aims to provide a principled set

Article title and mnemonic	Author(s)	Source	Word count
'EU referendum: England leads UK to exit' (BBC_REP)	Anonymous	http://www.bbc.co.uk/news/uk-politics-eu-referendum-36606245	1,241
'A less than United Kingdom' (BBC_OP)	Mark Easton	http://www.bbc.co.uk/news/uk-politics-eu-referendum-36605656	1,175
'Unlikely alliance between Labour heartlands and Tories in the Home Counties gives a slap in the face to the London political elite' (DM_REP)	Sam Greenhill, Ian Drury, Gerri Peev	http://www.dailymail.co.uk/news/article-3659162/Unlikely-alliance-Labour-heartlands-Tories-Home-Counties-gives-slap-face-London-political-elite.html	1,419
'Take a bow Britain' (DM_OP)	Anonymous	http://www.dailymail.co.uk/debate/article-3659143/DAILY-MAIL-COMMENT-bow-Britain-quiet-people-country-rise-against-arrogant-touch-political-class-contemptuous-Brussels-elite.html	1,255
'UK votes to leave EU after dramatic night divides nation' (GUA_REP)	Anushka Asthana, Ben Quinn, Rowena Mason	https://www.theguardian.com/politics/2016/jun/24/britain-votes-for-brexit-eu-referendum-david-cameron	1,150
'The vote is in, now we must face the consequences' (GUA_OP)	Anonymous	https://www.theguardian.com/commentisfree/2016/jun/24/the-guardian-view-on-the-eu-referendum-the-vote-is-in-now-we-must-face-the-consequences	1,363

Table 7.1 Overview of the data

of steps for classifying instances of language usage as metaphoric. These steps can then be carried out by different researchers, therefore making it, as far as possible, objective and transparent. The MIP method consists of several steps that enable the analyst to determine whether a word is being used metaphorically or not. The first step is to read the whole text to gain an understanding of it, followed by ascertaining the lexical units in the text. This is not always simply a case of looking at each word individually because the meaning of, for example, phrasal verbs, polywords and conventionalised phrases carry metaphorical meaning when combined, but not when analysed individually. Therefore, the analyst first needs to distinguish lexical units before looking into metaphoric meanings. Once done, the third step involves a number of questions about the lexical item being analysed:

- What is its meaning in context?
- Does is have a more basic contemporary meaning? ('Basic' can mean either more concrete, related to bodily action, precise or historically older.)
- Does the more basic meaning contrast with the meaning in the text and, if so, can the meaning in the text be understood in relation to the more basic meaning?

If the answer to the last two questions is yes, then the lexical item can be marked as metaphoric.

We used the MIP method to identify metaphors in our small corpus of news articles. As our particular interest is in the target domains of the British electorate and the UK political establishment, we restricted our coding to metaphoric expressions constructing those two groups. In the second stage of the analysis, we categorised those metaphoric expressions according to what embodied metaphors they realised. We looked at whether and how the metaphors were perspectivised through image schemas, meaning that particular image schemas, for example UP-DOWN, provide a certain perspective that adds further detail to embodied metaphors.[2] Next we investigated whether and how the metaphors were specified through other, less basic source domains, that is, what additional meaning was constructed by using, for instance, a Landmass source domain to make the ontological division metaphor more specific. The last stage, scenario analysis, meant investigating what scenarios the specific source domains motivate, including detail on actor, actions and evaluations. The next section will present the findings of our analysis.

5. Analysis

5.1. *Metaphoric Expressions for the Electorate and the UK Political Establishment*

While we originally identified spatial and ontological metaphoric expressions for four target domains – the electorate, the UK political establishment, future EU–UK relations and the referendum result – the first two showed more varied metaphoric expressions. We therefore decided to proceed only with those two target domains. Looking first at metaphors for the electorate, we can see that different metaphoric expressions are shared between genres and news outlets, suggesting not only a focus on the electorate but also a conventionalised way of construing the electorate. This contrasts with metaphoric expressions for the UK political establishment, which show no overlaps between genres and news outlets, indicating that there is no one conventional metaphoric way of writing about this target domain in media discourse. Tables 7.2 and 7.3 (see Appendix) show the metaphoric expressions for the two groups. (Shaded cells represent overlap across news outlets and genres. Where applicable, underlining indicates the relevant metaphoric expression.)

Tables 7.2 and 7.3 show that the journalists in our data use a wider range of different metaphoric expressions to refer to the political establishment – ninety compared to seventy-nine for the electorate – but that there is a lower degree of overlap: 13.33 per cent versus 20.25 per cent for the electorate. This suggests that the metaphoric construal of the electorate is more conventionalised than that of the political establishment in British media discourse.

5.2. *Embodied Metaphors, Images Schemas and Source Domains*

Relating the metaphoric expressions listed in Tables 7.2 and 7.3 back to their co-text, we can see that as individual groups, the electorate and the political establishment are mostly construed through an ontological metaphor, namely as objects that have been divided. Reflecting the very similar percentages of votes in the referendum, the metaphoric expressions construe differences of opinion among voters:

(1) 'It shows a country just split down the middle.' (GUA_REP)[3]

It is noteworthy that the Mail Online, rather than construing voters as a 'divided' group, focuses on how the Leave vote 'united' people from different socio-economic classes:

(2) Voters in the rich Tory shires and in Labour heartlands in the north were <u>united</u> in rejecting the threats and blandishments of their party leaders. (DM_OP)

The Mail Online is also the only news site to use the terms 'Leaver' and 'Remainer' as social category labels. This points to an identity – emergent before and immediately after the referendum and well-established at the time of writing (July 2018) – that is organised less around party allegiance, location or socio-economic background, and more around one's stance on the referendum question.

This reconfiguration of political identities is also reflected in the journalists using the ontological metaphor of division to refer to differences within political parties:

(3) Trust in politicians . . . is likely to have been damaged still further by a campaign that saw both <u>sides</u> accuse the other of bare-faced lies. (BBC_OP)

Division is not only represented as *within* the electorate or the political establishment but, crucially, also as *between* the two groups. For example:

(4) Door-knocking . . . will be important in <u>mending</u> the <u>link</u> between the electors of Britain, and the mostly pro-European representatives whom they elect. (GUA_OP)

More prominently, however, the relationship between the two groups is construed by means of a spatial metaphor, namely as distant.

(5) 'Decades of centralised control . . . has [*sic*] <u>distanced</u> our residents from the decisions that affect their everyday lives.' (BBC_OP).

The spatial (distance) metaphor is perspectivised by a number of image schemas, notably FRONT-BACK, CENTRE-PERIPHERY and UP-DOWN. All of these construe the relationship between electorate and establishment as one of unequal power, where UP/FRONT/CENTRE are the respective positions of privilege:

(6) all the towns and estates <u>left behind</u> by an international economic order which has not treated them well (GUA_OP)
(7) 'Many communities . . . feel very angry about the way they have been betrayed and <u>marginalised</u>.' (GUA_REP)[4]

(8) The quiet people of our country <u>rise up</u> against an arrogant . . . political class. (DM_OP)

It is interesting to note that the Mail Online uses the UP-DOWN image schema, where the establishment is on top and the (Leave) electorate is positioned below, but moving to change their position, that is, defy those who are more powerful. The writers of the Mail Online news report use the metaphoric expression 'groundswell' to express the same idea:

(9) Across the North, . . . the Leavers were overwhelmingly the winners. The same <u>groundswell</u> was in evidence in Tyneside. (DM_REP)

It has been noted (Mannheim 1992) that vertical spatial metaphors are a hallmark of hierarchically structured societies, meaning that democratisation is 'essentially a reduction of vertical distance, a de-distantiation' (Mannheim 1992: x). We can relate this notion to populist discourses, whose participants demand or promise to address a perceived democratic deficit by challenging 'elites'. The Mail Online clearly contributes to this discourse here.

Rather than being perspectivised, the ontological metaphor of division is specified by a number of source domains. Thus, we find the domain of Landmass interacts with collective nouns and place-for-people metonymies to construe the electorate as divided:

(10) The vista of a sharply divided country with particular <u>fault lines</u> <u>opening up</u> between London and other English communities was repeatedly raised by Labour MPs reacting to the results. (GUA_REP)
(11) The referendum has reminded us of a dangerous <u>division</u> that lies just beneath the <u>surface</u> of Britain. It is a <u>volcanic gulf</u> that has its origins in the furnaces of the industrial revolution. (BBC_OP)

Conceptualising differences among voter opinions as a geological phenomenon entails a sense of the age, scale and potentially destructive consequences of such differences of opinion within the electorate. In addition, the source domain reconstructs a social phenomenon as a natural one, thereby making it seem beyond human control, and invoking a sense of disaster (Charteris-Black 2006).

As well as drawing on the source domain of Landmass to specify the ontological metaphor, the author of the BBC News opinion piece also employs the source domain Body to highlight the problematic aspects of metaphorical division among voters. Indeed, the source domain is used to 'bracket' the article (see Koller 2004: 79, 107), occurring both in the opening and the closing paragraph:

(12) The EU referendum has revealed an ancient, jagged <u>fault line</u> across the United Kingdom. It is a <u>scar</u> that has sliced through conventional politics ... It is a <u>fault line</u> across the UK, a <u>scar</u> that has never been properly treated. (BBC_OP)

The conceptual metaphor THE NATION STATE IS A BODY has a long history in political discourse (Musolff 2016) and it is here adapted to negatively evaluate the fact that voters fall into two groups of roughly equal size but with very different views: this 'division' is seen as painful and destructive, but also as older than the current situation, which has *re*opened the divide. Although the source domain is slightly different – Fabric rather than Body – in particular Tissue – the ontological division metaphor is specified in similar ways by the writer(s) of the Guardian opinion piece:

(13) The deep strains on the nation's <u>fabric</u> ... must be addressed. (GUA_OP)

The conceptually related source domains – Landmass, Body and Fabric – all specify the ontological division metaphor and also endow it with negative value. This pessimistic view of difference of opinion is specified further by the source domain of War/Violence, which construes differences in opinion as leading to conflict, within both the electorate and the establishment, and between the two. The use of related lexis differs across the news sites, with BBC News using only two lexemes, 'campaign*' and 'victory', to refer to politicians and voters, respectively. The Guardian writers employ seven different lexemes, all to construe conflict among politicians as physical or military aggression:

(14) [O]thers have pointed the finger at Nicola Sturgeon, the SNP leader, saying that she spent too much time <u>attacking</u> the remain <u>camp</u> ... A source within the SNP <u>hit back</u> at what she called a 'poor attempt by Labour to deflect from its own <u>campaign</u>'. (GUA_REP)

The use of the War/Violence source domain by the Mail Online is of particular interest, as its writers foreground military strategy when talking about the (Leave) electorate but select lexemes of physical violence and hand-to-hand combat when construing an adverse relationship between voters and British politicians:

(15) The extraordinary <u>alliance</u> of voters who embraced 'Leave' also included many of the nation's suburbs. (DM_REP)

(16) [V]oters were <u>bombarded</u> with hysterical threats . . . Those who believed Britain could prosper as an independent nation . . . were <u>attacked</u> as 'Little Englanders'. (DM_OP)

(17) [Leave voters] had a common purpose: to give a firm <u>slap</u> in the face of the London political elite. (DM_REP)

While the source domains discussed above all specify the ontological division metaphor, they at the same time motivate particular scenarios. We will explore those in the next subsection.

5.3. Metaphor Scenarios

As we could see in the previous subsection, the ontological metaphor of division occurs across all three news outlets in the data. Although the referendum was about the UK leaving or remaining in the EU, the metaphorical divide that preoccupies the journalists is within Britain: they variously construe a divide in opinion within the electorate (BBC News and Guardian Online), within the political establishment (all news sites) or between the electorate and the establishment (Mail Online and Guardian). These are notably different construals of the participants in the referendum.

We also saw that the division metaphor is specified by a number of source domains, notably Landmass, Body, Fabric and War/Violence. (For metaphoric expressions realising other source domains, see Tables 7.2 and 7.3 in the Appendix.) Although the first of these construes differences among voters as a natural disaster, a specific *earthquake* scenario, while carrying negative value, features no human actors and actions. The Body and Fabric source domains both motivate a *tearing* scenario with continued negative evaluation, but also include actions and at least imply actors: looking again at Examples 12 and 13, we could ask who failed to 'properly treat' the scar and who exerts the 'strains on the nation's fabric', respectively.

However, it is in the *military/physical conflict* scenario motivated by the War/Violence source domain that we find explicit indications of actors, along with a sequence of actions and complex evaluation. That scenario is therefore the most developed one. As far as the electorate is concerned, BBC News differentiates between urban voters and those in rural areas, proclaiming that

(18) this was a victory for the countryside over the cities. (BBC_OP)

Example 19 indicates a scenario in which different parts of the voting population fight or at least compete with each other. Elsewhere though, the electorate is construed as forming an 'alliance' (see Example 15). This construal extends only to Leave voters though who are the focus for the Mail Online writers.

Remain voters receive comparatively little attention in the data. This is unsurprising, because the referendum result was both unexpected and a vote for change, and as such, it is cognitively profiled. (Of course, the winning vote is also more important in itself.) However, the metaphoric expressions that Mail Online writers use to refer to the areas where a majority of people voted for Britain to remain in the EU is clearly evaluative.

(19) In the map of the results London is a small, isolated <u>island</u> of euro-enthusiasm in a <u>sea</u> of blue. (DM_REP)
(20) Geographically, <u>pockets</u> of remainers included cities where universities loomed large. (DM_REP)

While 'sea of blue' is likely inspired by coloured maps in the election night coverage on television (on which Leave areas were blue and Remain areas were yellow), referring to London as 'a small, isolated island' diminishes the Remain vote. While this example is not part of a scenario motivated by the War/Violence source domain, Example 20 features a metaphoric expression ('pockets') that is usually found in war reports and has a negative semantic prosody. To corroborate this point, we searched for collocates of 'pockets of' in the Corpus of Contemporary American[5] and found that its most frequent collocate is 'resistance'. This construes Remain voters as resisting the prevailing opinion, invoking the concept of military invasion, but also calling into doubt the enduring strength of the minority vote.

It was noted above that the Mail Online writers use the War/Violence domain to specify both the ontological and spatial metaphors of distance and division between electorate and establishment. The writers employ those domains to motivate a scenario in which the establishment attacks Leave voters until they resist and return the physical aggression:

(21) [V]oters were <u>bombarded</u> with hysterical threats and terrifying scares – everything the Government machine, the mainstream party leaders and the global political and financial elites could <u>throw at</u> them. (DM_OP)
(22) Unlikely alliance . . . gives a <u>slap</u> in the face to the London political elite. (DM_REP)
(23) The biggest <u>punches</u> were dealt by voters in the Midlands. (DM_REP)

Interestingly, the metaphorical violence on the part of the political establishment is evaluated negatively ('hysterical threats'), while the aggression on part of Leave voters is evaluated as an act of self-defence that is further justified by the power imbalance between the two groups (see discussion of the UP-DOWN image schema above). The focus on the British, rather than EU, political establishment as an actor in this scenario construes the referendum as having been about domestic issues and dissatisfaction rather than a rejection of the EU.[6]

In the next, final section, we will answer the research questions by summarising our findings, and point out the theoretical and methodological contributions of the present chapter.

6. Conclusion

In sum, we found that writers on the three most popular British news sites used an ontological metaphor to construe both the electorate and the UK political establishment as divided. In addition, we found a spatial metaphor to construe both groups as being distant from each other. Interestingly, the referendum results and the EU itself were of lesser concern to the journalists in our data (RQ1). The embodied metaphor of distance was perspectivised by FRONT-BACK, CENTRE-PERIPHERY and UP-DOWN image schemas (RQ2). While all three construe the relationship between electorate and establishment as one of unequal power, the Mail Online stands out because its writers refer to voters as being 'below' the establishment but 'rising up' against them. The journalists here echo the populist trope of the people challenging the elites to further democracy.

The ontological metaphor of division is specified by a number of source domains, notably the conceptually related domains of Landmass, Body and Fabric. All three specify the idea of a social group as an object divided, with the writers referring to a 'fault line' and 'volcanic gulf', a 'scar' or 'strains on the nation's fabric', respectively. Furthermore, we find the source domain War/Violence specifying the division as leading to conflict (RQ2). While the Landmass, Body and Fabric source domains motivate *earthquake* and *tearing* scenarios, respectively, and as such involve negative evaluation, they either do not feature human actors or the writers leave them implicit. By contrast the War/Violence domain motivates a scenario of *military/physical aggression* that is conceptually rich and complex (RQ3). Using that scenario – which is largely eschewed by BBC News – the Guardian writers construe the UK political establishment as characterised by in-fighting, while the Mail Online refers to Leave voters as an 'alliance' that is 'united' in giving 'a slap in the face' to the elite. Such metaphoric violence is construed as a justified, positively evaluated reaction to a more powerful, negatively evaluated establishment that has itself 'bombarded' and 'attacked' Leave voters. This scenario signals a triumph for the electorate in the articles from the Mail Online, while it is a cause for introspection on part of the establishment, as represented by the Guardian.

This leaves us with the question of how Conceptual Metaphor Theory and metaphor scenarios can be employed in the analysis of discourse (RQ4). Taking the example of media discourse on political events, we have developed a model that sees embodied metaphors as being perspectivised by image schemas and specified by additional source domains, which in turn also motivate metaphor scenarios. The fact that this model emerges from our analysis of authentic data demonstrates the value of empirical research to further metaphor theory: it both adds conceptual complexity to the notion of metaphor scenarios (Musolff 2006) and refines the modelling of relations between embodied metaphors, image schemas, source domains and scenarios (Kövecses, 2017). In this chapter, we have therefore shown that cognitive linguistic approaches can enrich the analysis of text and discourse and, through their application, can be further developed themselves.

Notes

1 People who voted to leave the EU comprised 51.9 per cent, while 48.1 per cent voted to remain in the EU (The Electoral Commission 2018).
2 It seems apt to use the metaphoric expression 'perspectivisation' here because, in our data, image schemas mostly concretise embodied spatial metaphors.
3 We have included quotes as part of media discourse on the referendum, because a case can be made that quotes are strategically integrated into news texts to underline the paper's or writer's stance on an issue.
4 See also Koller and Davidson (2008) on spatial metaphors and image schemas for social exclusion.
5 No equivalent general corpus of British English was available at the time of analysis (latter half of 2017).
6 This construal contrasts with the motivations given in vox pops by people who intended to vote Leave, as they overwhelmingly constructed the EU, not the UK political establishment, as a negative Other (Miglbauer and Koller 2019).

References

Berry, M. (2016). Understanding the role of mass media in the EU referendum. In D. Jackson, E. Thorsen and D. Wring, D. (eds), *EU Referendum Analysis: Media, Voters and the Campaign*. Bournemouth: Centre for the Study of Journalism Culture and Community, p. 14.

Charteris-Black, J. (2006). Britain as a Container: Immigration metaphors in the 2005 election campaign. *Discourse & Society* 17 (5): 563–81.

Chilton, P. and Ilyin, M. (1993). Metaphor in political discourse: The case of the 'Common European House'. *Discourse & Society* 4 (1): 7–31.

Dancygier, B. and Sweetser, E. (2014). *Figurative Language*. Cambridge: Cambridge University Press.

Durović, T. and Silaški, N. (2018). The end of a long and fraught marriage: Metaphorical images structure the Brexit discourse. *Metaphor and the Social World* 8 (1): 25–39.

The Electoral Commission (2018). EU referendum results, <https://www.electoralcommission.org.uk/find-information-by-subject/elections-and-referendums/past-elections-and-referendums/eu-referendum/electorate-and-count-information> (last accessed 17 July 2018)

Farrell, N. (2016). Public personalities in the EU debate: Elites vs. the majority and Bullingdon resurgent. In D. Jackson, E. Thorsen and D. Wring (eds), *EU Referendum Analysis: Media, Voters and the Campaign*. Bournemouth: Centre for the Study of Journalism Culture and Community, p. 26.

Firmstone, J. (2016). Newspapers' editorial opinions in the EU referendum campaign. In D. Jackson, E. Thorsen and D. Wring (eds), *EU Referendum Analysis: Media, Voters and the Campaign*. Bournemouth: Centre for the Study of Journalism Culture and Community, pp. 36–7.

Fitzgibbon, J. (2016). How the Brexit outcome has changed our understanding of referendums. In D. Jackson, E. Thorsen and D. Wring (eds), *EU Referendum Analysis: Media, Voters and the Campaign*. Bournemouth: Centre for the Study of Journalism Culture and Community, pp. 16–17.

Gibbs, R. (2017). *Metaphor Wars: Conceptual Metaphors in Human Life*. Cambridge: Cambridge University Press.

Gifford, C. (2016). Brexit: The destruction of the common good. In D. Jackson, E. Thorsen and D. Wring (eds), *EU Referendum Analysis: Media, Voters and the Campaign*. Bournemouth: Centre for the Study of Journalism Culture and Community, p. 15.

Grady, J. (1997). *Foundations of Meaning: Primary Metaphors and Primary Scenes*. PhD thesis. Berkeley: University of California.

Hardt-Mautner, G. (1995). How does one become a good European? The British press and European integration. *Discourse & Society* 6 (2): 177–205.

Henkel, I. (2018). How the laughing, irreverent Briton trumped fact-checking: A textual analysis of fake news in British newspaper stories about the EU. *Journalism Education* 6 (3): 87–97.

Koller, V. (2004). *Metaphor and Gender in Business Media Discourse: A Critical Cognitive Study*. Basingstoke: Palgrave.

Koller, V. and Davidson, P. (2008). Social exclusion as conceptual and grammatical metaphor: A cross-genre study of British policy-making. *Discourse & Society* 19 (3): 307–31.

Koller, V., Kopf, S. and Miglbauer, M. (eds) (2019). *Discourses of Brexit*. Abingdon: Routledge.

Kövecses, Z. (2010). *Metaphor: A Practical Introduction*, 2nd edition. Oxford: Oxford University Press.

Kövecses, Z. (2017). Levels of metaphor. *Cognitive Linguistics* 28 (2): 321–47.

Lakoff, G. and Johnson, M. (1980). *Metaphors We Live by*. Chicago: University of Chicago Press.

Lakoff, G. and Johnson, M. (1999). *Philosophy in the Flesh: The Embodied Mind and its Challenge to Western Thought*. New York: Basic Books.

Levinson, S. (2003). *Space in Language and Cognition: Explorations in Cognitive Diversity*. Cambridge: Cambridge University Press.

Levy, D., Aslan, B. and Bironzo, D. (2016). The press and the referendum campaign. In D. Jackson, E. Thorsen and D. Wring (eds), *EU Referendum Analysis:*

Media, Voters and the Campaign p. 33. Bournemouth: Centre for the Study of Journalism Culture and Community, p. 33.

Mannheim, K. (1992). *Essays on the Sociology of Culture*, 2nd edition. London: Routledge.

Miglbauer, M. and Koller, V. (2019). 'The British people have spoken': Voter motivations and identities in vox pops on the British EU referendum. In V. Koller, S. Kopf and M. Miglbauer (eds), *Discourses of Brexit*. Abingdon: Routledge.

Musolff, A. (2004). *Metaphor and Political Discourse: Analogical Reasoning in Debates about Europe*. Basingstoke: Palgrave.

Musolff, A. (2006). Metaphor scenarios in public discourse. *Metaphor & Symbol* 21 (1): 23–38.

Musolff. A. (2016). *Political Metaphor Analysis: Discourse and Scenarios*. London: Bloomsbury.

Musolff, A. (2017). Truths, lies, and figurative scenarios: Metaphors at the heart of Brexit. *Journal of Language and Politics* 16 (5): 641–57.

Newsworks (2016). EU referendum boosts newspapers' print circulation and online traffic, <http://www.newsworks.org.uk/Media-Centre/eu-referendum-boosts-newspapers-print-circulation-and-online-trac/144041> (last accessed 19 July 2018).

Pragglejaz Group (2007). MIP: A method for identifying metaphorically used words in discourse. *Metaphor & Symbol* 22 (1): 1–39.

Press Gazette (2016). ABC figures: National press sees June Brexit vote boost in print and online, <http://www.pressgazette.co.uk/abc-figures-national-press-sees-june-brexit-vote-boost-in-print-and-online/> (last accessed 8 December 2017).

Semino, E. (2002). A sturdy baby or a derailing train? Metaphorical representations of the euro in British and Italian newspapers. *Text* 22 (1): 107–39.

Semino, E. (2008). *Metaphor in Discourse*. Cambridge: Cambridge University Press.

Sheridan Burns, L. (2013). *Understanding Journalism*. London: Sage.

Sowińska, A. (2009). A European identity on the periphery: A comparative study of representations of Europe in the 'awkward squad's' press. *Critical Approaches to Discourse Across Disciplines* 3 (1): 21–35.

Statista (2017). Monthly reach of national newspapers and their websites in the United Kingdom (UK) from April 2016 to March 2017 (in 1,000 individuals), <https://www.statista.com/statistics/246077/reach-of-selected-national-newspapers-in-the-uk/> (last accessed 8 December 2017).

Wring, D. (2016). From super-market to Orwellian super-state: The origins and growth of newspaper scepticism. In D. Jackson, E. Thorsen and D. Wring (eds), *EU Referendum Analysis: Media, Voters and the Campaign*. Bournemouth: Centre for the Study of Journalism Culture and Community, pp. 12–13.

Appendix

BBC_OP	BBC_REP	DM_OP	DM_REP	GUA_OP	GUA_REP
	against				
			alliance		
	back* (v.)		back* (v.)		back* (v.)
			bastions		
					bellwether
beneath the surface					beneath
				between	between
		bow* (n., v.)			
	build; builders of bridges and not barriers				
		camp (n.)	camp (n.)		
					centre of gravity
common ground					
concentrated					
		control (v.)			
	delivered				delivered
	distanced				
divide (n.), division	(deeply) divided	divide (n.)			(sharply) divided, divides
	driving force	drove			
				embarked	
embrace (v.)			embraced		
fault line					fault lines
				forces (n.)	
				frailty	
				fringes	

Table 7.2 Metaphoric expressions for the electorate

	gamble (v.)				
			gave		
	going				
			groundswell		
				handed	
healed					
			heavy		
		held			
				journey (n.)	
	leads (v.), led				
				left behind	
				link (n.)	
		little			
manifests					
					marginalised
		message (n.)			
				moved	
				opening up	
out of step					
out of touch					
outlook					
		outside			
				place (n.)	
				plunge (n.)	
			pockets		
potshots					
prism					
			punches (n.)		
		quiet			
regard (v.)					

Table 7.2 (*cont.*)

restore				
		rise up		
	roar (n.)			
	said, say		said	
saw, seen		saw		
scar (n.)				
		sides (n.)		side (n.)
		slap (n.)		
sliced through				
				split down the middle
			spoken	
	strong*	strong*		
	succumb			
support* (n., v.)	support (n.)	support* (n.)		supporters
				swing
	tak* back			
	taken out of			
tear apart				
treated				
unite	united	united		
			unleashed	
victory				
view (n.)	views (n.)			
volcanic gulf				
widespread				

Note: Asterisks indicate wildcards, for example 'campaign*' includes 'campaigns', 'campaigning' etc.

Table 7.2 (*cont.*)

BBC_OP	BBC_REP	DM_OP	DM_REP	GUA_OP	GUA_REP
		architect			
		asset			
				at the top	
		attacked			attacked
				bet his shirt	
				between	
				beyond	
		bitterness			
		bombarded			
				broken	
		brought			
		building bridges			
			camp (n.)		camp (n.)
campaign (n.)	campaign* (n., v.)	campaign (n.)	campaign (n.)	campaign* (n., v.)	campaign* (n., v.)
					captured
					close* (adj., adv.)
				control (n.)	
				cool (adj.)	
	cross-party				
damaged					
				defeat (n.)	
		descended			
		devaluing the currency			
				duck (v.)	
		emerge			
				enemies	

Table 7.3 Metaphoric expressions for the UK political establishment

					faces (v.)	
		followed			followed	
force (v.)					forceful	
		fought				
					gambled	
	gauged					
					generals	
					go down	
					grab the reins	
					grasped	
		held				hit back
					home front	
					in place	
	lead*, led	lead*, led	lead*, led	lead*, led	lead*, led	
left (n.)						
					link	link
	listen*				listen*	listen*
		lose				
		machine*			machine*	
					moves (n.)	
					navigate	
					opposed	
					outflanking	
					outgoing	
		out-of-touch				
		overturn (v.)				
pillars						
					point to	point (n.), pointed the finger

Table 7.3 (*cont.*)

		positioning	
			pressure
		prophes* (v.)	
		put	
			race (n.)
			raised
		reconnected	
			reflect
			replaced
right (n.)			
			robustly
		rush (n., v.)	
			shadow (adj.)
sides (n.)			
		smeared	
			sour
			source (n.)
	stand down		standing (n.), stand firm against
			step-by-step
	stressed		
		surrendered	
			take back
		throw (v.), threw	
		throw in his lot	
			touching (v.)
		turning his back	
			underpinning

Table 7.3 (*cont.*)

			victory	victory
	view (n.)			
			vision	
				vista
warm (adj.)				
			way out	
	win (v.)			
			wing (n.)	
		within		

Note: Asterisks indicate wildcards, for example 'campaign*' includes 'campaigns', 'campaigning' etc.

Table 7.3 (*cont.*)

8

'That's Just What We Hear on Telly All the Time, Isn't It?' Political Discourse and the Cognitive Linguistic Ethnography of Critical Reception

Sam Browse

1. Introduction

On 6 October 2015, the Conservative Member of Parliament and British Home Secretary, Theresa May, delivered her annual address to the Conservative Party Conference. The speech set out a number of government policies and positions but the section on immigration – in which she blamed economic problems such as falling wages, faltering public services and job losses on rising numbers of migrants – hit the headlines, causing outrage amongst the liberal and left-wing commentariat. Maurice Wren, chief executive of the British Refugee Council, called it a 'chilling' and 'bitter attack' (quoted in *The Guardian* 2015). Writing for the liberal *Guardian* newspaper, Alan Travis (2015) said that it marked 'a new low in the politics of refugees and migration'. Human rights organisations and liberal journalists were not the only ones to object to what May said, but also business leaders; Simon Walker, the director general of the UK's Institute of Directors, called the speech 'irresponsible' and said that May was 'pandering to anti-immigration sentiment' (quoted in *The Guardian* 2015). On the other side of the political spectrum, the right-wing *Daily Mail* (2015) called the conference address 'little short of magnificent' and claimed that May had 'found the courage to voice the thoughts of the vast, disenfranchised majority'. It is notable, however, that even on the political right the speech garnered criticism; for example, both the Conservative supporting publications, *The Spectator* and *The Telegraph*, ran opinion pieces condemning it for being 'tawdry' and 'contemptible' (Massie 2015), and 'ugly, misleading, cynical and irresponsible' (Kirkup 2015).

In this chapter, I investigate how it is audiences construct interpretations such as those quoted above. My analytical focus is on the critical responses of three municipal politicians to Theresa May's speech. All three are members of the British Labour Party and have a seat in local government representing a constituency in a large city in the north of England. To do this analysis, I employ a critical cognitive stylistic approach. It is 'critical' because I 'take an explicit sociopolitical stance' (van Dijk, 1993: 252); the first aim of this chapter is to amplify and support the critical voices raised in opposition to the speech and explain how it is these critical responses were produced – to describe how, based on the linguistic representation May proffers, these three discourse participants individually and collectively provide what Hall (1980) has called an 'oppositional reading' of the text (see also Brunsdon and Morley 1999). My approach is 'cognitive' insofar as it describes the knowledge and cognitive processes involved in the critical reception of the speech. Specifically, I use concepts from Text World Theory (Gavins 2007; Werth 1999) and Cognitive Grammar (Langacker 1987, 1991, 2008) to analyse audience responses. The second aim of this chapter is therefore to demonstrate the utility of these concepts in analysing oppositional reading. Finally, I use the term 'stylistic' because rather than attending to the processes involved in discourse production – as per most critical forms of discourse analysis (see Fairclough 1996: 51; Jeffries 2010: 11) – my approach to discourse is 'reception-oriented' (Carter and Stockwell 2008: 300). Indeed, more recently, work in stylistics has encompassed ethnographic methods of collecting reader-response data (for example, Norledge 2016; Peplow 2011, 2016; Peplow et al. 2015; Whiteley 2011a, 2011b). Like these researchers, I also use ethnographic methods – focus group discussions and interviews – alongside think-aloud and annotation exercises, to elicit response data from the three participants. The work presented here extends this stylistic research into a non-literary context. My third aim, then, is to demonstrate the efficacy of combining cognitive analytical frameworks with ethnographic methods in order to provide a fully contextualised, socio-cognitive description of the interpretive processes involved in critical reception.

To meet these aims, in Section 2, I outline a cognitive theory of oppositional reading using concepts from Text World Theory (Gavins 2007; Werth 1999); in Section 3, I provide a more detailed linguistic analysis of a passage from May's speech and the representation of immigration it proffers; in Section 4, I examine the participants' views of immigration and the knowledge and attitudes they bring to the discourse; in Section 5, I outline the protocols for eliciting audience response data from the participants; and in Sections 6 and 7 I analyse the audience response data using concepts from Cognitive Grammar (Langacker 1991, 1987, 2008).

2. A Cognitive Model of Critical Reception

The view of discourse I adopt to analyse the critical reception of Theresa May's speech is taken from Text World Theory (Gavins 2007; Werth 1999). As a 'cognitive discourse grammar' (Werth 1994: 90), this framework focuses on explaining the generation of complex, rich, discourse-level mental representations, or 'text-worlds' (for applications of the theory in a variety of different discourse contexts, see Gavins and Lahey 2016). Text-worlds are conceptual deictic spaces defined by world-building elements such as time and location, alongside the objects and the people (these are called 'enactors' in the theory) those deictic spaces contain (Werth 1999: 81; Gavins 2007). Importantly, discourse participants construct these mental representations in response to the texts with which they engage. From this perspective, discourse in reception can be viewed as a kind of 'text-driven' cognition (see Gavins 2007: 29). The text created by the speaker or writer provides a set of linguistic cues that cause audiences to access their pre-existing knowledge in order to create text-worlds of the events and situations described in the discourse. In Text World Theory, this pre-existing knowledge is modelled with the concept of a 'frame' (Werth 1999: 103–13, see also Filmore 2006). Frames are 'experiential models of (part of) human life which direct and influence human understanding of aspects of the world, as mediated through human perceptions and cultural knowledge' (Werth 1999: 107). The text-worlds discourse participants create from the linguistic cues they encounter in the text might straightforwardly instantiate a pre-existing frame stored in their long-term memory. Alternatively, world-building might involve creatively combining existing frames to create new novel representations (think, for example, of the fantastical fictional text-worlds readers construct as they engage with science fiction or fantasy literature). The creation of text-worlds is thus an active and dynamic cognitive process; participants bring their pre-existing repertoire of conceptual frames to the discourse situation in order to construct meaning from the linguistic forms they encounter.

For my purposes, the advantage of a text-world approach is that world-building necessarily involves recruiting the audience member's own conceptual frames in the process of constructing a text-world from the cues in the text. As experiential models, frames establish expectations about the kinds of objects, entities and relations that audiences encounter in the text-worlds they create (including the emotional or attitudinal valences we associate with these objects and entities). In the case of political discourse, there is much at stake ideologically in diverging from the conceptual frames that encode audience members' sense of reality. If these frame expectations are not met by the text-worlds discourse participants create – if the frame knowledge evoked in the process of world-building contradicts the text-world cued by the text – then there is a chance that the text-world representation will be resisted by the audience member (Browse 2018). From a text-world perspective, then, the potential for audience resistance is not an extrinsic feature of political discourse in reception, but is always an imminent possibility in every discursive event. In the process of world-building, the discourse prompts participants to access the very same knowledge that might well form the basis of their resistance to it. Thus resistance or opposition is dialectically built in to the very processes by which audiences construct meaning from spoken or written texts.

In his important discussion of television news, Hall (1980: 125–7) suggests that there are three ways in which audiences might position themselves in relation to news content: they might 'read' the news segment in the manner they perceive is intended by the news producers (Hall 1980: 125 calls this the 'dominant-hegemonic' position); they might accept the abstract values to which the producer seems to adhere, but object to the particularities of representation in the news segment (a 'negotiated' position); or, finally, they might occupy an entirely 'oppositional' position. Although Hall (1980) discusses responses to news discourse, rather than the speech of politicians, these different 'positions' are pertinent to any discussion of critical reception. For my purposes, the last – the 'oppositional position' – is especially germane. Hall (1980) defines an oppositional reading to a text as follows:

> It is possible for a viewer perfectly to understand both the literal and the connotative inflection given by a discourse but to decode the message in a globally contrary way. He/she detotalizes the message in the preferred code in order to retotalize the message within some alternative framework of reference. (Hall 1980: 127)

Although he writes in the vocabulary of Saussurean structuralism, with its (quite different) attendant view of communication as a process in which messages are 'encoded' by a 'sender' and 'decoded' by a 'receiver', this definition of oppositional reading can be reframed from a more contemporary, text-world perspective. Hall's (1980) account of oppositional reading entails two forms of representation: on the one hand, what he calls 'both the literal and the connotative inflection given by a discourse', and, on the other, 'some alternative framework of reference'. In keeping with Text World Theory, I will call the first of these representations the text-world proffered by the speaker or writer (or simply, 'the proffered text-world'), and the second the conceptual frame (or frames) associated by the audience with whatever topic is under discussion (I use the term 'audience' to encompass the readers of written texts and also the various addressees, over-hearers and eavesdroppers [Bell 1984] involved in the reception of spoken texts). An oppositional

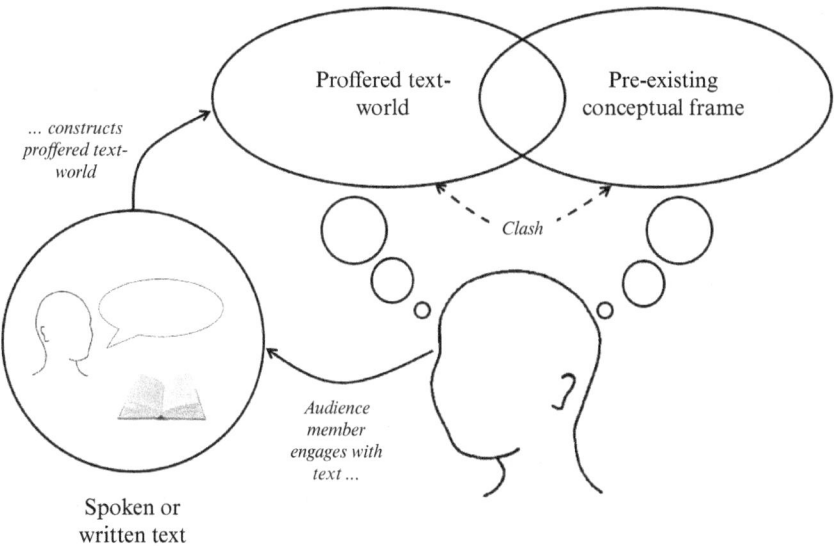

Figure 8.1 A model of critical reception

reading arises in the clash of these two competing conceptualisations – when a speaker or writer seems to proffer a text-world representation which breaks with the audience member's understanding of reality. I have diagrammed the relationship between text, proffered text-world and the audience member's own conceptual frame in Figure 8.1. Although I have suggested that oppositional positioning is the product of a clash between the proffered text-world and the audience member's pre-existing conceptual frame/s, there is also a sense in which the audience's preferred conceptualisation might overlap with the proffered text-world, even in the case of such a clash (I have represented this overlap in Figure 8.1 by overlapping the proffered text-world and pre-existing conceptual frame circles). So, to pre-empt my later discussion for the sake of example, the participants in this study all agree with Theresa May that wages in the UK are in relative decline – their understanding of reality 'overlaps' with hers in this sense – but, as I shall outline, the reasons they provide for this decline utterly contradict May's; she attributes it to the downward pressure on wages supposedly caused by immigration, they to unscrupulous bosses who want to exploit all workers (migrant or otherwise). The difference between proffered text-world and audience frame is thus not absolute, but the former should instead be seen as instantiating the latter to a greater or lesser extent. Of course, this raises the question of what counts as a significant enough difference for audiences to reject the text-world representation as an accurate depiction of reality and thus occupy Hall's (1980) oppositional position. There is not the space, here, to discuss such a complex issue. For the purposes of this chapter, it suffices to say that the participants in this study do, in fact, reject May's representation of immigration (which suggests that their own preferred conceptualisation is at least different enough to provoke their opposition). Here, I aim to describe how, rather than why, they do that. It is with this aim in mind that I now describe the representation of immigration proffered in May's speech.

3. The Speech

The political motivation, and therefore the motivation for the language used in the speech, should be understood in the context of the electoral insurgency of the populist, hard-right and anti-immigration UK Independence Party (UKIP), a political party whose base of supporters were overwhelmingly former-Conservative voters (see Ashcroft 2014). The speech can be read as an attempt to win these voters back by taking a harsher line on immigration, whilst at the same time adopting a 'common sense' rhetorical style in order to appeal to the broader, more moderate Conservative electoral coalition. This political strategy is reflected in the speech itself; May claims to occupy a 'middle-ground' position located between UKIP – who she calls the 'anti-immigration far-right' – and the supposedly 'open-borders liberal-left' (the reference, here, is presumably to the Labour Party): 'But people on both extremes of the debate – from the anti-immigration far right to the open-borders liberal left – conflate refugees in desperate need of help with economic migrants who simply want to live in a more prosperous society' (May 2015). In the speech, these two positions comprise two 'extremes'. May's rhetorical challenge was to elaborate a more hard-line, right-wing approach to immigration by criticising those to her left, whilst not, at the same time, appearing to succumb to the demagoguery of those further to her political right. The linguistic means by which she meets this challenge will be familiar to those acquainted with 'critical' forms of discourse analysis (for example, Fairclough 2001; Fowler et al. 1979; Jeffries 2010; Kress and Hodge 1979; Wodak and Meyer 2009). Take this passage of the speech, which forms the locus of several critical comments from the participants in this study, and also the journalistic coverage of the speech (for example, Travis 2015; Walker, quoted in *The Guardian* 2015; Younge 2015):

> Because when immigration is too high, when the pace of change is too fast, it's impossible to build a cohesive society. It's difficult for schools and hospitals and core infrastructure like housing and transport to cope. And we know that for people in low-paid jobs, wages are forced down even further while some people are forced out of work altogether. (May 2015)

As is well established in critical linguistic analysis, using nominalisations is a way of 'reducing' (Fairclough 2001: 103) the information available to audiences, thereby mystifying what might be important aspects of the situation or events being described (see also, Fowler et al. 1979; Jeffries 2010: 25–9; and for debate on this issue, see Billig 2008a, 2008b; Martin 2008; and van Dijk 2008). There are two nominalisations in the first sentence of this passage, 'immigration' and 'the pace of change'. Immigration is a nominalisation because it describes a process – immigrants crossing a border from one country to another – rather than a thing. Using this nominalisation places an emphasis on the process as a whole rather than making the immigrants the conceptually salient part of the adverbial. One might have instead used the adverbial 'when too many immigrants come here', which would have the opposite effect – it would foreground the human actors. The second nominalisation, 'the pace of change', similarly downplays the role of immigrants in the situation described. Perhaps a more direct 'translation' of this adverbial would be 'when communities change too fast'. However, this also seems to background immigrants (and even immigration, conceived holistically as a process). Indeed, for this reason, this nominalisation seems doubly euphemistic; it needs quite some conceptual unpacking before the human agents responsible for the changes – immigrants – are implicated at all in the representation May proffers. In both cases, then, the nominalisations background the immigrants themselves whilst blaming the more abstract, larger-scale process of immigration for making it 'impossible to build a cohesive society' and 'difficult for schools and hospitals and core infrastructure like housing and transport to cope'.

Another linguistic form that has received much attention from critical linguists is the passive (for example, Fairclough 2001: 104; Trew 1979), especially because one affordance of this grammatical construction is that it allows for agent deletion. In this extract from the speech, May can be seen to use the passive in the same way as she uses nominalisation – to blame immigrants for economic and social problems whilst simultaneously downplaying their culpability for these issues. In the final sentence of this passage from the speech, there are two passive constructions, 'wages are forced down even further' and 'some people are forced out of work altogether'. In both cases, the agent – immigrants – has been removed. Again, the effect is to background the human actors that May blames for wages being forced down and people being forced out of work.

Although both the journalistic coverage and the participants in this study were very critical of this passage, the language used in it is rather indirect, certainly by the standards of traditional critical linguistic analysis (as I hope to have demonstrated in my discussion of passives and nominalisations).

May could have adopted a far more polemical – overtly racist, even – tone by putting the blame squarely on immigrants; 'immigrants are stealing your jobs', 'immigrants are forcing down wages', 'it's difficult for schools and hospitals and core infrastructure like housing and transport to cope with all these immigrants' and so on. The point, here, is emphatically *not* to disagree with either the participants in the study or the journalists who called the speech 'tawdry' and 'contemptible'. The speech is both those things. It does, however, beg the question of how the journalists, the participants, and I constructed this oppositional reading from the relatively evasive language that May uses. To investigate this requires not only analysing the text produced by May, but also the conceptual frames that participants bring to the discourse in the process of constructing meaning from the linguistic cues provided by the speech. For this reason, I now describe the participants in this study and what they think about immigration.

4. The Participants

Three participants took part in the study, George, Cat and Emily (all pseudonyms). They were recruited on the basis of their dense multiplex connections to one another (Milroy 1987) and the fact that they are part of a social network that participates in various communities of practice (Wenger 1998) across the British labour movement and activist left. All the participants are linked by their participation in the institutions of local government. They are all extremely active Labour Party members and supporters of the Labour leader, Jeremy Corbyn (which at the time of collecting the audience response data was somewhat of a shibboleth issue in British politics). They are also active members of the GMB trade union, and they support local campaign groups, frequently speaking at public protests and rallies against issues such as the Conservative government's support for the US bombing of Syria and its 'austerity' economic agenda. One of the main things coordinating the group's activity across these different contexts is a shared political perspective. Following van Dijk (for example, 1998) we might model such a political perspective cognitively in terms of the social representations to which this group of political actors subscribes. Put in the text-world terminology I used to describe my approach to critical reception, the three participants share similar conceptual frames which they draw upon in order to construct meaning (see also Potter and Wetherall 1987).

Both the audience's prior conceptualisation of the speaker, and their prior knowledge of the discourse topic are important in determining the extent to which proffered representations are resisted by the audience (Browse 2018). For my purposes, this means describing the conceptual frames that the participants share of both May's topic – immigration – and May herself. Given constraints of space, in this chapter I focus on the former. In a group interview I conducted as part of the ethnographic research for this project, I asked participants what they thought about immigration. Of the three participants, Cat's response is perhaps the most 'pro'-immigration (she says 'it's mainly a really positive thing') and she notes that members of her own family were immigrants. She also brings up other people's perceptions of immigration, saying that 'a lot of the fear . . . is actually misplaced'. Similarly, Emily talks about how people perceive immigration and, although she does not say that these perceptions are wrong or, as Cat puts it, 'misplaced', she does say 'I don't think we need an overhaul of our immigration laws.' Emily also talks from her experience – she was a practicing solicitor – about the strain on the legal processes associated with immigration due to government underfunding. From the perspective of these participants, immigration is not an intrinsically problematic process. Instead, the problems relate to how immigration is perceived by the population or the manner in which immigration services are resourced by the government. Conversely, George has a much more agnostic approach to the process itself. George emphasises that he is 'pleased to live in a society which is multicultural', but says that immigration *may* – he is 'open minded' – have thrown up some 'challenges'. He suggests that twentieth-century immigration into Britain was of a different order to the free movement of people within the European Union and cites the migration of Polish workers as an example.

Whilst George is a little sceptical of immigration, his view can be differentiated from May's in three senses. The first is that he celebrates the UK's multiculturalism. This is not a view May appears to share (she says that 'the pace of change' in communities is too fast). The second is that George places an emphasis on the immigrants themselves in order to empathise with them (he says 'I wish [Polish migrants] could make a life – a good life in – in Poland and they have to come here, 'cause you don't get a sense from some of them that it's very pleasant'), whereas – as I demonstrated – May tends to background the human beings involved in immigration. Indeed, George later says that 'I thought [former Labour leader] Ed Miliband's immigration policy was spot on . . . he didn't just say, oh right, okay, you know immigration's great and let's have open borders, but he said it's actually where you have im-exploitation'. The concern here is for the exploitation of immigrants, rather than the effects of immigration on local communities. Again, this suggests empathy – rather than hostility – towards immigrants. Thirdly, whereas May advocates for a right-wing crackdown on immigration rules, George is 'open minded' about whether the rules just need to be better enforced, or whether they should be changed. There is a sense, then, in which George occupies a middle-ground position between Cat and Emily on the one hand – who think there is little wrong in principle with the immigration rules – and May, on the other.

Although Cat, Emily and George differ in their commitment to defending immigration policy as it stands, there is an overlap in their attitudes which is related to their wider political beliefs. In discussing their membership of the Labour Party, the participants all mention their background in campaigning for traditionally left-wing causes or their support for socialism. Emily said that before joining the Labour Party, she had always been 'campaigning on a left-wing agenda'. Cat, the only participant to have been a member of the Party under the former Labour leader and Prime Minister, Tony Blair, said that even at this time, 'I still felt that I was a socialist or I thought I was a socialist . . . and that the Labour party summed up my views' (the party under Blair was then much further to the right than under Corbyn). Similarly, George says 'through my family I developed a socialist, Labour outlook on the world, and they . . . were trade union members, and so . . . I thought about the world as a socialist'. The participant's attitudes to immigration are all coloured by this perspective. Cat is most explicit: 'the pressure that . . . Theresa May highlights . . . around services . . . is a scapegoat for why immigration is a bad thing, um, when actually it's about investment in public services for me'. Emily's discussion of under-resourcing in the immigration service is a good example of this; the problems with immigration are a product of cuts to government agencies (she says they have been 'cut, cut, cut, cut'). Notably, too, George also poses his disquiet around immigration in terms of workers' rights and exploitation. Funding public services and defending the rights of workers are all traditional concerns of the political left and the socialism to which all three participants adhere. Indeed, it is these concerns that form the locus of the group's critical responses to May's speech, responses to which I now turn.

5. Protocols

Audience response data was collected from the participants in three different ways. The first was an online, written form of 'think-aloud' task in which participants were shown one paragraph of the speech on a computer screen and then asked to type their immediate reactions to the passage in a comment box underneath (for discussion of this method, see Norledge 2016: 66–8; Short and van Peer 1989). The participants would then press the 'next' button, which would take them to the following paragraph and so on. There were sixteen paragraphs, rendering a corpus of forty-eight individual comments. Having completed the online task, participants were then invited to take part in a group discussion of the speech. In the first part of the discussion, participants were played a video of May delivering the speech and given a

CRITICAL RECEPTION AND POLITICAL DISCOURSE | 167

copy to annotate. These annotations comprised the second form of response data. Finally, the participants were asked a series of open-ended questions about their response to the speech. The group interview was transcribed and forms the third source of data. In what follows, I use all three sets of data to illustrate and describe the ways in which participants critically respond to May's address to the 2015 Conservative Party Conference.

6. Ways of Resisting

There are two main ways in which the participants oppose the representation of immigration May proffers. The first I will call 'top-down' opposition. These forms of critical reception involve a wholesale rejection of the proffered text-world on the basis of an out-and-out clash with the preferred representation encoded in participants' pre-existing frame knowledge. A good example of this is provided in Figure 8.2. Figure 8.2a is one of

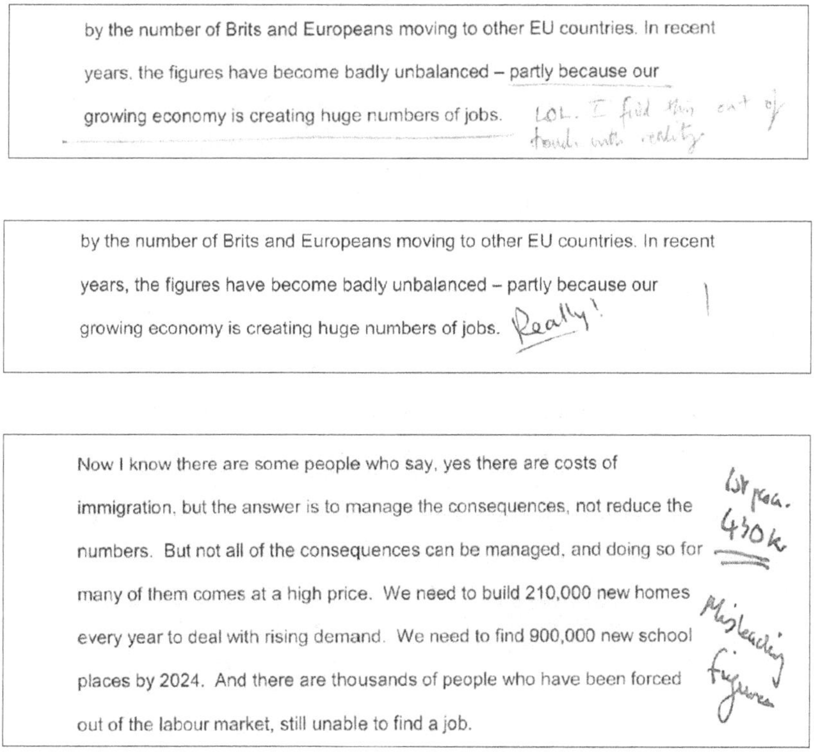

> by the number of Brits and Europeans moving to other EU countries. In recent years, the figures have become badly unbalanced – partly because our growing economy is creating huge numbers of jobs. *LOL. I find this out of touch with reality.*

a.

> by the number of Brits and Europeans moving to other EU countries. In recent years, the figures have become badly unbalanced – partly because our growing economy is creating huge numbers of jobs. *Really!*

b.

> Now I know there are some people who say, yes there are costs of immigration, but the answer is to manage the consequences, not reduce the numbers. But not all of the consequences can be managed, and doing so for many of them comes at a high price. We need to build 210,000 new homes every year to deal with rising demand. We need to find 900,000 new school places by 2024. And there are thousands of people who have been forced out of the labour market, still unable to find a job. *UK pop. 430k. Misleading figures*

c.

Figure 8.2 Annotations on the speech

George's annotations on the speech. George writes 'LOL. I find this out of touch with reality'. May's comments about the economy and job creation do not match George's conception of the economic situation. Indeed, the proffered text-world is so far from his preferred conceptual frame that it is funny; he writes 'LOL', which is short for 'laugh out loud'. Cat expresses similar disbelief. In her annotation (Figure 8.2b), she writes and underlines 'Really!' This sentiment is also expressed by Emily in her think-aloud comments. She writes 'absolute nonsense. We do not have a growing economy'. Both the annotations and Emily's comment amount to a complete rejection of May's proffered representation on the basis of a clash with the participants' understanding of reality. I call these 'top-down' forms of opposition because the participants' pre-existing frames simply overrule the proffered representation.

In many ways, these top-down forms of opposition are linguistically the least interesting type of critical response because they relate to matters of content rather than linguistic form. Rather than rejecting the proffered representation's ontological claims to veracity or accuracy, far more interesting are the participant's objection to *how* a situation has been represented in the proffered text-world. These I call 'bottom-up' forms of opposition. An example is provided by Emily in Figure 8.2c. Here, Emily accuses May of using 'Misleading figures'. This is echoed in her think-aloud comments on the same paragraph: 'I cannot accept that these figures can be directly attributed to just [the] needs of refugees and economic migrants. The speaker is trying to make me think that though. It is very misleading and manipulative.'

In his comments, George makes a similar point: 'Rising demand for housing isn't (can't be?) just because of migration'. Neither George nor Emily disagree that there might be a demand for 210,000 new homes, or 900,000 new school places. They do not, however, believe that this demand can be attributed only to immigrant communities. Indeed, although there is a strong implication that this apparent demand for housing and school places is a 'consequence' of immigration that 'comes at a high price', May does not explicitly say that 'immigrants require an additional 210,000 new homes and 900,000 new school places'. Instead, she uses the nominalisation, 'rising demand' – a nominalisation which obscures the agent doing the demanding. Clearly, though, Emily and George are able to 'unpack' this nominalisation; they notice that the 'rising demand' could well be attributed to the population in general, rather than migrants specifically.

These forms of bottom-up resistance to the proffered representation can be described using ideas from Cognitive Grammar (Langacker 1987, 1991, 2008), specifically the notion of 'construal':

> An expression's meaning is not just the conceptual content it evokes – equally important is how that content is construed. As part of its conventional semantic value, every symbolic structure construes its content in a certain fashion. It is hard to resist the visual metaphor, where content is likened to a scene and construal to a particular way of viewing it. (Langacker 2008: 55)

All linguistic forms evoke conceptual content at the same time as they construe that content in some manner. Langacker (1987, 2008) outlines four different dimensions of construal: specificity, focus, prominence and perspective. For the purposes of this chapter, I will focus on two of these dimensions: focus and prominence. I begin with focus.

6.1 Resistance as Rescoping

To continue Langacker's (2008: 55) visual metaphor, if grammatical forms entail some form of representation that can be likened to a scene, then 'focus' relates to what is included and excluded from that scene – what is included in the 'viewing frame', so to speak. Take, for instance, the noun, 'arm'. The immediate scope of 'arm' is represented in Figure 8.3a. However, we also understand that arms are part of larger structures, that is, bodies. We can therefore say that the maximal scope of 'arm' is the whole body, as

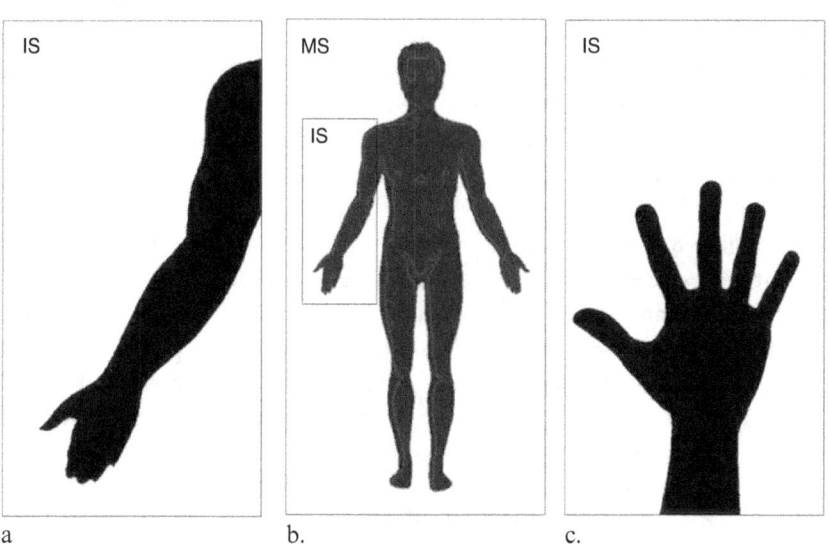

Note: IS = immediate scope; MS = maximal scope

Figure 8.3 The immediate and maximal scope of arm and hand

represented in Figure 8.3b. Compare, this, say, to a noun like 'hand'. The immediate scope of 'hand' is represented in Figure 8.3c, and includes space around the hand, and some portion of the wrist and lower arm, too. Thus, the focus of a linguistic form is determined by its scope – by what aspects of conceptual structure are included in the immediate scope of predication, and which aspects form the conceptual substrate backgrounded in the maximal scope of predication.

Focus can be 'scaled-up' to the clause. Cognitive Grammar is a usage-based approach to language (Langacker 2009). In our day-to-day lives we experience a number of energetic interactions between things – feet kicking balls, fingers pushing buttons, hands turning pages and so on. These iterative experiences of some entity affecting some other entity are encoded in the transitive clause structure. The transitive clause can thus be represented abstractly as in Figure 8.4a. In Figure 8.4a, some yet-to-be-specified entity (called the trajector) affects some other yet-to-be-specified entity (the landmark). Figure 8.4a represents the immediate scope of a transitive clause in the active voice. To be more concrete, in Figure 8.4b, I have designated the trajector as 'immigrants', the verb process as 'force down' and the landmark as 'wages', to yield the active transitive clause 'immigrants force down wages'. In Figure 8.4b, the immigrants and the wages are both included in the immediate scope of predication. As I have already noted, one of the affordances of the English passive is that it allows for agent deletion; as Theresa May says in the speech, 'wages are forced down'. The passive with agent deletion consequently entails removing the trajector from the immediate scope of predication. We can represent this as in Figure 8.4c. Here, the wages are acted upon (as per the arrow) but the immigrants are removed from the immediate scope. In this extract from the speech, May proffers a representation of immigration which, in the case of her use of passives, removes immigrants from the immediate scope of predication.

As Figure 8.5 demonstrates, passives such as these are a cause of concern to Cat who circles them all (she circles '[wages are] forced down even further', '[people are] forced out of work altogether' and at a later point in the speech, not included in Figure 8.5, she circles the phrase 'people who have been forced out of the labour market'). Indeed, one of the ways in which the participants resist this representation is by *rescoping* these passive grammatical forms. They perform this rescoping both with respect to the text-world representation May proffers and to their own conceptual frames for the economy. For an example of the latter, this is Cat's think-aloud comment on part of this section of the speech (the emphasis is mine): 'She identifies what government should do *but then blames immigration for job losses. Again trying to persuade the reader this is immigrations fault.*'

CRITICAL RECEPTION AND POLITICAL DISCOURSE | 171

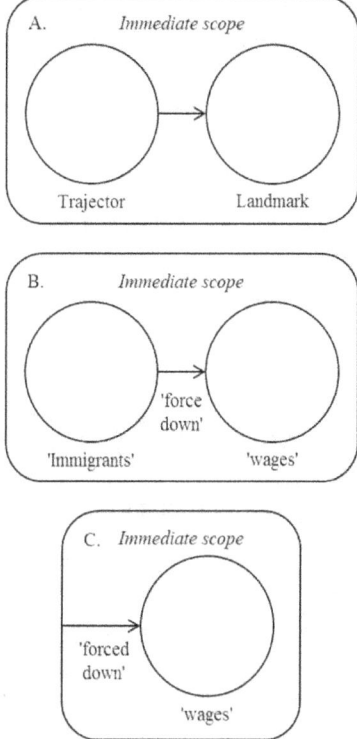

Figure 8.4 Focusing on the level of the clause

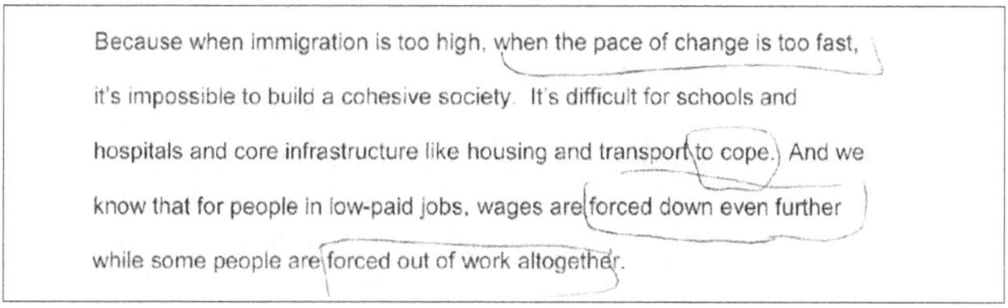

> Because when immigration is too high, when the pace of change is too fast, it's impossible to build a cohesive society. It's difficult for schools and hospitals and core infrastructure like housing and transport to cope. And we know that for people in low-paid jobs, wages are forced down even further while some people are forced out of work altogether.

Figure 8.5 Cat circles the passives

Despite May's use of the passive, Cat is able to rescope the proffered representation in order to identify that May 'blames immigration' and that she is 'trying to persuade the reader this is immigrations fault'. Participants also collectively rescope the passive in relation to their own frames for immigration and the economy, especially in relation to May's suggestion that 'wages are forced down even further'. Recall that earlier I said that as socialists, the participants were all committed to defending workers' rights. In the group discussion, this forms a collective basis on which to reject the proffered construal:

EMILY: And – and I mean – and again, you know, if it is – if it is British employers who are exploiting workers, then you know
CAT: [There's powers]
EMILY: [Then why not] you know, ta- take the – you know, there's already
SAM: Hm, mm
CAT: [They could – they could – yeah]
EMILY: [Things there that could bring them to account]
SAM: [There's laws and – mm]
CAT: And they could ra- raise the living wage, or raise the minimum wage, and
EMILY: And enforce people who don't pay it

Throughout this exchange, the discussion of wages is reframed as a workers' rights issue, rather than one that directly relates to immigration. Emily begins by saying, 'if it is British employers who are exploiting workers'. Rather than rescope in relation to the proffered text-world – in which it is immigrants that are forcing down wages – instead Emily does so in terms of her own conceptual frame. There is a point of connection between the proffered text-world representation and the participants' own background knowledge of immigration and the economy – earlier I called this an 'overlap' – but it is also a point of departure. The reframing of the issue is achieved by rescoping from this point. To use Hall's (1980) terminology, Emily 'detotalizes' the 'fact' of falling wages from the proffered text-world and resituates, or 'retotalizes' it (via a process of rescoping) in her own conceptual frame ('within some alternative framework of reference' [Hall 1980: 127]). This rescoping in relation to the participant's shared conceptual frame allows for alternative solutions to the problem of falling wages to be proposed. Cat says that government could 'raise the living wage, or raise the minimum wage' to which Emily adds 'and enforce people who don't pay it'. The participants, then, identify a number of methods – raising the minimum/living wage and enforcing existing laws – that could be used to stop a 'race to the bottom' on pay. In this shared conception it is not migrants that are responsible for this race to the bottom, but exploitative employers and the government for failing to crack down on them (indeed, Cat's written comments on this section from the speech say 'she is using examples that are a failure of government'). May's use of the passive has in this instance left a 'gap' which the participants have filled with their own frame knowledge.

6.2 Resistance as Reprofiling

The second of Langacker's (1987, 2008) construal operations which is useful to consider in light of the participants' responses to the speech is prominence. Prominence relates to how salient conceptual structure is within the immediate scope of predication. Prominence is thus a matter of foreground and background. The most foregrounded aspect of conceptual structure is said to be 'profiled'. Returning to Figure 8.3c, we can say that the nominal, 'hand', profiles the fingers, thumb and palm, but excludes the wrist, lower arm and surrounding space. In Cognitive Grammar, the concept of profile is integral to the difference between grammatical classes; for example, nouns profile things whereas verbs profile processes (Langacker 1991: 5). As in the case of the focus construal operation, it is possible to scale the notion of prominence up to the level of the clause. The prototypically profiled element in the clause is the trajector (for more detailed discussion see Langacker 1991: Chapter 7). This is certainly the case when a transitive verb is used in the active voice (so, in 'immigrants force down wages', it is the immigrants who are profiled). Conversely, the passive is a marked structure because it is the landmark that is profiled (thus, 'wages are forced down by immigrants' profiles the wages, not the immigrants. In the case of agent deletion, such as 'wages are forced down', the landmark is similarly the profile because the trajector is missing from the immediate scope of predication altogether.). Such a view of passives coheres with Trew's (1979) suggestion that even when passives do include an agent, that agent is backgrounded. What is and is not profiled in the clause is therefore an important part of how speakers and writers ideologically represent an event (indeed, see Hart 2014).

It is also possible to place a 'thing-like' construal on a clause by using a noun to describe a verb process; that is, by using nominalisation. Langacker (1991: 22–50) outlines a number of different kinds of nominalisation. The most pertinent for this discussion is what Langacker (1991: 24) calls an 'episodic' nominalisation. Episodic nominalisations profile a 'freeze-frame' moment of the verb process, or, as Langacker (1991: 25) puts it, 'the result [of this form of nominalisation] is a derived noun that profiles a region whose constitutive entities are the component states of a process'. The effect of this form of nominalisation is thus to construe those 'constitutive entities' of the process holistically as a thing-like assemblage. The nominalisation 'demand' in 'we need to build 210,000 new homes every year to deal with rising demand' is one such case. The verb process, 'demand', presupposes a 'demander', and goods or services that are demanded from someone. I have diagrammed the conceptual substrate of 'demand' in Figure 8.6a. The nominalisation places a holistic, thing-like construal on this process; the assemblage of conceptual

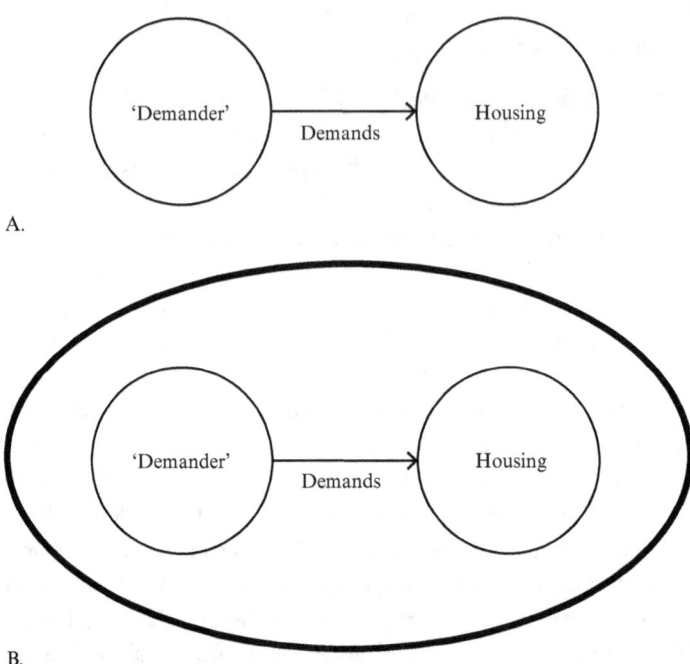

Figure 8.6 The conceptual substrate of 'demand' and its 'thing-like' construal

elements *as a whole* is profiled, with no one aspect of conceptual structure being the most salient. I have represented this with a thick ellipse in Figure 8.6b.

As I have already suggested, the participants are quite capable of unpacking this construal; they rightly ask who it is that makes the demand. This process of unpacking the nominalisation – of picking out a specific aspect of conceptual structure from amidst the holistic construal proffered by May – can be described as a form of *reprofiling*. As in the case of rescoping, the reprofiling is performed with respect to both May's proffered text-world and the participant's own preferred conceptual frames. The participants say that May is implying immigrants are the cause of the demand (the proffered text-world) at the same time as they voice their suspicions that the figure is actually the overall demand for housing (their own conceptualisation). The suspicion, of course, is just that – it is obvious from their comments that although George and Emily attribute the 210,000 to a larger group of people than just immigrants, they do not know the exact figures for the shortfall in housing (although George's parenthetical question, 'can't be?', suggests he has some idea about the numbers involved). Interestingly, although they dispute May's use of statistics, the numbers themselves are accepted as having some real-world validity; that is, they do not assume that May has simply made them up, but rather that she has employed some statistical trick in order to 'mislead' or 'manipulate' her audience (this is, of course, not an unreasonable assumption, given the level of media scrutiny the speech would have attracted). This is significant because it suggests that even a proffered text-world that is rejected by audiences can in some ways modify the knowledge that discourse participants already possess. Although the argumentative relevance of the figure is dismissed by the participants, it *is* integrated – via the process of reprofiling – into the discourse participant's preferred frame in such a way that it harmonises with their existing conception of reality (indeed, this integration is a form of what Garfinkel 1967 calls 'ad hocing').

7. That's Just What We Hear on Telly All the Time

The participants, then, are able to 'fill' the gaps in the proffered representation. They do this either by rescoping (in the case of passives) or reprofiling (in the case of nominalisations) the construal of immigration proffered by May. Indeed, this idea of identifying what is missing or backgrounded in the proffered text-world is raised more or less explicitly by Emily who says the problem with the speech is 'kind of what isn't in [it]' and 'what isn't said'. It is the participants who supply this missing information as part of the process of world-building. As I argued in the previous sections, they do this both in relation to their own preferred conceptual frames but also the conceptual substrate underpinning the proffered text-world representation. In the case of the latter, they reconstrue the proffered text-world so as to make May's relatively euphemistic anti-immigration rhetoric explicit. The agents supposedly responsible for forcing down wages, taking jobs and demanding houses – immigrants – are profiled in the participant's re-representations of the content of the speech. Even if they do not use technical vocabulary such as 'passive' or 'nominalisation', the three participants are clearly aware of May's indirect linguistic strategy:

EMILY: [That] which um I did put on my notes was – was that um, you know, what she's saying here is the anti-immigration far right, open borders liberal left
GEORGE: Mm
EMILY: But what you've got here is a very right-wing [immigration policy]
CAT: [(laughs)]
GEORGE: [Yeah, yeah, hm]
EMILY: This isn't in the middle, so
CAT: But I kinda think that's trying to moderate her own [views]

EMILY:	[Yeah]
CAT:	By saying, well I'm not the most extreme person on immigration and but – you know, you don't want those open door (.) liberal left
EMILY:	Mm
CAT:	Um, but what I'm saying here is somewhere in the middle actually, even though it's not, like you say

Cat and Emily perceive that May is 'trying to moderate her views', or at least appear to adopt a moderate stance on immigration. At the same time, however, their ability to reconstrue this proffered representation allows them to identify it as 'a very right-wing immigration policy'. May's attempt to look 'reasonable' consequently fails.

Given the difference in George's attitude to immigration, it is worth noting some of the dissimilarities between his responses and the other participants. Earlier in the interview, he says he began listening to the speech 'willing ... to follow ... [May's] train of thought'. It is notable that the passives that Cat and Emily rescope – 'wages are forced down even further while some people are forced out of work altogether' – occasion no comment from George in either his think-aloud remarks, or his annotations. He does refer to these in the group interview, however, saying 'I thought she halfway went in many ways towards, uh you know, trying to convince me ... You know, when she – when she pushes her buttons of people whose wages are cut, job security.' May's apparent concern for wages and conditions thus harmonise with George's own reservations about immigration and form a bridgehead, so to speak, between his own conception of immigration and hers. In fact, he later describes the paragraph in which May outlines the importance of occupying a middle ground between the 'open borders liberal left' and 'anti-immigration right' as 'actually pretty good and convincing'. In response to George's comments, Emily points to another part of the speech which says 'many of the people [who get into the Schengen area] will eventually get EU citizenship and the free movement rights that come with it'. She exclaims 'so what, what – why is that? – she's not qualified in any way to go on to say, and this would not be good ... it's just like – kind of like left hanging, isn't it?' George replies –

GEORGE:	Which is why – actually why I started off relatively open minded
EMILY:	[Right]
GEORGE:	[And then] became unconvinced because like that
EMILY:	Mm
GEORGE:	That second paragraph is quite carefully constructed and

EMILY: [Mm]
GEORGE: [There is] an argumentation in there, that she then just drops and starts firing points

George's annotations on the text shortly after the second paragraph evidence the sense in which he thinks the careful argumentation 'drops' and that May 'starts firing points'; he describes her use of figures as 'very cynical'. For George, May's 'cynical' use of statistics – which he is able to unpick by reprofiling the nominalisation, 'demand' – undermines her previous appearance of balance, the result being that George 'became unconvinced'. When asked why he became unconvinced, he says 'I just think – I think that she um – she told a fairly conventional story . . . that's just what we hear on telly all the time, isn't it?' Owing to his greater scepticism of immigration and its impact on the labour market, the textual prompts which cause George's opposition to the speech are different, but the opposition itself is rather similar to Cat and Emily's reasons for rejecting the speech; according to George, rather than a balanced, middle-ground view of immigration, May's speech articulates the kinds of arguments George is used to seeing in the media. In fact, Cat likewise notes that this is the kind of speech she would expect May to give. When asked why, she said, 'Just because of what the narrative is at the moment around immigration, and like how that's grown, and like Emily was saying about [the refugee] crisis and all that sort of stuff, that's what they want . . . people to think'. Here, the third person pronoun, 'they', refers to the Conservative Party, rather than the media, but the point stands; May's rhetorical strategy of occupying a middle ground fails because George, Cat and Emily see it as a (text-world) instantiation of an already widespread right-wing conceptual frame for immigration. Granted, this particular text-world proffers a euphemistic construal of this underlying right-wing, anti-immigration frame, backgrounding, as it does, immigrants. Nonetheless, the participant's ability to reconstrue the proffered text-world in relation to this underlying conceptual frame (in addition to their own preferred frames) allows them to make this identification between May's 'carefully constructed', 'moderate' construal and 'a very right-wing immigration policy'. Reconstrual is thus a cognitive process which is integral to the participant's construction of an oppositional position.

8. Conclusion

In this chapter, I have used Text World Theory and Cognitive Grammar to outline some of the bottom-up and top-down conceptual and linguistic processes involved in constructing George, Emily and Cat's oppositional reading of May's speech. These analytical frameworks have been useful because of their focus on the pre-existing knowledge audiences bring with them to the discourse in order to construct meaning. According to these perspectives, the potential for reader resistance is an intrinsic element of discourse processing. An important part of describing the participants' interpretative processes involved using ethnographic methods to determine their shared representations of, and attitudes towards, immigration. Indeed, the ethnography complemented the cognitive linguistic analysis of reader response data; it explains the nuanced differences in the way George constructed his oppositional position as compared to Cat and Emily, and how those differences were coordinated and integrated in such a way as to arrive at a shared group perspective on the speech – that May's speech was a novel construal of a fundamentally familiar right-wing conceptual frame for immigration. I thereby hope to have demonstrated the utility of combining ethnographic and cognitive approaches to describe the interpretive procedures employed in critical reception. In theorising the audience as active participants in the discourse, it seems to me that such an approach is invaluable in accounting for the critical responses of activ*ist* audiences.

References

Ashcroft, M. (2014). Post European election poll. Conservative Home, <http://www.conservativehome.com/wp-content/uploads/2014/05/LORD-ASHCROFT-POLLS-Post-Euro-Election-Poll-Summary-May-2014.pdf> (last accessed 6 September 2017).

Bell, A. (1984). Language style as audience design. *Language in Society* 13: 145–204.

Billig, M. (2008a). The language of critical discourse analysis: The case of nominalisation. *Discourse & Society* 19 (6): 783–800.

Billig, M. (2008b). Nominalising and de-nominalising: A reply. *Discourse & Society* 19 (6): 829–41.

Browse, S. (2018). *Cognitive Rhetoric: The Cognitive Poetics of Political Discourse*. Amsterdam: John Benjamins.

Brunsdon, C. and Morley, D. (1999). *The Nationwide Television Studies*. London: Routledge.

Carter, R. and Stockwell, P. (2008). Stylistics: Retrospect and prospect. In R. Carter and P. Stockwell (eds), *The Language and Literature Reader*. London: Routledge, pp. 291–302.

Daily Mail (2015). Magnificent Mrs May shows PM the way. *Daily Mail*, <http://www.dailymail.co.uk/debate/article-3262736/DAILY-MAIL-COMMENT-Magnificent-Mrs-shows-PM-way.html> (last accessed 6 September 2017).

Fairclough, N. (1996). A reply to Henry Widdowson's 'Discourse analysis: A critical view'. *Language and Literature* 5 (1): 49–56.

Fairclough, N. (2001). *Language and Power*, 2nd edition. Harlow: Longman.

Filmore, C. (2006). Frame Semantics. In D. Geeraerts (ed.) *Cognitive Linguistics: Basic Readings*. Berlin and New York: Mouton de Gruyter.

Fowler, R., Kress, G., Hodge, R. and Trew, T. (1979). *Language and Control*. London: Routledge and Kegan Paul.

Garfinkel, H. (1967). *Studies in Ethnomethodology*. Cambridge: Polity.
Gavins, J. (2007). *Text World Theory: An Introduction*. Edinburgh: Edinburgh University Press.
Gavins, J. and Lahey, E. (2016). *World Building: Discourse in the Mind*. London: Bloomsbury.
Hall, S. (1980). Encoding/decoding. In S. Hall, D. Hobson, A. Lowe and P. Willis (eds), *Culture, Media, Language*. London and New York: Routledge, pp. 117–27.
Hart, C. (2014). *Discourse, Grammar and Ideology: Functional and Cognitive Perspectives*. London: Bloomsbury.
Jeffries, L. (2010). *Critical Stylistics: The Power of English*. Basingstoke: Palgrave.
Kirkup, J. (2015). Theresa May's speech is dangerous and factually wrong. *The Telegraph*, <http://www.telegraph.co.uk/news/uknews/immigration/119913927/Theresa-Mays-immigration-speech-is-dangerous-and-factually-wrong.html> (last accessed 6 September 2017).
Kress, G. and Hodge, R. (1979). *Language as Ideology*. London: Routledge and Kegan Paul.
Langacker, R. (1987). *Foundations of Cognitive Grammar: Volume I: Theoretical Prerequisites*. Stanford: Stanford University Press.
Langacker, R. (1991). *Foundations of Cognitive Grammar: Volume II: Descriptive Application*. Stanford: Stanford University Press.
Langacker, R. (2008). *Cognitive Grammar: A Basic Introduction*. Oxford: Oxford University Press.
Langacker, R. (2009). A dynamic view of language acquisition. *Cognitive Linguistics* 20 (3): 627–40.
Martin, J. (2008). Incongruent and proud: De-vilifying 'nominalisation'. *Discourse & Society* 19 (6): 801–10.
Massie, A. (2015). Theresa May's immigration was as tawdry as it was contemptible. *The Spectator*, <https://blogs.spectator.co.uk/2015/10/theresa-mays-immigration-speech-was-as-tawdry-as-it-was-contemptible/> (last accessed 6 September 2017).
May, T. (2015). Theresa May' speech to the Conservative Party Conference – in full. *The Independent*, <http://www.independent.co.uk/news/uk/politics/theresa-may-s-speech-to-the-conservative-party-conference-in-full-a6681901.html> (last accessed 6 September 2017).
Milroy, L. (1987). *Language and Social Networks*. Oxford: Blackwell.
Norledge, J. (2016). *Reading the Dystopian Short Story*. Unpublished PhD thesis.
Peplow, D. (2011). 'Oh, I've known a lot of Irish people': Reading groups and the negotiation of literary interpretation. *Language and Literature* 20 (4): 295–315.
Peplow, D. (2016). *Talk about Books: A Study of Reading Groups*. London: Bloomsbury.
Peplow, D., Swann, J., Tremarco, P. and Whiteley, S. (2015). *The Discourse of Reading Groups: Integrating Cognitive and Sociocultural Approaches*. London: Routledge.
Potter, J. and Wetherall, M. (1987). *Discourse and Social Psychology: Beyond Attitudes and Behaviour*. London: Sage.
Short, M. and van Peer, W. (1989). Accident! Stylisticians evaluate: Aims and methods in stylistic analysis. In M. Short (ed.), *Reading, Analysing and Teaching Literature*. London: Longman, pp. 22–71.

The Guardian (2015). Theresa May's immigration speech strongly criticised – Conservative conference as it happened. *The Guardian*, <https://www.theguardian.com/politics/blog/live/2015/oct/06/conservative-conference-david-camerons-morning-interviews> (last accessed 6 September 2017)

Travis, A. (2015). Theresa May speech marks new low in politics of migration. *The Guardian*, <https://www.theguardian.com/politics/2015/oct/06/theresa-may-speech-new-low-politics-migration> (last accessed 6 September 2017).

Trew, T. (1979). What the papers say: Linguistic variation and ideological difference. In R. Fowler, G. K. Hodge, G. Kress and T. Trew (eds), *Language and Control*. London: Routledge and Kegan Paul, pp. 117–56.

van Dijk, T. (1993). Principles of critical discourse analysis. *Discourse & Society* 4 (2): 249–83.

van Dijk, T. (1998). *Ideology: An Interdisciplinary Approach*. London: Sage.

van Dijk, T. (2008). Critical discourse analysis and nominalisation: Problem or pseudo-problem? *Discourse & Society* 19 (6): 821–8.

Wenger, E. (1998). *Communities of Practice: Learning, Meaning and Identity*. Cambridge: Cambridge University Press.

Werth, P. (1994). Extended metaphor: A text world account. *Language and Literature* 3 (2), 79–103.

Werth, P. (1999). *Text Worlds: Representing Conceptual Space in Discourse*. London: Longman.

Whiteley, S. (2011a). Text World Theory, real readers and emotional responses to *Remains of the Day*. *Language and Literature* 20 (1): 23–42.

Whiteley, S. (2011b). Talking about 'an accommodation': The implications of discussion group data for community engagement and pedagogy. *Language and Literature* 20 (3): 236–56.

Wodak, R. and Meyer, M. (2009). *Methods of Critical Discourse Analysis*. London: Sage.

Younge, G. (2015). No Theresa May – Immigration is not the real threat to national cohesion. *The Guardian*, <https://www.theguardian.com/commentisfree/2015/oct/06/theresa-may-immigration-threat-britain> (last accessed 8 January 2019).

9

Spatial Properties of ACTION Verb Semantics: Experimental Evidence For Image Schema Orientation in Transitive Versus Reciprocal Verbs and Its Implications for Ideology

Christopher Hart

1. Introduction

Research in Cognitive Linguistics has argued extensively for the pervasive role played by space in structuring the concepts and conceptualisations associated with linguistic items and language usages. Space is a fundamental area of human experience. It is therefore not surprising to find that spatial cognition is exploited in the architecture of other cognitive systems like language. A key claim of Cognitive Linguistics has been that many of the meanings encoded by language are represented in the mind in the form of *image schemas* – spatially laid out representations of the recurrent structural properties of scenes and events (Lakoff 1987; Langacker 1987, 1991, 2008; Talmy 2000). Many of these schemas emerge from our bodily location in and interaction with space (Johnson 1987). This embodied view of language is developed in opposition to amodal or symbol-manipulation approaches to representation (Fodor 1975; May 1985). The motivation for a modal rather than an amodal account of meaning stems partly from commonalities perceived between language and the visual 'parsing' of a scene (Landau and Jackendoff 1993) and partly from the nuanced meaningful distinctions that a spatial representational format is able to capture between alternative linguistic structures (Langacker 1987: Talmy 2000). A further finding from Cognitive Linguistics has been that these experientially derived image schemas frequently serve as models for understanding more complex and abstract areas of experience in conceptual metaphors (Lakoff and Johnson 1980, 1999). In this way, much of the conceptual system, as reflected in repeated patterns of language use, is grounded metaphorically in our knowledge and understanding of space.

A considerable body of work extending Cognitive Linguistics to the analysis of discourse has shown that image schemas derived from spatial experience, such as CONTAINER, UP/DOWN, PROXIMAL/DISTAL and FORWARD/BACKWARD MOTION, are mobilised to structure areas of contested social experience where they come to function ideologically (Charteris-Black 2006; Chilton 1996, 2004; Chilton and Lakoff 1995; Dirven et al. 2003; Goatly 2007; Hart 2010, 2011). For example, the CONTAINER schema is frequently exploited in discourses of migration and national identity where it acts as a principle of division and promotes exclusionary behaviour (Charteris-Black 2006; Chilton 2004; Hart 2010).

When language directly describes spatial relations or spatial markers such as prepositions are used explicitly to signal a spatial understanding of the target situation, it is not surprising that the conceptual representations invoked should be spatial in format. What is perhaps more interesting is that spatial forms of representation seem also to be a feature of language in areas which are not directly concerned with space or where no explicit spatial grounding is provided. For example, Richardson et al. (2001) showed that a number of both concrete action and more abstract verbs and psychological predicates include a spatial component as part of their meaning. Richardson et al. (2001) presented subjects with twenty target verbs hypothesised to encode images schemas in either a horizontal (e.g. *push, pull, argue, offend*) or vertical (e.g. *lift, sink, hope, respect*) orientation. Verbs were embedded in rebus sentence in past tense form (e.g. □ lifted ○). For each sentence, subjects were asked to select the image schema, presented in four orientations, which best depicted the scene described by the sentence. The results showed a high degree of consistency among subjects in assigning horizontal or vertical orientations as postulated for each verb. The same paradigm was adapted by Meteyard and Vigliocco (2009) and extended to account for both orientation and direction of motion in a larger-scale study of 299 verbs. Again, a high degree of consistency was demonstrated among subjects. The results of these studies are insightful because convergence among speakers suggests common, underlying forms of representations constitutive of linguistic knowledge or meaning. A number of other experimental paradigms have also been exploited to provide further evidence for spatial properties of verb semantics (Bergen et al. 2007; Meteyard et al. 2007, 2008; Richardson et al. 2003).

That the meaning of these verbs includes a spatial dimension, at least in the case of concrete action and motion verbs, is likely motivated by the fact that the events they designate unfold in space. Correspondingly, the image schemas attached to verbs should not be thought of as static representations but dynamic simulations with spatio-temporal properties. There is now a growing body of empirical evidence suggesting that language understanding involves a mental perceptual or motor simulation of the scenes and events described in utterances (Bergen et al. 2004; Glenberg and Kaschak 2002; Stanfield and Zwaan 2001; Zwaan et al. 2002). From an embodied simulation perspective, different points of view, specified in the semantics of the utterance, guide the reader toward assuming different roles and positions as an 'immersed experiencer' in a rich and dynamic mental model of the situation (Zwaan 2004).

While the ideological implications of spatial forms of representation have been widely studied in relation to figurative language, this is not the case for literal language usages (cf. Hart 2015). This chapter investigates (i) image schema orientation in transitive versus reciprocal action verbs (e.g. *attack* vs *clash with*) and (ii) the ideological implications that arise from contrasting spatial configurations associated with these verb types.

The study is motivated by previous research (Hart 2013a, 2013b) which found that, in reporting political protests, newspapers on the political right, as in (1), prefer to report violence between police and protesters using transitive verbs with protesters as the sole agent while more liberal newspapers, as in (2), favour reciprocal verbs which encode both participants as agentive. Interestingly, it was further found that when right-wing newspapers did use reciprocal verbs, as in (3), it was with a marked difference in information sequence compared to more liberal newspapers.

(1) A number of police officers were injured after [they $_{PATIENT}$] [came under attack from $_{ACTION}{}^T$] [youths $_{AGENT}$], some wearing scarves to hide their faces. (*Telegraph*, 10 November 2010)
(2) [Police wielding batons $_{AGENT}{}^1$] [clashed with $_{ACTION}{}^R$] [a crowd hurling placard sticks, eggs and bottles $_{AGENT}{}^2$]. (*Guardian*, 10 November 2010)
(3) Twenty-three people were arrested as [protestors $_{AGENT}{}^1$] [clashed with $_{ACTION}{}^R$] [police $_{AGENT}{}^2$] around the Bank of England. (*Telegraph*, 1 April 2009)

Hart (2015) analysed these competing formulations as evoking image schemas which not only have slightly different internal structures (representing a one-sided action event vs a two-sided action event in transitive vs reciprocal verbs respectively) but which occur in different orientations relative to the conceptualiser. According to this analysis, while for both verb types the associated image schema is represented in the horizontal dimension, the schema associated with transitive verbs is represented on the sagittal axis while the schema associated with reciprocal verbs is represented on the transversal axis. In line with embodied theories of language, this analysis suggests that the body itself, with its three intersecting axes (Tversky 1998; Tversky et al. 1999), provides a frame of reference for egocentric meaning construction.

Contrasts in voice (transitive verbs) and information sequence (reciprocal verbs) represent the schema in 180° rotations on the primary axis.

The analysis presented by Hart (2015) is based on intuition and assumptions drawn from the literature in Cognitive Linguistics. It is not yet clear whether naïve subjects will share in these intuitions or behave in such a way as to betray the underlying spatial forms of representation proposed. If, as is the claim, transitive versus reciprocal verbs encode image schemas in alternative orientations, then it is reasonable to assume that there will be commonalities across speakers in respect of which orientation is encoded for a given verb. We should therefore expect, in an experimental setting, to find convergence among subjects when asked to judge the image schema orientation for different verbs and verb types. Any evidence for this kind of consensus among speakers can be taken as support for the hypothesis (Richardson et al. 2001).

2. Experiment 1

2.1. Methods

Participants

Fifty-five participants took part in the study, recruited from the undergraduate population at Lancaster University. Two participants were excluded for having failed to complete the task. All participants were native speakers of English, defined as speaking or learning English since birth and currently using English as their primary language. Culturally, the participant sample was predominantly Western/European.

Materials and design

Following Richardson et al. (2001), participants completed a forced-choice sentence–picture matching task. Participants were presented with a single A4 sheet of paper containing a list of thirty-two 'action' sentences beneath an image schema presented in four orientations labelled A–D.

The action sentences were of four types (eight items per type): (i) transitive active voice; (ii) transitive passive voice; (iii) reciprocal sequence AB; (iv) reciprocal sequence BA. Sentences were presented in simple past tense form. To avoid interference from personal politics and to target specifically the semantics of the verbs and constructions presented, agents and patients were given as 'the circle' and 'the square' rather than 'police' and 'protesters'. In transitive constructions, the agent was always 'the circle'. Full sentences rather than rebus sentences were used in order to mitigate any potential for visual bias in picture selection (Meteyard and Vigliocco 2009).

The image schema was made up of two main elements, a circle and a square, connected by a line. The schema was presented at 90° rotations so that

IMAGE SCHEMA ORIENTATION AND IDEOLOGY | 185

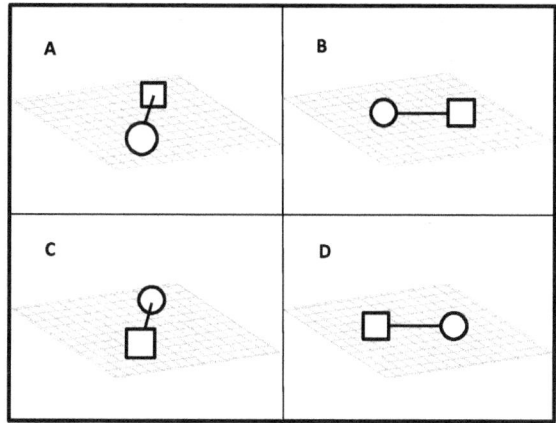

1. The circle attacked the square   [ ]
2. The circle clashed with the square [ ]
...

Figure 9.1 Example of questionnaire in Experiment 1

two ran sagittally and two ran transversally with the order of elements on each axis presented as mirror images (see Figure 9.1). To create a sagittal sense (i.e. an illusion of depth in a two-dimensional format) four steps were taken: (i) all four schemas were presented against a meshed quadrilateral which provided a horizontal reference plain; (ii) elements in the sagittal schemas were arranged on a mild diagonal line; (iii) the nearest element in sagittal schemas was slightly enlarged; (iv) the line connecting elements in sagittal schemas was drawn extending to the centre of the furthest element.

For each sentence, participants were instructed to select the image schema that best represented the event described in the sentence. Four randomised versions of the task sheet were created with different orderings for both sentences and images. The four versions were then randomly distributed to participants. Participants gave their selection by writing A, B, C or D inside empty parentheses on the same line as the target sentence (see Figure 9.1). The independent variable was therefore the verb and sentence types being judged and the dependent variable was consistency across picture choices. The design was within subjects.

2.2. Hypotheses

The primary hypothesis is that transitive versus reciprocal action verbs encode image schemas in orientations which follow sagittal versus transversal axes respectively. Secondary hypotheses are that constructional differences in the form of voice and information sequence are associated with opposite orientations on the primary axes.

2.3. Results

Participant responses are summarised in Table 9.1. The table shows the percentage of participants choosing each image for each verb and sentence type. For each item, the value for most frequently selected image schema is in bold. On average, for any given item, the image schema orientation that was most

Construction			Verb	Sagittal		Transversal	
				▢◯ (above/below 1)	◯▢ (above/below 2)	◯—▢	▢—◯
Transitive	Active *Circle VERBED square*		Attack	**74.5**	12.7	10.9	1.8
			Strike	**67.3**	14.5	18.2	0
			Hit	**69.1**	5.5	23.6	1.8
			Assault	**69.1**	16.4	7.3	7.3
			Beat	**69.1**	10.9	12.7	7.3
			Kick	**67.3**	12.7	18.2	1.8
			Punch	**72.7**	9.1	14.5	3.6
			Whack	**76.4**	10.9	12.7	0
	Passive *Square VERBED by circle*		Attack	**70.9**	16.4	10.9	1.8
			Strike	**70.9**	12.7	10.9	5.5
			Hit	**67.3**	21.8	9.1	1.8
			Assault	**74.5**	7.3	12.7	5.5
			Beat	**67.3**	14.5	9.1	9.1
			Kick	**69.1**	14.5	10.9	5.5
			Punch	**70.9**	14.5	9.1	5.5
			Whack	**70.9**	12.7	9.1	7.3
Reciprocal	Sequence 1 *Circle VERBED with square*		Clash	29.1	16.4	**50.9**	3.6
			Fight	23.6	5.5	**65.5**	5.5
			Battle	27.3	5.5	**58.2**	9.1
			Collide	27.3	10.9	**54.5**	7.3
			Struggle	20	20	**50.9**	9.1
			Scrap	38.2	12.7	**40.0**	9.1
			Trade punches	14.5	3.6	**67.3**	14.5
			Exchange blows	12.7	7.3	**78.2**	1.8
	Sequence 2 *Square VERBED with circle*		Clash	7.3	41.8	7.3	**43.6**
			Fight	5.5	25.5	10.9	**58.2**
			Battle	9.1	25.5	0	**65.5**
			Collide	10.9	25.5	12.7	**50.9**
			Struggle	12.7	20	9.1	**58.2**
			Scrap	7.3	**49.1**	1.8	41.8
			Trade punches	5.5	14.5	10.9	**69.1**
			Exchange blows	7.3	23.6	1.8	**67.3**
			Means	43.3	16.1	22.5	18.1

Table 9.1 Percentage of participants choosing each image schema orientation

IMAGE SCHEMA ORIENTATION AND IDEOLOGY | 187

Transitive		Reciprocal	
Active voice	Passive voice	Sequence AB	Sequence BA
16°	14°	59°	57°

Table 9.2 Mean axis angles for transitive versus reciprocal verbs

frequently selected was chosen by 64 per cent of participants (the figure was higher for transitive verbs [70 per cent] than for reciprocal verbs [58 per cent]). This indicates a substantial degree of agreement between participants.

Following Richardson et al. (2001), to further test the primary hypothesis concerning the main axis of transitive versus reciprocal verbs, the forced choice data was converted into axis angles. Sagittal choices were assigned an angle value of 0° while transversal choices were assigned an angle of 90°. A mean axis angle was then calculated (see Table 9.2). Values show how far, on average, the verb types steer toward a sagittal or transversal conceptualisation. This is visually depicted in Figure 9.2 which shows transitive verbs close to the sagittal axis and reciprocal verbs closer to the transversal axis. Binary logistic regression analysis reveals a significant relationship between verb type and main axis ($\beta=-2.1219$, $SE = 0.115$, $\chi2 (1) = 373.46$, $p<.001$).

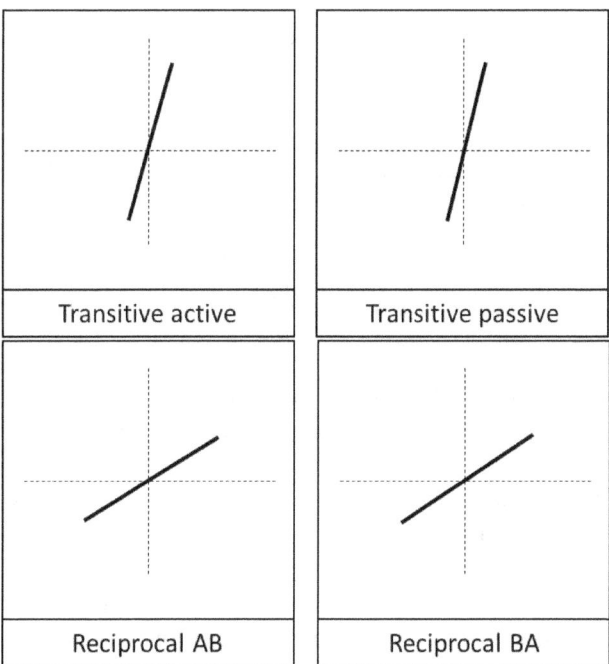

Figure 9.2 Visual depiction of mean axis angles for transitive versus reciprocal verbs

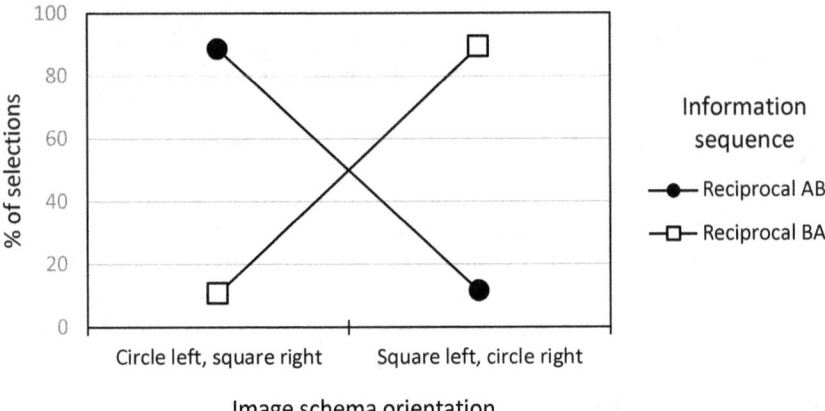

Figure 9.3 Left–right orientation of transversal schema for reciprocal verbs

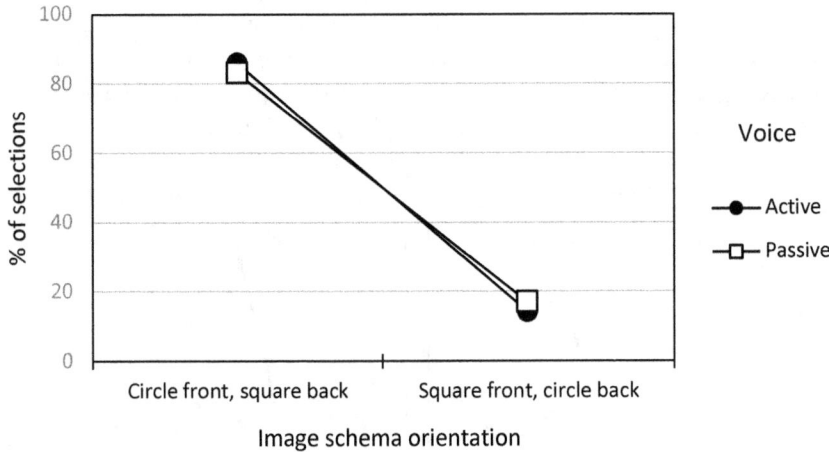

Figure 9.4 Front–back orientation of sagittal schema for transitive verbs

For reciprocal verbs, there was a strong tendency to select the transversal schemas whose left–right orientation was congruent with information sequence (see Figure 9.3). Thus, for reciprocal sentences of the form 'circle VERBED *with* square', 88.6 per cent of transversal selections were for the schema locating the circle on the left while for sentences of the form 'square VERBED *with* circle' only 10.7 per cent of transversal selections had the circle on the left (β=-4.133, SE = 0.268, χ^2 (1) = 238.31, p<.001). Contrary to the hypothesis, however, no equivalent pattern was found for voice in transitive verbs (see Figure 9.4). Sagittal selections for transitive verbs tended to locate the circle as the nearest element in both active (85.9 per cent) and passive (83.1 per cent) voice constructions (β=-.218, SE = 0.205, $\chi2$ (1) = 1.131, p=.228, ns).

2.4. Discussion

The results show an impressive degree of convergence among subjects on the orientation of image schemas associated with transitive versus reciprocal verbs. This evidence suggests there is indeed a spatial dimension to the underlying mental representations indexed by these verb types with orientation a crucial parameter. In so far as orientation is concomitant with viewpoint, the study provides empirical evidence for linguistic theories in which point of view, as a fundamental feature of conceptualisation, figures in the semantic specifications of linguistic units (Hart 2015; Langacker 1987, 1991, 2008; Talmy 2000).

The study shows that transitive action verbs are conceptualised along the sagittal axis while reciprocal action verbs are conceptualised along the transversal axis. One explanation for this may have to do with the fact that reciprocal verbs encode mutual action, whereby both participants are equally agentive. Reciprocal verbs may therefore motivate a construal of the situation as 'balanced' and we tend to make judgements concerning balance based on a twin-pan schema conceived along the transversal axis – rooted in our embodied experience of judging relative weights and pressures in our left and right hands (Johnson 1987). By contrast, transitive verbs are distinctly one-sided and so may encourage a perspective aligned with one or other of the participants in the scene.

For reciprocal verbs, the left-right orientation of the schema was found to follow the information sequence of the sentence. This suggests an iconic relationship between the linearity of the clause and resulting mental representations of events (Perniss et al. 2010) and raises interesting questions for languages with different writing directions. For example, in the semantic domain of time, which typically receives conceptual structure from the domain of space, it has been shown that the specific spatial configurations used to conceptualise time depend on writing direction (Bergen and Chan Lau 2012; Fuhrman and Boroditsky 2010; Tversky et al. 1991). For transitive verbs, by contrast, the front–back orientation of the image schema did not change in active versus passive sentences. In both cases, subjects selected the orientation that placed the agent as the nearest participant. On a dynamic simulation account, it may be that in processing transitive verbs, readers have to adopt the perspective of the agent in order to simulate the action designated in the sentence. This raises questions concerning the function of the passive voice if not for switching perspective between agent and patient as is usually assumed (Bergen 2012).

Now, point of view and relative spatial values like left, right, front and back are not interpersonally or ideologically neutral. For example, an extensive body of research in visual social semiotics suggests that the spatial layout of a text or image engages the reader in different ways and confers different evaluations on the actors and actions represented (e.g. Kress and van Leeuwen 1996; O'Halloran 2004; van Leeuwen and Jewitt 2001). Here, as Kress and van Leeuwen (2006: 146) state, 'the addition of perspective adds nothing to the representational meaning [of images] but it does add attitudinal meaning'. For example, the functional difference between a frontal angle (and thus sagittal arrangement) and an oblique angle (and thus transversal arrangement) on the horizontal plain is said to be the difference between *involvement* and *detachment* (Kress and van Leeuwen 1996: 136). For Kress and van Leeuwen, the frontal angle places a demand on the viewer that they enter into some form of relationship with the actors depicted in the image. The oblique angle, by contrast, merely offers the content of the image to the viewer as a neutral observer. The oblique angle, however, is not an entirely neutral point of view because spatial positions left and right carry symbolic associations. According to Kress and van Leeuwen, the left region of an image is associated with 'given' information while the right region is associated with 'new' information (following a systemic functional analysis of typical English clause structure where given information is presented sentence-initially in the Theme while new information follows in the Rheme). These different information values mean that objects located in the left region of an image are treated as part of common ground while objects located in the right region are subject to contestation. The validity of extending functional linguistic categories to the analysis of images in this way has been questioned (Bateman et al. 2004; Stöckl 2004). Indeed, Kress and van Leeuwen (1998: 218) themselves concede that

> the major challenge to our approach is the epistemological status of our claim . . . [H]ow can we know that left and right, and top and bottom, have the values we attribute to them, or more fundamentally, have any value at all?

However, there is evidence to suggest that spatial values are associated with ideological values. This comes from two sources, both suggesting an embodied basis to the connection. In the first, lexical evidence points to conceptual metaphors, such as SOCIAL DISTANCE IS PHYSICAL DISTANCE or MORALITY IS UP/IMMORALITY IS DOWN, in which social and ideological domains are structured in terms of spatial schemas (Feng 2011; Feng and Espindola 2013; Hart 2014). Here, the inference is that if interpersonal or ideological 'positions' are conceptualised as positions in space, then via some process of metaphor feedback, positions in space connote interpersonal or ideological evaluations. These metaphors are ultimately grounded in situated experiences of affective states correlating with physical locations and relations in space (Grady 1997). The second line of evidence comes from experimental studies. For example, there is some empirical support for the kind of bidirectional metaphor transfer effect alluded to above whereby spatial configurations in real-world situation types are shown to influence social judgements in ways predicted by conceptual metaphors (Winter and Matlock 2013; Winter et al. 2018). This reversed transfer effect is discussed in social psychology as part of what researchers refer to as 'metaphor-enriched social cognition' (Landau et al. 2010). Specifically in relation to left and right, Casasanto (2009) has shown that for right-handers (who vastly outnumber left-handers) rightward space is associated with positive valence and leftward space is associated with more negative valence while the opposite is the case for left-handers. This pattern was observed for judgements across a range of character traits including goodness, intelligence, attractiveness and honesty. According to Casasanto, these body-specific associations emerge from the positive experiences we have in controlling and manipulating objects on the dominant side of our body. Casasanto and Jasmin (2010) have similarly shown that politicians tend to produce spontaneous co-speech gestures using their dominant hand (usually the right hand) when communicating positive messages but their non-dominant hand when communicating more negative messages. Casasanto's findings run counter to Kress and van Leeuwen's analysis showing that, for most people, the positive versus negative value associations of left versus right are the other way around, with right having positive valence and left having negative valence, and rooted in embodied experience rather than cultural or linguistic conventions. All of these findings, however, point to a general mapping between spatial values and subjective evaluations.

This has implications for the ideological potentials of language (see Hart 2016a for extended discussion). Since there is no principled reason to suppose that spatial parameters should function differently across communicative modalities, then, if language is spatial, linguistic units may confer subtle ideological evaluations as a consequence of the spatial forms of representation they encode. In the case of transitive versus reciprocal verbs, any ideological effects arising from their use may, in part, be due to the contrasting viewpoints and relative image schema orientations that are constitutive of their meaning. Support for this claim would come from studies which show that the ideological effects of transitive versus reciprocal verbs in context are the same as for their visual analogues in the same context.

The ideological effects of transitive versus reciprocal verbs in media reports of political protests was investigated in an experiment which has previously been published (Hart 2016b) and is summarised here.

In Hart (2016b), participants read the lead paragraph of an online news article reporting violence at a recent protest in the fictitious city of Southfield. There were four conditions in a between subjects design. Each report contained two target descriptions of violent encounters between police and protesters. The independent variable was whether the violence was described using a transitive verb (with protesters as agent) or a reciprocal verb as well as voice and information sequence respectively. The texts were otherwise identical across conditions. The text is reproduced below, shown in the transitive active voice condition by way of example (emphasis added).

> A protest against local council policy turned violent yesterday in the city of Southfield. *Protesters attacked police officers* amid scenes of chaos outside City Hall. The protest later moved to the central square where *protesters continued to assault police officers*. Police officers used batons to control the crowds, which eventually dispersed around 9pm. 10 people received treatment for injuries.

After reading the article, participants were asked where they would place the blame for the violence that occurred and how aggressive they thought the different actors involved were. The question of blame was answered on a 5-point Likert-type scale <protesters fully to blame – protesters mainly to blame – both parties equally to blame – police mainly to blame – police fully to blame>. Aggression of the actors was judged on a 7-point semantical differential scale <not at all aggressive – extremely aggressive>. Results showed a significant difference in how blame was apportioned that depended first and foremost on whether the violence was described using transitive or reciprocal verbs ($\chi^2=32.3911$, $p<.001$). Participants given transitive verbs (with protesters as agent) were more likely to see the protesters as fully (22 per cent) or mainly (54 per cent) to blame and less likely to assign equal blame (18 per cent). Conversely, participants given reciprocal verbs were much more likely to apportion equal blame (45 per cent). Moreover, of those participants given reciprocal verbs who did assign blame to one party over the other, there was a fairly even distribution (protesters mainly to blame = 25 per cent, police mainly to blame = 23 per cent). Where blame was disproportionately assigned in response to reciprocal verbs, this depended on information sequence with participants in the protester-first version more likely to assign blame to protesters (46 per cent) than police (11 per cent) and participants in the police-first version more likely to assign blame to the police (36 per cent) than to protesters (11 per cent) ($\chi^2=13.5761$, $p<.01$).

For perceptions of aggression, police were ranked as more aggressive in response to reciprocal verbs ($M=5.1$), where they are agentive, than in response to transitive verbs where they are the patient ($M=3.87$) ($U=1436$,

$p<.001$). Conversely, protesters were ranked as less aggressive in response to reciprocal verbs ($M=4.66$) than transitive verbs where they were the sole agent ($M=5.4$) ($U=1893$, $p<.001$). Within reciprocal verb constructions, perception of aggression depended on information sequence. Actors were judged as more aggressive when they occurred first in information sequence ($M=5.125$) than when they occurred second ($M=4.63$) ($U=2.5949$, $p=<.01$). Contrary to the hypothesis, however, within transitive verb constructions, voice had no significant effects on perception of aggression.

The results of this experiment show that the choice of transitive versus reciprocal verbs and information sequence within reciprocal verb constructions affect blame assignment and perception of aggression. The effects observed can be attributed to the alternative image schemas evoked by transitive versus reciprocal verbs (one-sided versus two-sided action schemas respectively). When there is only one agent, the agentive actor attracts blame and actors are perceived as more aggressive when they are encoded as agents than when they are encoded as patients. Similarly, within reciprocal verbs, the effects of information sequence may have to do with levels of agency ascribed to actors. Although, semantically, reciprocal verbs ascribe equal levels of agency to the actors involved, grammatically the subject nominal is closely associated with agenthood. The first agent in a reciprocal construction may therefore be judged as more agent-like. However, the effects found may also arise as a function of viewpoint and relative image schema orientation. The 'involved' perspective encoded by transitive verbs may encourage an action-based simulation in which the conceptualiser imagines themselves performing the action designated. Such an engaged perspective may then facilitate blame and aggression judgements based on a recognition of the subjective intentional and affective mental states that would accompany such an action. By contrast, the 'observer's' perspective encoded in reciprocal verbs may encourage a perception-based simulation in which the conceptualiser imagines themselves as a more neutral witness to the scene described. Within reciprocal verb constructions, the effects of information sequence may be due to the relative left–right orientation of the image schema invoked. The first agent may be judged as more aggressive because they occupy the left region of the schema and, as Casasanto (2009) has shown, leftward space is associated with negative character traits. Within transitive verb constructions, the fact that voice alternates had no similar ideological effects is consistent with results from Experiment 1 where voice was found not to encode contrasting image schema orientations on the sagittal axis. The extent to which the ideological functions of transitive versus reciprocal verbs and information sequence within reciprocal verb constructions are a consequence of image schema orientation, as well as differences in the internal structure of the image schemas invoked, remains an open question. However, evidence supporting the claim that image schema orientation is a semiotically consequential factor would come if congruent ideological effects are found for actual images where viewpoint or relative orientation is the only variable.

3. Experiment 2

If viewpoint and relative orientation is a functional semantic feature of the conceptualisation invoked by transitive versus reciprocal verbs, then we should expect to observe the same ideological effects arising from corresponding viewpoints presented by images in the same discursive context. In other words, if the ideological effects arising from viewpoint in actual images (within the same social context) are congruent, by the hypothesis, with the ideological effects of transitive versus reciprocal verb constructions, then this can be taken as further evidence that viewpoint is a semiotically significant feature of the conceptualisations invoked by these linguistic forms. Experiments 2a–b therefore investigated the ideological effects, in blame assignment and perception of aggression, of viewpoint and relative orientation in images of violent encounters between police and protesters. Experiment 2a investigated the effects of viewpoint on blame assignment while Experiment 2b investigated the effects of viewpoint on perception of aggression.

3.1. Methods

Participants
For Experiment 2a, 106 participants were recruited from the undergraduate student population at Lancaster University. For Experiment 2b, 115 participants were recruited via Amazon's Mechanical Turk (https://www.mturk.com) (Buhrmester, et al. 2011; Crump et al. 2013; Mason and Suri 2012; Paolacci et al. 2010). Participation was restricted to users registered in the UK, the US, the Republic of Ireland, Canada and Australia. To ensure high quality participants, only 'Turkers' with a HIT Approval Rate of 98 per cent or above were eligible. This rating indicates that participants had completed at least 98 per cent of previous tasks satisfactorily. Participants in both experiments were native speakers of English (by self-report). This was important to avoid potential interference from language systems with different writing directions.

Materials and design
Experiment 2a was conducted online as part of a package of other unrelated experiments. Instructions informed participants that they would see an illustration of a violent encounter at a recent political protest and be asked a follow-up question about the image. Participants were then presented with a

Figure 9.5 Stimulus images used in Experiments 2a and 2b

single image of a violent encounter between a police officer and a protester. The experiment followed a between subjects design in which participants were auto-randomly assigned to one of four conditions presenting the image in contrasting orientations corresponding with the image schema orientations in Experiment 1. In order to ensure that viewpoint was the only variable introduced, illustrations rather than photographs of real-life protests were used.[1] The stimulus images are shown in Figure 9.5. To measure blame allocation, participants were asked to indicate, on a 5-point Likert-type scale, where they would place the blame for the violence that occurred: <protesters fully to blame – protesters mainly to blame – both parties equally to blame – police mainly to blame – police fully to blame>.

Experiment 2b was conducted online and followed a within subjects design. In Experiment 2b, participants saw pairs of images in six trials per pair. Images were paired by primary axis so that images A and C in Figure 9.5 were presented together as were images B and D. Paired images were presented simultaneously in each trial. Transversal images B and D were presented on the screen one above the other in order to avoid any interference from values associated with a left–right positioning of the images themselves. This was counter-balanced so that half of participants saw image B above image D and half saw image D above image B. Similarly, sagittal images A and C were shown side by side on the screen so as to avoid any interference from values associated with top and bottom regions of the screen. This was also counter-balanced between participants.

Participants were instructed that they would be shown a series of paired illustrations depicting violent encounters at a political protest and asked to make a judgement about the images. In each trial, participants were asked to give a judgement, based on six adjectives relating to aggression, indicating in which image the protester was most *aggressive / unfriendly / intimidating / frightening / threatening / hostile*. The protester rather than the police officer was chosen as the social actor whose status and legitimacy is typically at issue in media discourses of political protest. The twelve total trials were presented in random order to minimise any potential carry-over effects between conditions.

Transversal and sagittal conditions were analysed separately. For the transversal images, the binary choices made by participants were used to categorise them as either 'left=aggressive' or 'right=aggressive' coders. Participants were categorised as left=aggressive coders when the image selected in 4/6 or more trials showed the subject character on the left. Participants were categorised as right-aggressive coders when the image selected in 4/6 or more trials showed the subject character on the right. Participants who showed no directional preference, that is, selected the image with the subject character on the left in 3/6 trials and on the right in 3/6 trials, were excluded from the analysis. The same method was employed for the sagittal images categorising participants as 'front=aggressive' or 'back=aggressive'.

3.2. *Hypotheses*

The primary hypothesis, tested in Experiment 2a, is that blame allocation will be a function of viewpoint such that blame will be assigned more evenly in transversal images than in sagittal images. The secondary hypothesis, tested in Experiment 2b, is that spatial values on the transversal and sagittal axes are differentially associated with aggression. For transversal images, it is hypothesised that spatial left is more strongly associated with aggression than spatial right. For sagittal images, it is hypothesised that the distal, ego-opposed position will be more strongly associated with aggression than the proximal, ego-aligned position.

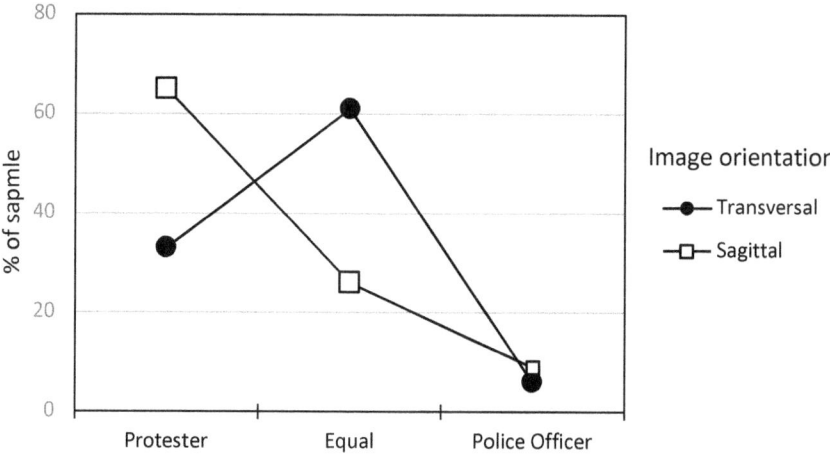

Figure 9.6 Blame allocation in transversal versus sagittal images

3.3. Results and Discussion

Results from Experiment 2a confirm that viewpoint and relative orientation is a significant factor in blame allocation for images of violence at political protests. Participants presented with transversal images were much more likely to assign equal blame (61 per cent) for the violence depicted than participants presented with sagittal images (25 per cent) (χ^2=13.7414, p<.001). Results from Experiment 2a are shown in Figure 9.6. As discussed earlier, the transversal arrangement may encourage more equal blame assignment based on the typical 'twin-pan' concept of BALANCE which is conceived in terms of a transversal schema (Johnson 1987). The effect may also arise due to feedback from a general conceptual metaphor STANCE IS POSITION IN SPACE (Hart 2014). In the transversal images, the viewer's sagittal line intersects the midpoint between actors in the image. And, as evidenced by linguistic expressions such 'occupy the middle ground', this spatial position is associated with neutrality. Based on the same metaphor, we might then expect participants given sagittal images to assign blame differently depending on whose 'side' the image asks them to take. However, in all conditions, when blame was unequally assigned, it was most often assigned to the protester, regardless of position on the primary axis, suggesting an entrenched discourse of deviance in relation to political protest (Hall 1973). This points to the competing influences of conceptual metaphors and pre-existing beliefs and value positions in the social perception of images.

Results from Experiment 2b (see Figure 9.7) show that opposing viewpoints in both sagittal and transversal images does affect perception of

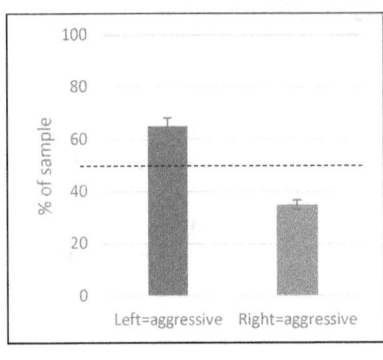 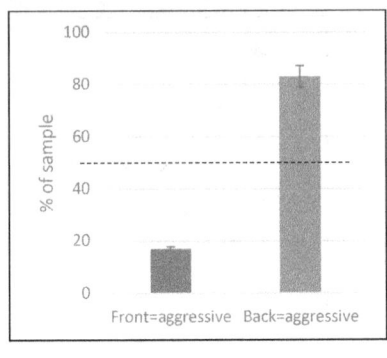

(a) Transversal images   (b) Sagittal images

Figure 9.7 Spatial discrimination in perception of aggression

aggression. For transversal images, 65 per cent of non-neutral participants exhibited a tendency to code the subject character as more aggressive when they appeared in the left region of the image (six participants were excluded as neutral, $n=109$). The result is significantly above chance ($\chi^2=4.8144$, $p<.05$) and seems to confirm Casasanto's (2009) claim that for the majority of people spatial left is symbolically associated with negative valence (86 per cent of participants were right-handed, identified by self-report).[2] For sagittal images, 83 per cent of non-neutral participants exhibited a tendency to code the subject character as more aggressive in images where they appeared as distal and ego-opposed (nine participants were excluded as neutral, $n=106$). This result is highly significant when measured against chance ($\chi^2=25.9415$, $p<.001$) with the effect more pronounced than for left versus right positions in transversal images.[3] This shows that near and far positions in sagittal images are highly evaluatively laden with the distal position judged much more negatively. As suggested earlier, this may be a result of some general association between GOOD/BAD and PROXIMAL/DISTAL which is encoded across conceptual metaphors such as SOCIAL DISTANCE IS PHYSICAL DISTANCE, MORALITY IS DISTANCE and SIMILARITY IS DISTANCE (Chilton 2004; Winter and Matlock 2013; Winter et al. 2018). However, it is not only position but also orientation in space that is likely to account for the effect. In the sagittal images, the nearest actor is presented ego-aligned with the viewer. By contrast, the furthest actor is presented ego-opposed. And, as suggested in the etymology of words like *confrontation*, the ego-opposed orientation is associated with antagonism. Moreover, on a dynamic simulation account of how we understand images, whereby viewers 'complete' the scene depicted by a static image inside a mental situation model (Proverbio et al. 2009; Winawer et al. 2008), the distal, ego-opposed actor may be perceived as more aggressive as they are imagined moving toward the viewer.

4. General Discussion and Conclusion

In summary of this chapter, I have presented data from three experiments which, taken together, suggest that (i) transitive versus reciprocal verbs and differences in information sequence within reciprocal verb constructions include as part of their meaning a viewpoint specification and that (ii) the alternative viewpoints associated with these linguistic forms, when used in contexts of reporting violent interactions between police and protesters, may be responsible for ideological effects in blame assignment and perception of aggression. The three experiments, thus, provide convergent evidence for hypotheses made within cognitive linguistic approaches to critical discourse analysis (e.g. Hart 2015).

In Experiment 1, a sentence–image matching task showed an impressive degree of convergence among participants in selecting image schemas in different orientations as best representing the meaning of transitive versus reciprocal sentences. This consensus is taken as betraying common underlying representations constitutive of native speaker knowledge and thus offers further evidence that ostensibly non-spatial language usages include as part of their meaning a spatial component (Richardson et al. 2001). It could be argued, however, that the results reflect the limited, forced-choice nature of the task rather than a deeper level of commonality in participants' mental representations. It should also be noted that the task is a reflective one, based on metalinguistic intuitions, and therefore does not necessarily indicate that these spatialised forms of representation are activated in real-time language processing (see Richardson et al. 2003). Future work might look to corroborate these results using a free-form task or paradigms explicitly intended to access online language processing such as the image-sentence compatibility effect (ICE) (Stanfield and Zwaan 2001; Winter and Bergen 2012; Zwaan et al. 2002) or eye tracking, where eye movements have been found to 'follow' the spatial locations, orientations and directions implied in language usages (Matlock and Richardson 2004; Richardson et al. 2007; Spivey and Geng 2001; Spivey et al. 2000).

Further evidence to support the claim that viewpoint and relative orientation is a meaningful feature of the conceptualisations invoked by transitive versus reciprocal verb constructions, it was argued, would come from studies which show that the same ideological effects arise from language usages and images which are, by the hypothesis, congruent. This works on the assumption that, if understanding language involves the activation of mental imagery, the mental imagery invoked by specific language usages will have similar framing effects to comparable concrete images (Hart 2017). This was tested across two experiments – Experiment 2 and a previously reported experiment (Hart 2016b). The results of these two experiments were indeed consistent with one another. Images of violent interactions between police and protesters where viewpoint was the only variable produced ideological effects in the same direction as their purported linguistic counterparts. The only exception was in relation to voice alternates in transitive verb constructions. While opposite viewpoints in sagittal images significantly affected the level of aggression ascribed to actors in the image, no equivalent effect was found for the active versus passive voice, which was originally hypothesised as involving a perspective-switch on the sagittal axis. However, the fact that the same effect is not reproduced across modalities here is in fact consistent with results from Experiment 1, which defeated this hypothesis and suggested that voice does not involve such a shift in viewpoint. We should therefore not expect to find equivalent effects in this case.

To conclude, at a more general level, the chapter has demonstrated at least one way in which cognitive linguistic analysis can be usefully extended to the realm of text and discourse where it can illuminate the ideological qualities of conceptualisations associated with attested language usages. Further, by exploiting experimental methodologies, as is consistent with the most recent developments in COGNITIVE LINGUISTICS, I hope to have shown empirically the validity of such an approach to text and discourse analysis.

Notes

1 It should be noted that one potential confound is the handedness of actors in the transversal images where one actor is left-handed and the other is right-handed. However, maintaining consistency in handedness for actors in the image, as well as in the body poses assumed, would necessarily result in an obscuration of one or other of the actors' faces. And while it is possible that handedness may influence participant judgements, visible facial expression is much more likely to be a significant factor affecting social perception (Willis et al. 2011).
2 Parametric tests with a dependent variable created from the number of left selections made by each participant also produce significant results when measured against chance ($t=3.111149$, $p<.01$).
3 Again, parametric tests with a dependent variable created from the number of back selections made by each participant also produce significant results when measured against chance ($t=9.049638$, $p<.0001$).

References

Bateman, J., Delin, J. L. and Henschel, R. (2004). Multimodality and empiricism: Preparing for a corpus-based approach to the study of multimodal meaning-making. In E. Vetonla, C. Charles and M. Kaltenbacher (eds), Perspectives on Multimodality. Amsterdam: John Benjamins, pp. 65–87.

Bergen B. (2012). *Louder than Words: The New of Science of How the Mind Makes Meaning*. New York: Basic Books.
Bergen B., Chang, N. and Narayanan, S. (2004). Simulated action in an embodied construction grammar. In *Proceedings of 26th Annual Conference of the Cognitive Science Society*. Mahwah, NJ: Erlbaum, pp. 108–13.
Bergen, B., Lindsay, S., Matlock, T. and Narayanan, S. (2007). Spatial and linguistic aspects of visual imagery in sentence comprehension. *Cognitive Science* 31: 733–64.
Bergen, B. K. and Chan Lau, T. T. (2012). Writing direction affects how people map space onto time. *Frontiers in Psychology* 3: 109, http://doi.org/10.3389/fpsyg.2012.00109.
Buhrmester M. D., Kwang, T. and Gosling, S. D. (2011). Amazon's Mechanical Turk: A new source of inexpensive, yet high-quality, data? *Perspectives on Psychological Science* 6 (1): 3–5.
Casasanto, D. (2009). Embodiment of abstract concepts: Good and bad in right- and left-handers. *Journal of Experimental Psychology* 138 (3): 351–67.
Casasanto, D. and Jasmin, K. (2010). Good and bad in the hands of politicians: Spontaneous gestures during positive and negative speech. *PLoS ONE* 5 (7): e11805.
Charteris-Black, J. (2006). Britain as a container: Immigration metaphors in the 2005 election campaign. *Discourse & Society* 17 (6): 563–82.
Chilton, P. (1996). *Security Metaphors: Cold War Discourse from Containment to Common House*. New York: Peter Lang.
Chilton, P. (2004). *Analysing Political Discourse: Theory and Practice*. London: Routledge.
Chilton, P. and Lakoff, G. (1995). Foreign policy by metaphor. In C. Schäffner and A. I. Wenden (eds), *Language and Peace*. Aldershot: Ashgate, pp. 37–60.
Crump, J. C., McDonnel, J. V. and Gureckis, T. M. (2013). Evaluating Amazon's Mechanical Turk as a tool for experimental behavioural research. *PLoS ONE* 8: e57410.
Dirven, R., Frank, R. and Pütz, M. (2003). Introduction: Categories, cognitive models and ideologies. In R. Dirven, R. Frank and M. Pütz (eds), *Cognitive Models in Language and Thought: Ideology, Metaphors and Meanings*. Berlin: Mouton de Gruyter, pp. 1–24.
Feng, D. (2011). Visual space and ideology: A critical cognitive analysis of spatial orientations in advertising. In K. L. O'Halloran and B. A. Smith (eds), *Multimodal Studies: Exploring Issues and Domains*. London: Routledge, pp. 55–75.
Feng, D. and Espindola. E. (2013). Integrating functional and cognitive approaches to multimodal discourse analysis. *Ilha do Desterro* 64: 85–110.
Fodor, J. (1975). *The Language of Thought*. New York: Crowell.
Fuhrman, O. and Boroditsky, L. (2010). Cross-cultural differences in mental representations of time: Evidence from an implicit nonlinguistic task. *Cognitive Science* 34: 1430–51.
Glenberg, A. and Kaschak, M. (2002). Grounding language in action. *Psychonomic Bulletin and Review* 9: 558–65.
Goatly, A. (2007). *Washing the Brain: Metaphor and Hidden Ideology*. Amsterdam: John Benjamins.

Grady, J. (1997). *Foundations of Meaning: Primary Metaphors and Primary Scenes*. Unpublished PhD dissertation. Berkeley: University of California.

Hall, S. (1973). A world at one with itself. In S. Cohen and J. Young (eds), *The Manufacture of News: Deviance, Social Problems and the Mass Media*. London: Constable, pp. 147–56.

Hart, C. (2010). *Critical Discourse Analysis and Cognitive Science: New Perspectives on Immigration Discourse*. Basingstoke: Palgrave.

Hart, C. (2011). Force-interactive patterns in immigration discourse: A cognitive linguistic approach to CDA. *Discourse & Society* 22 (3): 269–86.

Hart, C. (2013a). Event-construal in press reports of violence in political protests: A cognitive linguistic approach to CDA. *Journal of Language and Politics* 12 (3): 400–23.

Hart, C. (2013b). Constructing contexts through grammar: Cognitive models and conceptualisation in British newspaper reports of political protests. In J. Flowerdew (ed.), *Discourse and Contexts*. London: Continuum, pp. 159–84.

Hart, C. (2014). *Discourse, Grammar and Ideology: Functional and Cognitive Perspectives*. London: Bloomsbury.

Hart, C. (2015). Viewpoint in linguistic discourse: Space and evaluation in news reports of political protests. *Critical Discourse Studies* 12 (3): 238–60.

Hart, C. (2016a). The visual basis of linguistic meaning and its implications for CDS: Integrating cognitive linguistic and multimodal methods. *Discourse & Society* 27 (3): 335–50.

Hart, C. (2016b). Event-frames affect blame assignment and perception of aggression: An experimental case study in CDA. *Applied Linguistics*. doi.org/10.1093/applin/amw017.

Hart, C. (2017). 'Riots engulfed the city': An experimental study investigating the legitimating effects of fire metaphors in discourses of disorder. *Discourse & Society*. doi.org/10.1177/0957926517734663.

Johnson, M. (1987). *The Body in the Mind: The Bodily Basis of Meaning, Imagination, and Reason*. Chicago: The University of Chicago Press.

Kress, G. and van Leeuwen, T. (1996) *Reading Images: The Grammar of Visual Design*, 2nd edition. London: Routledge.

Kress, G. and van Leeuwen, T. (1998). Front pages: (The critical) analysis of newspaper layout. In A. Bell and P. Garrett (eds), *Approaches to Media Discourse*. Oxford: Blackwell, pp. 186–219.

Kress, G. and van Leeuwen, T. (2006). *Reading Images: The Grammar of Visual Design*, Second edition. London: Routledge.

Lakoff, G. (1987). *Women, Fire and Dangerous Things: What Categories Reveal about the Mind*. Chicago: The University of Chicago Press.

Lakoff, G. and Johnson, M. (1980). *Metaphors We Live By*. Chicago: The University of Chicago Press.

Lakoff, G. and Johnson, M. (1999). *Philosophy in the Flesh: The Embodied Mind and its Challenge to Western Thought*. New York: Basic Books.

Landau, B. and Jackendoff, R. (1993). 'What' and 'where' in spatial language and spatial cognition. *Behavioral and Brain Sciences* 16: 217–65.

Landau, M. J., Meier, B. P. and Keefer, L. A. (2010). A metaphor-enriched social cognition. *Psychological Bulletin* 136: 1045–67.

Langacker, R. W. (1987). *Foundations of Cognitive Grammar: Volume I: Theoretical Prerequisites.* Stanford: Stanford University Press.
Langacker, R. W. (1991). *Foundations of Cognitive Grammar: Volume II: Descriptive Application.* Stanford: Stanford University Press.
Langacker, R. W. (2008). *Cognitive Grammar: A Basic Introduction.* Oxford: Oxford University Press.
Mason, W. and Suri, S. (2012). Conducting behavioural research on Amazon's Mechanical Turk. *Behavioural Research Methods* 44: 1–23.
Matlock, T. and Richardson, D. C. (2004). Do eye movements go with fictive motion? *Proceedings of the 26th Annual Conference of the Cognitive Science Society.* Mahwah, NJ: Erlbaum.
May, R. (1985). *Logical Form.* Cambridge: The MIT Press.
Meteyard, L. and Vigliocco, G. (2009). Verbs in space: Axis and direction of motion norms for 229 English verbs. *Behaviour Research Methods* 41 (2): 565–74.
Meteyard, L., Bahrami, B. and Vigliocco, G. (2007). Motion detection and motion verbs: Language affects low-level visual perception. *Psychological Science* 18: 1007–13.
Meteyard, L., Zokaei, N., Bahrami, B. and Vigliocco, G. (2008). Visual motion interferes with lexical decision on motion words. *Current Biology* 18: R732–R734.
O'Halloran, K. L. (ed.) (2004). *Multimodal Discourse Analysis.* London: Continuum.
Paolacci, G., Chandler, J. and Ipeirotis, P. G. (2010). Running experiments on Amazon Mechanical Turk. *Judgement and Decision Making* 5: 411–19.
Perniss, P., Thompson, R. and Vigliocco, G. (2010). Iconicity as a general property of language: Evidence from spoken and signed languages. *Frontiers in Psychology* 1: 227.
Proverbio, A. M., Riva, F. and Zani, A. (2009). Observation of static pictures of dynamic actions enhances the activity of movement-related brain areas. *PLOS ONE* e5389.
Richardson, D. C., Dale, R. and Spivey, M. J. (2007). Eye movements in language and cognition. In M. Gonzalez-Marquez, I. Mittelberg, S. Coulson and M. J. Spivey (eds), *Methods in Cognitive Linguistics.* Amsterdam: John Benjamins, pp. 323–44.
Richardson, D. C., Spivey, M. J., Barsalou, L. W. and McRae, K. (2003). Spatial representations activated during real-time comprehension of verbs. *Cognitive Science* 27: 767–80.
Richardson, D. C., Spivey, M. J., Edelman, S. and Naples, A. D. (2001). 'Language is spatial': Experimental evidence for image schemas of concrete and abstract verbs. *Proceedings of the 23rd Annual Conference of the Cognitive Science Society.* Mahwah, NJ: Erlbaum.
Spivey, M. J. and Geng, J. J. (2001). Oculomotor mechanisms activated by imagery and memory: Eye movements to absent objects. *Psychological Research* 65: 235–41.
Spivey, M. J., Richardson, D. C., Tyler, M. J. and Young, E. E. (2000). Eye movement during comprehension of spoken scene descriptions. In L. R. Gleitman and A. K. Joshi (eds), *Proceedings of the 22nd Annual Conference of the Cognitive Science Society.* Mahwah, NJ: Erlbaum, pp. 487–92.
Stanfield, R. A. and Zwaan, R. A. (2001). The effect of implied orientation derived from verbal context on picture recognition. *Psychological Science* 12: 153–6.

Stöckl, H. (2004). In between modes: Language and image in printed media. In E. Ventola, C. Charles and M. Kaltenbacher (eds), *Perspectives on Multimodality*. Amsterdam: John Benjamins, pp. 9–30.
Talmy, L. (2000). *Toward a Cognitive Semantics*. Cambridge, MA: The MIT Press.
Tversky, B. (1998). Three dimensions of spatial cognition. In M. A. Conway, S. E. Gathercole and C. Cornoldi (eds), *Theories of Memory II*. Hove, East Sussex: Psychological Press, pp. 259–75.
Tversky, B., Kugelmass, S. and Winter, A. (1991). Crosscultural and developmental-trends in graphic productions. *Cognitive Psychology* 23: 515–57.
Tversky, B., Morrison, J. B., Franklin, N. and Bryant, D. J. (1999). Three spaces of spatial cognition. *Professional Geographer* 51: 516–24.
Van Leeuwen, T. and Jewitt, C. (eds) (2001). *The Handbook of Visual Analysis*. London: Sage.
Willis, M. L., Palermo, R., and Burke, D. (2011). Social judgements are influenced by both facial expression and direction of eye gaze. *Social Cognition* 29 (4): 415–29.
Winawer, J., Huk, A. C. and Boroditsky, L. (2008). A motion aftereffect from still photographs depicting motion. *Psychological Science* 19: 276–83.
Winter, B. and Bergen, B. (2012). Language comprehenders represent object distance both visually and auditorily. *Language and Cognition* 4 (1): 1–16.
Winter, B. and Matlock, T. (2013). Making judgements based on similarity and proximity. *Metaphor and Symbol* 28: 1–14.
Winter, B., Daguna, J. and Matlock, T. (2018). Metaphor-enriched social cognition and spatial bias in the courtroom. *Metaphor and the Social World* 8 (1): 81–98.
Zwaan. R. A. (2004). The immersed experiencer: Toward an embodied theory of language comprehension. In B. H. Ross (ed.), *The Psychology of Learning and Motivation, Volume 44*. New York: Academic Press, pp. 35–62.
Zwaan, R. A., Stanfield, R. A. and Yaxley, R. H. (2002). Do language comprehenders routinely represent the shapes of objects? *Psychological Science* 13: 168–71.

Index

action chain, 32–3, 47–50, 183
agency, 32–3, 45–9, 104, 193
aggression, 80, 85–6, 143–5, 146, 192–200
ambience, 20–35
atmosphere, 22, 26, 38, 40, 44, 50
attention, 2, 3, 7, 10, 32, 44–5, 47–9, 98–100, 102, 105, 108
axiology, 107, 117, 120, 124–6

blame, 163–4, 170–1, 192–200
body-specificity hypothesis, 191

Cognitive Grammar, 4–5, 8, 22–4, 37–8, 40–50, 96, 158, 169–78, 181
Cognitive Stylistics, 6–9
conceptual blending, 7, 81–3, 121–3, 126
Conceptual Metaphor Theory, 3, 7, 74–5, 77–89, 131–7, 147
construal, 2–3, 22, 40, 116–17, 168–9
context model, 115–16, 118, 126
Corpus Linguistics, 9, 21, 24–5, 27–30, 34, 76–7, 145
creativity, 54, 57, 66–70, 77, 79, 80–3, 135, 159
Critical Discourse Analysis, 6–9, 21, 34, 56, 199
critical reception, 158–61
current discourse space, 4–5

deixis, 2, 7, 22, 33, 42, 62, 94–5, 97, 100–8, 113, 117–20, 123–7
Discourse Space Theory, 7, 94–5, 97–8, 100–8, 114, 116–17, 120
disorientation, 40–6
distance, 32–3, 78, 101–2, 119–20, 124, 127, 134, 141–2, 145–6, 190, 198
dominion, 8, 22–5, 28–30, 34
dynamic systems, 87–8

embodiment, 1, 6, 10, 37, 79, 85, 94, 97, 108, 134–6, 140–4, 146–7, 181, 183, 189, 191
emotion, 111, 116–17, 124, 134, 159
evaluation, 63–9, 108, 112, 116, 120, 125, 127, 136, 144–6, 190–1; *see also* stance

focus, 169–71, 173
frames, 7, 115, 133, 135–6, 159–61, 164, 168, 170–2, 174–5, 177

genre, 4, 5, 8–10, 27, 57, 137, 140

iconicity, 31–2, 189
ideology, 21, 100, 114, 121, 159, 173, 182–3, 190–4, 199–200
image schema, 27, 48, 94–100, 102–8, 135–6, 139–44, 146–7, 181–200

immersion, 38–9, 42–4, 46
information sequence, 183–4, 186, 188–9, 192–3, 199
intersubjectivity, 3, 74, 84–5, 88
invariance principle, 94

K-device, 115, 126
keyness, 27–8
knowledge, 62, 65–7, 85, 87, 111–27, 135, 158–60, 164, 167, 172, 175, 178

lacuna, 30

mental models, 42, 93–7, 100, 102, 108
mental space, 82, 97, 116, 119, 122–3, 135–6
metaphor, 7, 32, 39, 50, 67, 73–89, 94, 100, 102, 108, 119–23, 125–7, 131–47, 181, 190–1, 197–8
metaphor combinations, 79–81
metaphor feedback, 190–1
metaphor identification procedure, 137–9
metaphor scenarios, 79, 80, 83–5, 88, 131–7, 144–7
metaphor-enriched social cognition, 191
metonymy, 74–6, 80, 85, 87, 121, 142
mind-modelling, 63–9
modalisation, 22, 32–4, 45, 48–9, 126
modality, 45, 48, 101, 117, 120, 124–7
multimodality, 10, 67, 111, 127n

narrative urgency, 46
negation, 32, 33, 107
nominalisation, 163, 168, 173–5

objective construal, 22, 32, 45–6
oppositional reading, 159–60, 177

passive voice, 163, 170–1, 173
perspective, 22, 30, 32, 38, 42, 117, 125, 139, 169, 189–90, 193, 200

point of view, 2, 10, 22, 47, 101–2, 116–17, 127, 181–200
primary metaphor, 77–9, 80, 84, 86, 88, 134, 191
profiling, 7, 8, 47, 173–5
prominence, 49, 169, 173–5
prosody, 145
proximity, 27, 33, 78, 106–7, 112, 117, 119, 120–1, 124–7, 134, 182, 196, 198

reciprocal verbs, 183–200
reprofiling, 173–5
rescoping, 169–72

scenario, 42–5, 50, 115
scope, 43, 169–70, 173
simile, 73–88
simulation semantics, 10, 85, 182–3, 189, 193, 198
space builders, 98–100, 108, 122
specificity, 43–4, 61, 169
stance, 133, 135, 141, 176, 197; *see also* evaluation
stylistics, 6, 158
subjective construal, 22, 32–3, 44–6

text-worlds, 22, 40, 42, 44–6, 59–69, 118–25, 164, 167–8, 170, 172, 174–5, 177
Text-World Theory, 7, 37, 58–9, 64, 70, 97, 112, 114–18, 126–7, 158–62
tone, 10, 22, 26, 40, 44, 46, 81, 87, 164
transitive verbs, 173, 181–200
transitivity, 10, 170–1

valance, 10, 159, 191, 198
vectors, 94, 102, 104–6
viewpoint *see* point of view
visual social semiotics, 190–1
voice, 170–3, 175–7, 184, 185–9, 192–3, 200

world builders, 44
world building elements, 62, 114–18, 120, 122–6, 159

EU representative:
Easy Access System Europe
Mustamäe tee 50, 10621 Tallinn, Estonia
Gpsr.requests@easproject.com

www.ingramcontent.com/pod-product-compliance
Lightning Source LLC
Chambersburg PA
CBHW071841230426
43671CB00012B/2035